Joseph Glackin hails from Motherwell in the West of Scotland, a former steel town where the common experience of fighting over football and religion were, he says, a good preparation for his working life in Africa. This included twelve years in the West African country of Liberia at the height of its infamous civil war where, as a priest, he worked directly with child soldiers, street children and other victims of a disintegrating society.

He has also worked in child protection and youth development in Sudan and South Sudan, Sierra Leone, South Africa, Rwanda and Eritrea. He presently works as Head of Programme Development for Hope and Homes for Children, a charity working to end institutional care of children worldwide.

By the same author:

A Lone Star Weeps, Thirsty Books (2013)
Freedom's Shadow, Thirsty Books (2015)

A Patchwork of Darkness

An Inspector Gloria Mystery

JOSEPH GLACKIN

THIRSTY NOIR

First published 2021 by Thirsty Books, Edinburgh
thirstybooks.com

ISBN: 978-1-9161112-2-6

The paper used in this book is recyclable.
It is made from low chlorine pulps produced in a low energy,
low emission manner from renewable forests.

Printed and bound
by Bell & Bain Ltd., Glasgow

Typeset in Adobe Garamond
by Main Point Books, Edinburgh

In memory of Clementine Rhodes Momo (1967–2020),
colleague and friend of many years.

Chapter One

There were times when Inspector Gloria Sirleaf regretted her appointment as the head of Liberia's Family and Child Protection Unit. Her regrets had nothing to do with the dangers her work exposed her and her nephew to but the fact that, as a woman in this job, she was still expected to be the 'softer' side of the police. That was why she was spending her Saturday standing on the sidelines of the Antoinette Tubman stadium preparing to watch the finals of the National Child Protection Football Tournament. Even the title made her cringe. She really would have preferred to be at home drinking a few cold beers. But instead, here she was waiting to make a speech before the final match started.

She could see her nephew, Abu, making his way across the field towards her. This was the other reason she could not have avoided the tournament. Having encouraged Abu to be a bit more socially responsible she could only express delight when he and his friend Morris managed to put together this project, bringing together football teams from across the city, holding workshops on children's rights culminating in the tournament itself. Of course she admired his ability to garner sufficient resources to put the tournament on and his natural aptitude for publicity, she just wished she didn't have to be here. The tournament was being supported by international agencies, various government ministries and by the President's office, so there was no way Gloria could avoid it. She looked around the stadium again, amazed at the momentum the project had gathered – the stands were full and there were still people pouring in. Everyone wanted to be seen to be part of such a worthy cause.

Gloria wasn't especially fond of football, and certainly didn't believe one tournament was going to change very much. On the other hand, it had kept Abu and his friends busy and looked like being a fun day for a lot of children. How could she complain about that?

The lead up to the tournament had been marked by the usual complaints and accusations; some of the entry fee money had disappeared, volunteer referees and officials had been accused of partiality, one game had been cancelled because a visiting team claimed the opposition was using witchcraft and the trophy had been stolen – twice.

The trophy had also been recovered twice and was now being guarded by two smartly uniformed soldiers. Gloria had donated the trophy and she knew it was not worth more than twenty dollars – one of her friends had bought it in a trophy shop in Accra according to Gloria's instructions that she wanted something 'big, shiny and cheap'.

She strongly suspected that Abu, with his newfound talent for publicity, knew more about the theft and subsequent recovery of the trophy than he was letting on. It had been stolen from Abu and his committee while they were taking it around town to different media houses to discuss the project; lifted once from the back of the taxi they were in and snatched right out of his hands, the second time, as they were leaving the offices of The Eye newspaper.

The trophy had been recovered both times by groups of street children who had variously 'found it' in the cemetery and 'snatched it back' from the thieves. The result had been the widest possible coverage for the tournament. They had been on the front page of most of the local newspapers, been interviewed on radio and, on a slow news day, had even got a mention on the BBC World Service. Gloria was more than a little suspicious about the timings of the thefts and the swift recoveries but Abu had denied knowledge of any publicity stunts. Well actually, she realised afterwards, he had said he wouldn't do 'nothing to spoil the competition' which wasn't nearly the same thing. Interest in the tournament had rocketed, resources had poured in and there were rumours that the Ministry of Youth and Sports were thinking of making it an annual event. She admired his enterprise, but decided she was going to have to keep a close eye on her nephew.

Bursting with excitement and importance, Abu finally made it through the crowds and bounded up to her with a gaggle of fellow officials in his wake.

'Aunt Glo, are you ready to speak now? You'll have to talk loud, the sound system is not working properly, it keeps hissing and then going off.'

'Oh great, I'll just shout then shall I?'

'Yes, that'll be fine, thanks.' He was more than a little harassed so she didn't press him.

The sound system wasn't the only problem they had; Liberia's most famous footballer, Abraham Kanneh, had turned up unexpectedly with a crowd of his fans, creating havoc at the gate, half of the refreshments had disappeared en route to the stadium and, to cap it all, the Executive Mansion had just sent a message to say that the President herself was coming to present the trophy to the winning team. Gloria wasn't surprised; President Helen Sirleaf was a big supporter of youth initiatives and was also very shrewd about being seen to be so, but Gloria was not looking forward to the increased security. After her grandson had been kidnapped, security around the President and her family had become very tight. But anyway, it wasn't her responsibility. She waved to Inspector Barnyou, the Head of CID, who was making his way through the crowd to her. Now here was a man with a tense day ahead of him.

'Morning Gloria, this is a great way to spend a Saturday eh!' Barnyou had been confirmed in his post as Head of CID and Gloria sensed that he was finally beginning to enjoy the job.

'And to think I've got my own nephew to blame for this. I should have known he would never be satisfied with a few teams playing football. No, Abu has to have everyone and their wife here.'

Barnyou looked around the stadium. It did look like a 'Who's Who' of Liberia. The Ministers of Education, Youth and Sport, Social Welfare and Health were all there along with the directors of international agencies, the sporting elite and representatives of Monrovia's oldest families. 'How did he persuade all of them to turn up for this?'

'Oh you know what it's like. Once one signs up they all have to be seen here and demonstrate how committed they are to children.'

'I hate to spoil your day Gloria but is that Africanus Varley who has just come in?'

She looked over and saw the unmistakeable figure of Varley going up to the VIP section with a large entourage. As well as being a very successful businessman from a powerful family and a close confidante of the rich and powerful, Africanus Varley was also a murdering, power-hungry, misogynist sociopath – in Gloria's humble opinion. He had narrowly escaped Gloria's clutches during her last investigation but she hadn't given up on him, not by a long shot.

'Yes, that's him. He seems to have recovered quickly from his son's imprisonment and losing custody of his grandson.'

'Yes, and none of that has dented his place in society I see. Those VIP seats are not easy to get.' Barnyou looked disgusted. 'What about the grandson, how is he doing?'

Gloria shrugged. 'He made it clear he wanted to stay with Lawrence's mother so Peter Dennis has made it an official foster placement.'

Barnyou laughed. 'You mean you told the Minister of Social Welfare what you wanted to see happen!'

Gloria said nothing; she was still staring at Africanus Varley. Every time she saw him it reawakened her fury that someone like him was still treated with such deference. She gave herself a shake and laughed. 'Oh, Peter is ok. He actually cares about people and he's doing a good job. But someone needs to talk to him about his clothes.'

She pointed to a figure in a white suit and purple bow tie standing a few rows down from them. Peter Dennis was never seen without a suit and his signature bow tie, but on a Saturday morning at a stadium he did stand out from the crowd. The press had a lot of fun with that but, as he said himself, the result was that everyone knew who the Minister of Social Welfare was and, in that quirky Liberian way, support for the work of the Ministry had increased enormously. Everyone was a politician here.

'While you've gone for the very casual look I see.' In her grey sweatpants, white t-shirt and baseball cap Gloria looked unusually relaxed. He gave a mock salute. 'And I like the cap Gloria.' The baseball cap, which Gloria had found in the market in Waterside, bore the legend 'Oslo Eurovision' in bright red letters.

'Mmm well, I thought it was something to do with a collective political vision for a united Europe, so I got it in preference to all the ones with the names of American football teams on them.' Barnyou made a puzzled face. 'Turns out though, it's actually some awful singing competition. So why it's called Eurovision instead of Eurovoice I don't know. Just another strange thing about Europeans, I suppose. And really not a suitable cap for me.' Barnyou laughed. Gloria's off-key singing was almost as famous as her legendary bad cooking.

'Well, I'll see you around. I better go and check on my people Gloria, before the old ma arrives.'

The 'old ma' or the President, as she was more properly known, would not arrive until the tournament was almost finished but Gloria knew Barnyou would want to check on his men. The public image of the police had suffered some serious blows recently and he would not want any mistakes today.

'I'm going over to make my speech now anyway,' she rolled her eyes. 'Luckily the sound system isn't working so no-one will hear my carefully prepared words.'

'Oh, right, so you haven't actually thought about what you're going to say yet?'

She just nodded. Preparing speeches was something Gloria hated doing and always put off until the last minute, in this case the very last minute. She made her way through the crowd shaking hands and shouting greetings at people. It was all very good-natured. Monrovia on a sunny Saturday morning, with the prospect of hot food, cold beer and football, was a great place to be. She reached the podium, where Abu was ushering people to their seats.

'Aunt Glo,' he was definitely flustered now, 'please wait a minute. Abraham Kanneh is here.'

Gloria nodded. 'I saw him arrive.'

'Well, I want to ask him to say something too, is that fine with you?' Gloria nodded again. Abraham Kanneh was Liberia's best-known celebrity, of course he should say something. Abu disappeared again and came back a few minutes later with the man in tow.

Kanneh flashed his famous smile at her and shook her hand. 'Inspector Gloria,' he had more than a touch of an American drawl about his speech, 'it is great to meet you.'

Gloria was suddenly conscious how short she must look next to this rangy footballer. 'And great to meet you too, a real celebrity.'

Kanneh laughed. 'Come on Inspector, celebrity comes in all shapes and sizes in Liberia.'

Gloria stared at him 'And today we've got the tall and the short, is that it?' They both laughed then.

'But seriously Inspector you must know that celebrity can be a really bad thing here.'

The Liberian public were famous for their quick changes of mood, and adulation could turn into aggression very easily. Kanneh's house had been attacked and set on fire the last time the national team had lost an international game.

'Oh yes, lose a game or lose a case and we're both finished.'

Abu prevented any further discussion by arriving with a sheet of paper and announcing they were going to start. Kanneh was to go first and then Gloria would open the tournament.

Gloria sat back, trying to string some thoughts together but she was distracted by Kanneh's antics. He hadn't given a speech; instead he had issued a challenge to any girl in the stadium to take him on at nafu, a game which was played almost exclusively by girls. It involved two people hopping, skipping and clapping in various complicated sequences until one was declared the winner. Abraham Kanneh was very good at it and had the whole stadium laughing, clapping and cheering as one after the other girls came up onto the podium and then left again. He ended his performance with just a few words and then sat down to huge cheers.

Great, thought Gloria, I get to follow the star performance of Liberia's tallest national hero. She went to the microphone, determined to get it over quickly. 'I want to say thank you to the organisers of today's events and,' she looked over to the VIP seating hoping to catch Africanus Varley's eye, 'I hope that today will remind us that we all have the responsibility to make our communities and our schools safe places for children.' She was going to add more but she could see the crowd were already getting restless so, before she lost their attention completely, she wished all the teams a good days sport and stood back while the army band struck up their creaky version of the national anthem.

Before the last notes of 'All Hail Liberia, Hail' had died away the podium was swarming with people, most of them heading for Kanneh, to shake his hand or ask for a favour. Gloria stepped back into the crowd. She had spotted her deputy, Captain Moses Anderson, waving at her from a few feet away. Moses was just back from a six-week vacation in Philadelphia which, he maintained, would have been more enjoyable if it had just been about six weeks shorter.

'Good speech boss.'

'You mean short, I presume.'

'Yeeesss,' he stretched it out as if unwilling to admit it, 'that as well. Are you staying for the day?'

Gloria nodded. 'Not much choice really. Abu will not be pleased if I disappear, plus the fact everyone seems to think that being head of Family and Child Protection means I have to attend every programme and event with the word 'child' in it. Have you any idea how many invitations I have on my desk?'

'Twenty-seven.' He looked at her. 'I was just catching up with things, you know, all the cases I've missed. There doesn't seem to be anything too interesting.' They looked at each other for a few seconds until Gloria spoke.

'I suppose we should be grateful really Moses. Maybe Mama Liberia is finally on the road to recovery.' She would have cause to remember those words a few hours later.

By two in the afternoon the noise of the sirens coming down the hill announced the arrival of the President. The large gates of the stadium were standing open and the outriders swept in followed by several cars and finally the armoured jeep of the President. The relaxed atmosphere stiffened as Monrovians reacted with their usual mixture of awe and resentment at this display. But the President waved cheerily to the crowds as, in jeans and t-shirt, she climbed up to the VIP area and sat down with very little ceremony. Gloria breathed a sigh of relief when she heard Leo, one of Abu's closest friends, invite the finalists to get onto the field. The day was almost over.

It didn't take long to see there was something wrong however. Even Gloria knew that there could not be three teams in a football final, but there were definitely three teams on the pitch. She saw Abu go on to speak to the referee. The referee was Hassan Black, the national coach for the u-18 team and a well-respected figure, but even his remonstrations were having no effect and, after ten minutes discussion in the centre of the field, there were still three teams milling around. Well, it wouldn't be a Liberian final without some controversy, but Gloria's heart sank when she eventually saw Barnyou's uniformed officers come onto the pitch and escort one of the teams off. Admittedly it was all done very easily, with no fuss, but she could already see the headlines in Monday's newspapers, Police arrest children at child protection football tournament. As the whistle went for the delayed kick-off, she decided she had better go down and see what was happening.

There was a lot of noise in the dressing room but Barnyou was laughing so she guessed it wasn't too serious. The children were all milling around Abu who was trying to make himself heard above the general clamour. Barnyou came over to her laughing out loud now.

'I think we can just observe Gloria, I don't think we need to arrest anyone here unless you want to rescue Abu?'

'Rescue him? Oh no, he'll do fine, just watch. What happened anyway?'

'Oh the usual, these are the New Kru Town Defenders and they claim that they should be in the final, even though everyone else agrees they lost their last game.'

Abu was not shouting above the noise of the protest. Instead, Gloria noticed, he was standing with his arms folded looking at the crowd of angry players. He was waiting. And he carried on waiting until eventually the team got tired of shouting out the same things over and over and they fell silent. Still he waited a bit longer. When he started to talk it was in a quiet voice.

'Let me tell you something, the way you all acted today was not good,' he paused when the muttering started again until it died down. 'You say we cheated you but let's leave that one for now. Let's look at today. We organised this football tournament and we brought all the big people together to watch you, so we can prove that we, the youth, are responsible, respectful, and now you people are acting just like old rebels.' Gloria cringed but the boys didn't react. 'So what do you think they will be saying about us now?' He sucked his teeth and shook his head. 'Tha so so rebel children we got in this town now,' he mimicked the harsh cries of the market women and the boys laughed. They knew he was right, that's just what they would be saying. 'So, forget about your grumbles, I beg you, we can look at that after. For now, I want all of you out in the stadium clapping and cheering for one of the teams in the final. Do you get me?'

There was a silence, until a short boy at the front who had been leading the protest piped up. 'Big brother, sorry-oh but the people did cheat us... but anyway you are right. We not supposed to act like this, not today. Even the old ma is here watching.' He turned to his teammates and with a simple 'Leh go now' he led the way back into the stadium.

Abu grinned at Gloria across the room and put his thumbs up. Then he was out into the stadium himself.

'Impressive,' Gloria recognized Lawrence's voice and turned round, 'that nephew of yours is some organiser.'

Gloria smiled and shrugged. 'Well if we ever get to host the Olympic Games or the World Cup then we'll know who to ask. Shouldn't you be hovering around your vehicle?'

Lawrence, Head of Traffic and also in charge of the presidential motorcade, showed her a tiny earpiece. 'I'll know as soon as anything happens.'

'Well I hope so, as all the senior police officers in the stadium are currently standing in this smelly changing room.'

Barnyou laughed. 'I'm out of here. See you later.'

'We better go too I suppose,' Gloria adjusted her cap, 'although I am not officially on duty.'

'Really? I can see most of your team out there, including Alfred and Izena and it's their engagement party tomorrow.' Lawrence always knew things like that.

'Oh, Alfred had to be here, Abu's orders. He's a senior match official.'

'What does a senior match...'

'Don't know Lawrence and really don't care.' They were back in the main stand now. She grinned. 'Let's hope we don't have to find out. I'll see you later, maybe this evening?' He smiled warmly and nodded.

The game finally ended in a 1-0 victory for the Congo Town Lions and Gloria made her way back to the podium, along with Abraham Kanneh, for the presentation. She eyed the sky anxiously. There were huge dark clouds massing and it looked as if they might be in for one of September's spectacular end-of-rainy-season thunderstorms. Abu and his officials had wisely abandoned any more speeches and the President and her entourage joined them on the podium.

It was hard to make conversation above the howling of the wind but Gloria managed to get a hug from Prince, the President's grandson, and a smile from the President who was struggling to keep her cap on. 'You are always in the middle of some storm or other Gloria, aren't you?' Gloria grinned. 'What to do ma'am… at least this should be over quickly.'

People were already streaming out of the stadium by the time the team had lined up to accept the trophy and their medals. They might just make it, Gloria thought, before the cloudburst. The sky had darkened and there was now a strong wind blowing. She could see the roof over the podium swaying as the team walked towards the President who lifted the cup high, for a cheer from the crowd, and then turned to present it to the team captain. Even as she was fighting to hold on to the trophy, while papers, cups and leaflets were all blown off the podium, there was a definite murmur around the stadium, audible even over the keening of the wind. The team were staring upwards and all eyes in the stadium were now on the swaying podium roof. At first Gloria thought the sheets of zinc were coming loose but it wasn't just that. On the edge of the flapping sheet of zinc something long was flailing in the wind. The team were now pointing, cup and medals forgotten, and even the President looked up. With one last mighty gush of wind the sheet of zinc flipped up and over and tipped the odd-shaped bundle, the cause of everyone's curiosity, off the roof. It was a body.

The world froze for a second and the President, trophy still in hand, could only stare in horror as the body thudded down onto the table right in front of her, knocking the cap off her head and cracking the table legs, sending it collapsing down the podium steps, carrying the body with it. Gloria pulled Prince out of the way while the President's security team surged forward surrounding her, shouting orders and pulling out guns. There was a collective scream around the stadium and the winning team scattered back off the podium, jumping the short distance to the field. Gloria handed Prince to a nearby security officer and ran down the steps to the broken table and the shattered body still splayed out on it. It was a child, lying on her back staring up with open unseeing eyes. She shivered, knowing the chill on her back had nothing to do with the wind or the rain. Then the President's security team started moving again, Colonel Toweh half carrying the President to her vehicle in their anxiety to get her away from the scene, while the rest of them scattered around the podium to make sure no-one else came near. There was no danger of that, however; people were climbing over the fence and squeezing through the gates in a panicked evacuation. Then with a deafening crack of thunder the clouds opened and a torrent of rain poured down.

Chapter Two

It only took an hour for the stadium to clear and some kind of order to be restored but it felt like a lifetime. The President and Prince had been taken away but some of her security had remained behind to assist with the clearing up. Abraham Kanneh's team had been almost as efficient, and he had been whisked away at the same time. Miraculously enough, no-one else had been injured. The downpour had quenched the panic somehow and people had slowed a little to get through the mud that formed instantly on all the paths out the stadium. No-one had looked back.

The only positive, thought Gloria, was that with several senior police officers already in the stadium, there was no need to send for anyone. This dead child had been seen by a lot of people, although thankfully most of them only from a distance. It was a shocking sight. A girl of about eleven or twelve, her wounds were obvious and violent; long straight gashes on both sides of her body, deep wounds which had gouged out flesh and bone leaving her body terribly disfigured but her face untouched. The fall from the podium roof had obviously broken more bones and the body still lay at an impossible angle. But it was the face Gloria came back to. The girl had been very pretty, that was obvious even in death, and she was wearing carefully applied make-up; lipstick in a vivid purple and eye makeup in the same colour with glitter on her cheeks and tiny little beads and jewels woven into her elaborate hairstyle. She looked like a little doll which the family dog had chewed up and spat out.

It was still raining and the rumbling thunder boomed out above the stadium. Barnyou's officers were holding large pieces of tarpaulin over the body to shield it from the pounding rain, but everyone else was soaked through to the skin. They had agreed to send for Dr Armah before moving the body. Dr Armah was one of Ghana's foremost forensic pathologists and he was on secondment to the Liberian government for three months to train and upgrade their pathology laboratory services. Unfortunately, speed did not seem to be one of his many attributes and it was an hour and a half before he was found and persuaded to come down to the scene.

Dr Armah was short and very fat but he smiled at everyone as he arrived, as if he was going to give them a guided tour of some ancient monument. As soon as he saw the body, however, his face changed. He took off his jacket and knelt down in the sopping grass beside it, and for the next ten minutes studied the body in silence. He then proceeded to talk out loud, as if they were a class of students.

'Is this how you found her?'

Barnyou explained the circumstances and that they had not moved the body at all. Armah nodded encouragingly as if he was addressing an unexpectedly bright student in one of his classes. 'Very good, very good.' He didn't seem to notice the rain, which was pouring onto his legs, and feet where they stuck out of the tarpaulin, absorbed in the close examination of the wounds. 'Um, well the cause of death would seem to be obvious; internal damage, loss of blood and shock of course but the wounds are very interesting.'

Gloria frowned. 'Interesting' just sounded like the wrong word here.

'The only times I see wounds like these in Ghana are on farmers, hunters or children who have been attacked by some kind of animal.'

'What kind of animal?'

'Well, I can't say here but something big and powerful. I will need to examine the body more closely. You can take the body to the morgue now. The child was not killed here though, I can tell you that; there would have been a lot more blood. She was killed somewhere else and then placed up there.' He looked up at the roof, narrowing his eyes against the wall of rain and muttered to himself. 'Very strange.' He leaned down and very gently closed the girl's eyes at the same time rubbing his finger across her eyelids. He stood up and stepped back into the full downpour and started shaking hands with them all. 'I will take a closer look when the body is in the morgue. And bring the sheet of zinc, I need to look at that as well.' Barnyou indicated the zinc sheet covered by another piece of tarpaulin already on the back of a pickup. 'Good. Now,' Armah seemed to notice for the first time that he was soaking wet, 'I better get some dry clothes before I do anything else.' And with a cheery smile he was off.

Moments later the body was being driven off to the newly refurbished morgue at the government's JFK Medical Centre. Barnyou gathered Moses and Gloria under the sparse shelter of the remaining podium roof where they stood in silence for a few moments staring gloomily at the rain.

'Well Barnyou we are all tired and wet so…'

Barnyou looked exhausted. 'I know Gloria but I just want us to agree on some things before we leave.'

'We can agree it's a murder of a child.'

'It's a killing all right but by a human being or an animal?' He shrugged and then pulled his damp jacket tighter around him. 'I'm not sure I like the idea of a wild animal on the loose any better than a murderer.'

Gloria glared at him. 'That was no animal Barnyou, just the human kind.'

'Well Dr Armah…'

'Dr Armah was just being careful. You saw the way he traced the length of both of the wounds. They were too straight and too even. No animal claws are like that.' Gloria hesitated, 'Well, as far as I know.' Her experience with wildlife was quite limited and her actual confrontation with it even more so. 'But yes, we better wait until he examines the body more carefully.'

'Ok, but I want us to agree that you, and your team of course,' he added hurriedly looking at Moses, 'will stay involved in the case, whatever he finds.'

Given his previous resistance this should have felt like a victory but all Gloria could think about was that small doll-like figure lying broken in the rain. She gave herself a mental shake and nodded agreement to Barnyou. 'Of course. And right now we need to try and identify her.'

'All that make-up on a young girl, I can only think she was working the streets.' Moses said.

'Right, good point Moses. That's where we'll start. I have some photos,' Gloria took out her digital camera, 'I'll print these off and go round the streets tonight and have a word with the girls. I know a lot of them. And with their madams.' Moses looked at her. 'I'll be fine on my own Moses and it will be easier for them to talk to me. I better get home first and see how Abu is. He put a lot of work into this tournament. I'm sure he's beginning to think that death and disaster follow me around.'

'I'll clear up here Gloria,' offered Barnyou, 'and if Moses stays we can work out our next moves. We can't wait till Monday on this one. The President's security chief is still here.'

'Toweh?'

Barnyou nodded glumly. Toweh had not forgiven him for his false arrest in their last case so their relationship remained uneasy. 'They'll want to know if it was an attack on the President or a threat.'

'Too clumsy I think. No-one could predict the body would fall off at that precise moment, and not much of an attack. Besides, there were other people there. Kanneh for example attracts a lot of attention.'

'Or maybe it was just some child who crossed the wrong people.' She thought of Varley again. 'Either way we better move quickly. The story will be all over the papers on Monday so that only gives us tomorrow for a start.'

As she walked to her car Gloria remembered guiltily that only hours earlier she and Moses had been lamenting the lack of any interesting cases. She was pretty sure the discovery of a dead child in these circumstances could not be described as interesting but it was a sharp reminder that the work of re-building Liberia into a safe place for children still had a long way to go.

The rain had eased off by the time she got home which was good as her red Polo did not like getting wet, but the sky remained dark with thick banks of clouds and wispy trails over the grey sea. The post-rain humidity was always more oppressive too so Gloria was soaked through again by the time she reached her apartment. Abu, Morris, Rahul and Leo were sitting around the table deep in serious discussion.

'Hey guys, how are you doing? I thought you might be feeling bad at how your tournament ended.'

'Bad for the girl Auntie but our tournament was over, and we still have the cup because Congo Lions got scared and ran away,' they laughed, 'we are calling them Congo Kittens now, and if they want the cup they will have to come for it.'

That didn't sound very sporting to Gloria but she knew the politics and culture of Liberian football, even youth football, was way beyond her.

'Who is the girl Aunt Glo?' The boys hadn't seen the wounds or the state of the body so she could forgive them their light tone but she really didn't want to discuss it. 'We don't know yet.'

'There was a scout at the tournament today, Aunt Glo, a real one.' So that was the cause of the excitement she thought.

'Oh, and what does a scout do?'

'You know, finds teams for young players, abroad.'

Gloria didn't pursue that. 'Well congratulations, you all did a great job. I have to go out tonight Abu but I've arranged for your grandma to send up food, so you can celebrate.' She caught his look, 'Yes it's jollof rice, and I'll leave money for soft drinks.'

She took a shower, sat down with a cup of coffee and by six thirty she was ready. She had to time it right. If she went too early, there wouldn't be anyone around, too late and, well, all the girls would be busy or, if they weren't, they wouldn't be keen to talk to a police officer, and Gloria was too well known now to try and go incognito. She printed off some headshots of the murdered girl and drove down to Gurley Street.

It was already getting dark and Gurley Street was buzzing. Small bars lined both sides of the road, the loud tinny music from each one forming a cacophony that was more an assault on the eardrums than an invitation to dance. There were five video clubs all advertising very nasty-looking adult films – all African judging by the lurid posters Gloria glanced at – and lots of people selling roasted meat and fish on the coal pots by the side of the road. And there were the girls, lots of them, in the bars, on the side of the road, leaning out of windows and doorways. Gloria had been down here many times but she never failed to feel defeated by it all. The cheap glitter of Gurley Street on a Saturday night just emphasised for her how far they still had to go to improve life for children especially. There were children everywhere; serving in the bars, watching adult movies, selling food and worst of all standing at the side of the road trying to attract men. The night was full of noise, and the smells of cheap perfume, frying oil and sewage from the open pipes hung in the humid air.

Gloria pushed all that to one side and made her way to a small flight of steps leading down to a very dark porch and a battered wooden door. She knocked the door calling 'Bentu, it's me, Gloria.' The door opened immediately and a tall thin girl smiled out at her. When she was sure it was Gloria the door swung all the way open and Bentu came out.

'Gloria, it's a bit late for you to be here is it not?' Bentu Stewart, at twenty-three, was a veteran of the streets and a consummate survivor. She had come to Monrovia when her village near Ganta was attacked by rebels during the war. A rebel commander had taken her as a 'wife,' when his forces overran the city, and she stayed with him until the peacekeepers had retaken control. Since then she had been the girlfriend of a UN official, a deputy minister of Lands and Mines and even, it was rumoured, one of Liberia's famous footballers. By her own admission she had enjoyed her life; the clothes and perfumes, the fine apartments, the jewellery and the attention. But her growing drug habit and her fading looks had set her firmly on a familiar but depressing path. She now lived in a windowless room in the ghetto of Gurley Street, about three quarters of the way down the ladder to complete destitution, Gloria reckoned. But tonight, at least, she was sober and calm; Gloria had arrived just in time.

They sat on a rickety bench at the door; there was no question of going into the room. Gloria had known Bentu for a few years and tried to help her or at least slow down the inevitable decline. Two weeks ago Bentu had come to see her at the station, very angry and distressed. She had spent the night with a man from the Indian peacekeeping contingent. In the morning he refused to pay her the paltry sum he had promised, and when she persisted in demanding her money he had beaten her and thrown her out. Gloria still remembered his shocked expression when he opened his door later that day to find Bentu, accompanied by a furious Gloria in full uniform. He had paid then, double what he had promised and extra for Bentu to go to a clinic, while his fellow officers sniggered and laughed at him. Not a great triumph, Gloria thought, but very satisfying.

She explained to Bentu what had happened at the stadium that day and showed her the picture. Bentu looked at it for a long time but shook her head. 'Sorry ma, I don't know her. I can show the picture around if you want but I don't think that girl is from around here.' She looked at Gloria and pointed at the photograph. 'That high-class make-up, the hair… It's too good for around here you know. She looks high class.' Gloria looked at the picture again. It was true, even in death the girl's face looked in better condition than many of the girls on Gurley Street.

'Thanks Bentu, that's useful but show the picture around anyway just in case. I'm going to see Madam Walker, maybe she can tell me something.' Bentu nodded again 'For a price maybe!' Gloria agreed, Madam Doreen Walker did nothing without a payment.

Doreen Walker was not called madam as a term of respect; it was also her job title. She had set up one of the first brothels on Gurley Street years before the war and her empire had grown ever since. She now controlled most of the official brothels on Gurley Street and, Gloria heard, had expanded outside the city for richer clients. Her wealth and her client base had also given her enormous influence and access to a lot of information. But she was no warm-hearted stereotype. Doreen Walker looked at the whole world from the viewpoint of her own advantage.

The street was even noisier when Gloria got back up. Lines of UN and aid agency vehicles had joined the taxis and cars parked outside the bars and clubs. Business was going to be good tonight. Gloria walked across the road and passed between two of the bars where customers were packed in from the bar to the door and the volume of the laughter and shouting was already drowning out the music. Gloria saw a few faces she recognised and waved in at a group of ex-pats who had commandeered the tables closest to the bar. Hans, clearly the leader of the party, came over to her.

'Gloria, how are you?'

'I'm all right Hans. What's the celebration, someone at IRS having a birthday or something?' The International Rescue Service was one of the biggest agencies working in the country. Gloria liked some of the staff and a few of their projects. Hans coordinated their work in Monrovia and sat on the Child Safety Committee with her.

'No, better than a birthday it's a leaving party for Kopius.' John Kopius was the IRS director and he hadn't come out well of Gloria's first investigation.

'Really, I don't see him.'

'Oh he's not been invited; we are celebrating the fact that he is going. He has become more and more irrational these past few months. I don't think he ever recovered from the discovery that some of his friends were associated with a trafficking ring. It's not a good image for us.'

'It wasn't very good for the children either,' Gloria raised an eyebrow at him, 'but John wasn't involved, they fooled him as they fooled a lot of people.'

Hans shrugged. 'Whatever it was, he has been getting worse and worse, impossible to work with. They are pulling him out next week. Come and have a beer with us.'

Gloria thought that a cold Club beer sounded like heaven but she shook her head.

'Can't tonight Hans. Following up on something. I'll see you in the week though.'

She left them to their noise and walked into the dark alley between the bars, careful where she placed her feet. There could be anything down there, literally anything. Or nothing, she thought, as her flashlight picked out a huge hole where the drainage system had collapsed. The noise subsided a little as she went down the alley but the heat and the smells were suffocating. Gloria had been brought up in Westpoint so she was well used to both of those but tonight they seemed to be affecting her more, maybe she was tired after the day.

She was concentrating so much on the road that she almost fell into the yard at the end of the alley. There was one house there, a large two-storey building that would not have looked out of place with the mansions of Mamba Point and Congo Town. The courtyard in front of the house was small but spotlessly clean. A plum tree with a small wooden bench under it dominated the space and there was even a cool breeze although Gloria could not, for the life of her, see where it could be coming from.

'Welcome to my little oasis Inspector. I heard you were looking for me.'

Gloria didn't know if this was true or if Doreen Walker was just good at making the most of a situation. She liked to be in control, that Gloria did know from previous encounters with her.

'Please sit down. Let me get you a drink.' Doreen loved to play the part of gracious hostess. She was a small woman, always neatly dressed but without being showy. But she reminded Gloria of her school principal, easy to overlook but with a core of steel.

Gloria looked around; the place was so tidy and ordered, in stark contrast to the work Doreen was involved in. Her eye caught a small painted picture which was nailed just above the door. It was a religious icon, she could see that, but not the details.

'Ah, I see you looking at my picture Inspector,' Doreen spoke with clear unaccented and very proper English, 'do you know her?'

Gloria shook her head. 'I'm not very strong on religious art.'

'It's an icon of St Mary of Egypt.' This didn't set off any lightbulbs in Gloria's head. 'She was the most famous prostitute in Egypt; rich, beautiful, independent. Then she went on a pilgrimage to Jerusalem, mostly to seduce the other pilgrims, and had a great time. Finally she tried to enter some famous church there but couldn't, an invisible force kept her from going in. So she went off into the desert and spent the rest of her life in penance.'

Gloria didn't know what to say to this. Doreen laughed loudly and harshly. 'I just think if there's anyone in heaven who might have some time for me it will be her, plus we do have some things in common. I mean I may not be beautiful but if I tried to get into any church in this town I am sure there's a lot of people would stop me.' She laughed again.

'Most of them your customers I suspect,' Gloria added.

Doreen only smiled at this. 'True Inspector, but that kind of information is only to be shared when you absolutely need to, otherwise people will stop using my services.'

Gloria snorted, 'I don't think so. Anyway I need some information from you Doreen.' She saw her stiffen. Information was Doreen's stock in trade.

'Information is as much my business as my girls are Inspector. You don't just give it away.'

I bet you say that to all the girls, Gloria thought to herself and smiled. 'I just want you to look at a photo and tell me if you know the person. Only that. It may be in your interest. If she is one of your girls it could mean problems for you.

Doreen looked at her. 'Alright, just a look then.' She took the photo from Gloria and stared at it. 'Very beautiful.' Gloria could see from her face this was no aesthetic appreciation, this was Doreen the madam measuring beauty in terms of profit.

'And very young Doreen, don't you think.'

Doreen put the photo on the table but close to her as if she wanted to keep it. She shrugged. 'I don't know her, never seen her before.'

'Look Doreen, forget the age, if this is one of your girls…'

Doreen shook her head again. 'I don't know her. But I should know her.' She picked up the photo again. 'This girl has been carefully prepared which means someone else is running a business on my territory without my permission. Where is she from?'

'We don't know, that's why we are asking. She was found dead today at the stadium, dropped in on us you might say.'

'If someone else was running a business around here I would hear about it Inspector so I suspect this girl was not for the domestic market.'

'The domestic market…'

'I mean, she was being sent abroad, trafficked, sold whatever you call it, it's obvious. A girl like this would make a lot of money for someone.'

'Then why kill her?'

'There could be any number of reasons. Many girls who are trafficked think they are going to get married or get a job or an education. They are enticed not forced, the forcing starts when they are out of their own country. And sometimes it even happens by accident. If she changed her mind before she left…' She let the sentence hang in the air.

'You sound very knowledgeable Doreen, how do you know so much about trafficking?'

Doreen looked at her. 'Not knowledge Inspector, personal experience. You want to hear a story of accidental trafficking?' Gloria leaned back, this had been an unusual conversation so far, she might as well get the rest of it. She nodded. Doreen filled her glass again and the opened her bag. 'Let me show you a picture.' She handed Gloria a small faded photograph. In it three young African women were standing with a European woman in front of St Peter's Basilica in Rome. Gloria recognised it from a print in her mum's house. The European was in the full outfit of a nun: long dress and veil, rosary and cross. The three young women were wearing white dresses and short white veils with a small cross on a silver chain. The middle one was unmistakably Doreen Walker. Gloria looked up at her, waiting for the story.

'Yes, that's Sr Doreen, if only for a short time. Some nuns came to my school way back and talked to us about joining them. We were poor, very poor, and I thought it looked like a great life and eventually I went to Rome with those two,' she pointed to the others, 'and we joined the Sisters of Compassion Order. I loved it until Mother Superior came to my room one morning and told me they had decided I did not have a vocation and they were sending me back home. To make the story short I knew I could not come back to live in a village here so I ran away. There's not much work in Rome for poorly educated Africans so I joined the other girls on the streets… doing whatever I had to do to survive. When I finally saved enough money and came back here I used my experience to open my own business. So I consider myself to have been accidentally trafficked. You do see how people can end up in all kinds of situations for many different reasons.'

Gloria nodded but couldn't help adding, 'Interesting story Doreen but how does that make your business ok? I would have thought you would have wanted to help other girls.'

Doreen's face hardened. 'I am helping them, I run establishments which are clean and where girls are safe and protected. And yes, I am making money but that is business. None of my girls have ever been killed.'

There was a silence and then Gloria picked up the photo again. 'Well, will you at least help me? If you hear anything will you let me know?' But Doreen had obviously taken offence and just pursed her lips.

As she was leaving Gloria thought she probably could have handled the interview better, like many of her other interviews. It wouldn't have taken much to pander to her a little, make her feel interesting and important. That's what Doreen would have liked, but Gloria was tired and, whatever her background story, as far as Gloria was concerned Doreen was just another abuser.

Saturday night party time was in full swing when Gloria reached the road again. She could see it was going to be impossible to get sense out of anyone else. It was time to go home.

Chapter Three

It was late on Sunday morning before Gloria woke up and it was the door buzzer that eventually dragged her out of sleep. It was Lawrence looking bright and shiny. He gave her that 'Do you need some time to get ready' look which really meant 'Please go and get ready.'

Gloria had forgotten Lawrence was coming round. It had become a regular Sunday morning thing; Abu and Rahul from downstairs went off to football practice and she, Lawrence and Rohit, Rahul's uncle, had breakfast together. Rohit brought most of the food, Gloria supplied the coffee and Lawrence came with all the latest news from around town, as supplied to him by his many and varied sources. It usually lasted until the boys came back from practice.

By the time Gloria joined them Rohit had spread the food out, a mixture of Indian and Liberian dishes, and Lawrence had made the coffee. They were sitting on her small balcony watching the early birds arriving at Mickey's Bar for their brunch. It was surprisingly cool, as if the storm had washed the oppressive humidity away for a while. The sky was blue and the breeze from the ocean strong enough to keep the curtains moving gently, all helping to make a very relaxing atmosphere. No-one mentioned the previous day's events until they had eaten most of the food. It wasn't until he was pouring Gloria her third cup of coffee that Rohit finally brought up the subject.

'You had a busy day yesterday Inspector ma'am.' Rohit was always unfailingly polite. 'The boys were telling me about the body. Very dramatic.' His tone also implied that at least this time the drama had taken place somewhere outside the apartment block. Rohit had come to her rescue on a number of occasions.

'Of course, everyone is asking how it could happen that a dead body could be dropped right in front of the President.'

Gloria looked at Lawrence. 'Well it was just bad luck. No-one knew the President was going to be there until the last minute and the body only dropped because the wind took part of the roof off otherwise it could have been there for days.'

'Bad luck! When was that ever taken as an explanation here? No, a lot of people are saying it's a conspiracy to scare her. Others are saying it's witchcraft.'

Gloria rolled her eyes. 'I wondered how long it would take before witchcraft was brought in. The point is she was a girl of eleven or twelve who was murdered in a terrible way and then dumped on a roof.' They fell silent until her phone's 'Sweet Liberia' ringtone made them jump. It was Barnyou.

'Sorry to disturb your Sunday Gloria but Dr Armah is going to the morgue to look at the body. I just wondered if you wanted to come down.'

'I won't Abraham. I drew a blank yesterday on Gurley Street but I want to go back this evening and talk to some of the girls again. You can give me the report on Armah's findings.' Barnyou agreed and rang off.

When she looked up both Rohit and Lawrence were staring at her with genuine amazement. 'Oh don't start you two, I made a promise to Abu that we would visit my mum this afternoon so I can't be at the morgue can I?' Neither of them said anything. 'But I will just see what Moses is doing.' She called him up and glared at Lawrence as she heard him say to Rohit: 'Have you noticed that it doesn't matter where you are with her Rohit, you always spend a lot of the time listening to one half of a phone conversation?'

Moses answered as he usually did on the second ring.

'Morning boss, any news?' Moses was always ready for work and his holiday in America with his wife's family had only made him keener to get back to it. Gloria told him about her previous night's work and asked him if he could go to the morgue while Dr Armah did his examination. Of course he could.

Lawrence couldn't resist provoking her. 'Another family Sunday broken up then Gloria? Could you not just get the report from Barnyou?'

'Actually Lawrence, Moses wife is working today, and his mother has taken the children to some church over at Seventy Second, so he's on his own and is glad to have something to do. What about your mother, is she not missing you this morning?'

Lawrence laughed. It was hard to get one over on Gloria. 'She and Richard have gone to church as well and Fatu…'

'Has gone to football practice with the boys, I know. How did she ever persuade your mother to allow that?' Fatu was Lawrence's young sister.

'How did Fatu ever persuade the boys to allow her is what I'd like to know.'

Rohit laughed. 'My nephew says Fatu is a better player than half the boys so they put up with her.'

As if on cue the apartment door behind them burst open and Abu came in. He was on his own.

'Good practice Abu?' Lawrence always asked although he wasn't that interested. Abu nodded absently, he was already eyeing the remaining samosas.

'Must have been, judging by the amount of sand he's managed to bring in.' Gloria looked at the floor 'Can't you shake it off before you come up? Or is that too much thinking?'

'I think you got most of the brains in your family Gloria, it happens like that.' Lawrence was laughing.

'Yeah, and your sister got all the sports skills in your family Lawrence,' Abu came straight back and then looked up, worried that he had just been rude, but Lawrence was laughing. Only Rohit looked a bit disapproving but the party was breaking up anyway and there was no further comment.

Sunday afternoon dragged by for Gloria. She never could understand how a visit to her family in Westpoint was always dominated by a discussion about how she never visited enough. But she had learnt from past experience that it was better to just let it flow over her. She was family and they loved her but she had moved far from Westpoint, in every sense, and that made her different, so they had to keep reminding her that she was not better than them. In Liberia doing too well was almost as bad as not doing well enough. Even in families love could quickly turn to jealousy with terrible consequences.

She roused herself from these thoughts; she was, she reminded herself, supposed to be enjoying her family. Her mother had prepared mountains of food and her aunts eventually started dishing up huge bowls of fufu and soup. Abu was in deep discussion with his cousins and the numbers on the porch had grown as neighbours drifted over. And so the afternoon passed in a haze of heat, food and loud stories and arguments. By five Gloria was exhausted so she made her excuses and got up to go. She could see Abu was still explaining to anyone who would listen how successful his football tournament had been so she left him to make his own way back.

Moses called her as she was getting into her car. 'Can you talk now boss?'

'Yes, go on Moses.'

'Dr Armah has just finished his examination.' Gloria looked at her watch. He must have been there for hours. 'Yes, he is very thorough… very!' Moses added as if he could read her mind. 'But I think I can put his report into a few words.' That was one of Moses best qualities as far as Gloria was concerned. 'His initial assessment was right. The girl died from massive bleeding; despite the terrible wounds and the damage to her internal organs she bled to death, slowly and in agony.'

'What caused the wounds, was it some kind of animal?'

'Just getting to that boss. He is very sure the wounds were not made by an animal. A superficial look at them might make people think of an animal but to an expert like him – his own words by the way – the wounds were manmade. With a very sharp blade with a serrated edge. The serrated edge gives the wounds the appearance of claws. The other thing he is sure of is that the make-up was added after the girl died.'

Gloria nodded. She hadn't really subscribed to the theory of some large animal on the loose in Monrovia. She drove off after telling Moses to get some additional photos of the wounds.

An hour later she was back on Gurley Street. It was quieter tonight. The bars were open but the music was more muted and a lot of the tables were empty. A few couples were having a quiet drink and there were groups of people sitting talking. There was even a man with a bible sitting with a group of girls in the corner of Honey's Bar. But Gloria had arranged with Bentu to meet some of the girls in a quiet food shop near the end of the street. Ricoh's Chop Shop served decent food at reasonable prices but was also out of public view so Gloria hoped the girls would feel freer to talk with her.

They were all there waiting for her with Bentu at the head of the table sitting like the school prefect. There were eleven girls and they all looked exhausted. Bentu insisted on introductions so it was another twelve minutes until all that had been done, food had been ordered and they all had a soft drink. Gloria took out the photos she had and put them on the table.

'Thank y'all for coming. You all looking tire-o.' They nodded. Gloria explained that she was looking for the girl in the photo and she wanted them to tell her anything that might help her to find her. The food arrived as she was talking. 'Leh we eat first, and then please anything you able to tell me eh.' Eating didn't take long; the girls looked as if they were starving. One girl, Gloria thought her name was Sugar, put her hand up as if she was in a classroom.

'Old ma, I want to ask something first.' Gloria nodded. 'This girl here,' she pointed to the photo, 'where you find her?'

Gloria explained what had happened; it would be in all the newspapers tomorrow anyway. Sugar nodded. She looked as if she might be fourteen but the tell-tale signs, the sores on her mouth, the cracked skin, reddened eyes, were all there. Sugar would not last too many more years in this life.

They all looked at the photo, some of them studying it hard, others just giving it a glance. In the end they all shook their heads. 'She not from here.'

'Ok, but have you heard anything about children being taken away, anything at all.' She knew they had an informal network which warned the girls of people or places which could be dangerous for them. They started calling out names of bars or hotels where it was not safe to go, and names of people they were afraid of. The list was depressingly long but they were all characters or places in the neighbourhood. Gloria mentally added the names to her list of future investigations, but there was nothing really new here. It was right at the end that a small girl who had sat quietly for most of the discussion put her hand up. Gloria couldn't remember her name but smiled at her to speak. The girl whispered something but it was too quiet for Gloria to catch it although she saw the girls sitting near her looked nervous.

'Come here my dear.' Motherly sympathy was not something that came easily to Gloria but she held out her hand to the child who walked down to her. She looked even younger than the girl in the photo. Surely she was not on the street. As if reading her mind Bentu piped up.

'This is Babygirl Gloria. She lives with Sugar and sells food on the road.' For now, thought Gloria looking at the child.

'Ok Babygirl, tell me what you said.' She gently pulled the girl towards her, feeling the thin shoulders tense beneath the dress. She leant close into the girl and heard her whisper. 'Never-Die.'

'Never-Die, what's that?' Some of the girls laughed, some of them looked worried.

'That's where Babygirl came from Gloria.' It was Bentu again. 'She ran away from the church, somewhere in Nimba, and came to town.'

'It's a church then?' They all nodded.

'The Never-Die Church. They were in Nimba and now they moved to some place near the St Paul River. That's why she is so scary, in case they come for her.'

'They do bad things to children,' Babygirl was whispering again, 'very bad things.' Gloria nodded wondering how she had never heard of it before. She was supposed to know all about these places.

There wasn't much more after that. Some of the girls had already fallen asleep at the table so Gloria thanked them and let them go. 'Bentu, I need to speak some more to Babygirl, could you bring her to the station tomorrow?'

Bentu shook her head. 'We can't go to the police station ma, it not possible.'

'Well if I send an officer down to talk to her will you make sure she's around. He is nice and he won't scare her.'

Bentu thought about that and reluctantly agreed and she promised to have Babygirl at Ricoh's the next morning.

Chapter Four

It was Monday morning and the newspapers were full of the story of the body 'dropped from heaven' as one of them put it. Speculation was rife, most of it wild and very ill-informed. There were reports that a strange animal had been seen in the vicinity of the stadium, that 'medicine' had been found under the podium and, best of all in Gloria's opinion, *The Investigator* newspaper had eye witness accounts of the body of the girl turning into an animal right in front of the police and running off into the undergrowth.

She stopped her car to let the presidential motorcade speed by, catching Lawrence's wave from the lead vehicle, and arrived in the quiet police headquarters. The Family and Child Protection unit had still not been redecorated but at least the power was a lot more reliable so the fans worked and she could use her illegal electric kettle to make a coffee before everyone else arrived. Well, everyone but Moses who was already at his desk.

'Still the first one in I see, Moses.'

'Just checking the attendance records ma'am, some of our team are not too serious I think, and what about Paul, I hear he's gone?'

Gloria sat down. 'Yes, Paul decided he wanted to play with the big boys so he's gone over to CID.' She managed to make it sound like the Dark Side. 'But it's the way he did it, it wasn't correct.' She told him how Paul had become so arrogant and had made some very bad judgment calls. 'Anyway, Barnyou trusts him.'

'And those new guys?'

Gloria had to remind herself who he was talking about. She didn't really think of Christian, Ambrose or Lamine as the new guys anymore. 'Ah well, Lamine and Christian started acting up a bit after you left for your holiday but they did well in the end.' Moses was writing something down which didn't bode well for them today. 'I want to send Christian down to talk to Babygirl this morning.' She explained the circumstances.

Moses was surprised. Christian had been a tough, surly ex-fighter when he had been foisted on them as a new recruit. Not the first choice to talk with a scared little girl.

'Trust me on this Moses, he's still surly with us but with children, old people, in fact anyone except us, he is very good.' Moses shrugged.

There was a lot of hand shaking when the others got in as most of them were seeing Moses for the first time since he had come back. 'We thought you might stay captain, you know, enjoy the sweet life over there.' Moses just shook his head. Loyalty to his wife wouldn't allow him to say too much but America, loud, brash and overweight, would never suit him.

'Well I might have if you guys could be left on your own, which you can't be. I go for six weeks and one leaves, two start making up their own working times and another two get engaged. If I had stayed another two weeks there might have been none of you left.' They all laughed but Christian and Lamine looked at each other, they knew they were in for trouble later.

They had all heard about the dead girl, in fact most of them had been in the stadium, and Gloria brought them up to date with what had been happening since. 'Christian.' He looked up wondering if he was going to get disciplined now. 'I want you to go and talk to Babygirl. I know you will be gentle but find out everything you can about this Never-Die Church. You can go now, she will be at Ricoh's.' Christian nodded. 'Now, the rest of you, any ideas?'

A few months ago that would have been followed by a long silence but not now. Ideas, questions and disagreements came thick and fast but it was old Alfred, a veteran officer who still did not entirely approve of Gloria's age or sex as his boss, who hit on something. 'It's Leopard Men, it has to be.' It took him a little while to grasp that most other people in the room had no idea what he was talking about. 'Deliberate wounds made to look like some kind of animal claws, that is something we saw a lot of when I was growing up in Lofa.'

Gloria had no idea how old Alfred actually was but he was certainly a good deal older than anyone else in the room. She had heard vaguely of Leopard Men and their activities but for almost everyone else in the room their experience of Liberia started with the war. Anything that happened before Charles Taylor and the rest of the warlord gang was so much dusty history.

'Alfred, I think you'll have to explain it a bit.'

Alfred stood up and cleared his throat. For once he had everyone's attention. 'I grew up in the high forest in Lofa. In our village we were hunters and farmers.' Gloria cleared her throat and Moses jumped in.

'Alfred this is very interesting but we just need to know about the Leopard Men for now.' He blinked as if coming back from somewhere else in his head. 'Oh, the Leopard Men, well they were a secret society, men who could take on the form of leopards and go hunting at night. Sometimes we would find the body of one of our villagers slashed and cut and parts eaten away, someone who had made the Leopard Men angry. We found out of course that most of them could not really change into leopards; they just wore masks and had these special blades that fitted on their hands like claws. It was all done to terrify people.'

'Most of them…' Ambrose asked the question they were all thinking.

'Yes, the real Leopard Men were only few, the ones who could really change. Most of them were just rogues, as usual.'

Gloria cut in. She didn't want to get caught up in a discussion as to whether people really could change into leopards, interesting as the idea was.

'Thanks Alfred, this little girl was killed by blades made to look like claws so there could be some connection. But why would Leopard Men be operating in Monrovia now?'

Alfred shrugged. As far as he was concerned Monrovia was full of crazy people, you didn't need to look for a reason. Gloria looked over at Lamine who was laughing. 'It's the best connection we have so far. The explanation actually fits the facts we have and is not just a storyline from the latest action movie you've been watching.' Lamine had suggested that maybe the girl had accidentally fallen out of a plane. 'We need to investigate the 'why' now.'

'Excuse me ma'am.' Young Alfred was desperate to prove that becoming engaged to Izena had not made him any less serious about being a police officer.

'What about Paul? He told me he had studied cults, magic, ritual killings etc. at the university.'

Gloria remembered him telling her that too. 'Good idea. Have a word with him Alfred, see if he knows anything about Leopard Men.'

She left Moses to divide out tasks, grateful she didn't have to do that anymore. He was back in minutes, shaking his head. 'I don't think we have enough people now boss. It really is impossible.'

'Well they're not going to give any more at the moment. The Chief, or the Director I should say, will just tell me to stop doing Barnyou's job. Like that would work.'

'So are CID allies or enemies?'

'Oh they're allies, or at least Barnyou is. He is doing his best but the constant reorganisation is making his life very hard. One week he is in charge of just about everything, the next week he's only got a team of detectives to manage. Anyway, I have a meeting this morning with the Child Safety Committee. I better not miss this one.'

'You need to meet Barnyou before you go.' Gloria raised an eyebrow at him. 'Well you told me to make arrangements so I did. And that footballer is also here to see you.'

'Which one?'

'Lord, boss, when we say "that footballer" in Liberia we can only mean one person, Abraham Kanneh.'

'Kanneh? What does he want?'

'Well I don't know because he wants to speak to you and apparently the fact that he has turned up himself is a great honour for us.'

Gloria sucked her teeth. 'He can wait a little while then. Let's go see Barnyou first.'

She was shown straight into Barnyou's office and marvelled again at how tidy and ordered it was. Her office, as far as she could remember, looked like a cross between a store cupboard and a detention cell. She made another mental note to get it sorted out.

'Gloria, come in.' They sat around his small conference table and he showed them the photographs. He was obviously about to launch into a detailed explanation of what Dr Armah had said but Gloria stopped him.

'Thanks but Moses explained most of it. What do we do next? I've got some people looking at any connections between the crime and Leopard Cults and at the Never-Die Church. I'll leave the actual murder investigation to you of course.'

Barnyou laughed briefly. 'Of course you will Gloria, like the last time. Ok, well we are doing a massive sweep of the area to interview as many people as possible who were in the stadium that day and those who live around there. Someone must have seen something, it's not that easy to get a body onto the roof.' Gloria wasn't so sure; there was a lot of selective amnesia around. But a short meeting was always welcome, so she just nodded.

'I'll see Kanneh now Moses and then I think you better come to the Child Safety Committee with me, make sure you catch up on the new faces and all the new strategies we are developing.' It was one of Gloria's biggest frustrations that the committee seemed to spend more time talking and writing rather than doing. Strategy was not one of her favourite words. That and the constantly changing membership of the committee made it very hard to get concerted action.

She decided to meet Kanneh in the conference room where there would at least be enough chairs for them to sit on. She was sure he would have a group with him; footballers seemed unable to attend anything without bringing a gang with them. But she was surprised when Kanneh came in with just a single companion who had a notebook and a pen and everything

– almost like a real secretary thought Gloria.

Abraham Kanneh looked healthy shiny and full of energy and his smile was on full power again. Gloria felt tired just looking at him. 'Inspector Gloria thanks for seeing me.' Gloria was a bit wrong-footed by his polite tone. She smiled back and extended her hand. She didn't know what to call him; using his first name was too familiar, calling him 'Mr' seemed just funny as he was only about twenty and calling him by his last name might sound as if she was somehow putting him down. She did what she usually did in these situations and called him nothing.

'That's no problem, sorry for keeping you waiting but you will realise it's very busy here today.' She noticed the companion was not introduced. 'So how can I help?'

'Well it's two things Inspector and maybe I can help you. The first is the incident on Saturday. I know a lot of people are saying it was an attack on the President but I need to know if you think it might have been aimed at me instead.' Gloria was already shaking her head before he finished. She explained again how the body dropping on them at that moment had been more due to nature than any plan. Kanneh nodded as if that was the answer he had expected. 'Well then maybe I can help you.' He looked at her expectantly and Gloria stared back, not knowing what reaction he had wanted. 'I just want to volunteer while I am here, put my weight' – for 'weight' read popularity and influence thought Gloria – 'behind any initiatives you might want to develop to keep kids safe.'

Gloria thought he sounded as if he had memorised a text prepared by someone else but she was cautiously appreciative of his gesture. Maybe she would mention it to the Child Safety Committee; it might spur them on to do something. 'Thank you, that's very kind. I will keep it in mind.' There was an awkward pause and then he got up.

'And just call me AK Inspector, most people do.' The brilliant smile hadn't faltered for an instant.

As the door closed behind them Moses sighed loudly and said 'Ah, the room feels a bit darker without him.' Gloria looked at him and then they both laughed long and loud.

'Just for a second I thought you had gone soft on me Moses. Mr AK is a bit of a charmer.'

'But he might be useful.'

Ten minutes later they were on their way to the Child Safety Committee meeting. It was being held today at the IRS office which meant that Hans would be chairing it.

The Child Safety Committee had been formed on the President's orders after a big trafficking case earlier in the year. It had been set up with a flourish of agency directors and senior government ministers but was now run by people who really wanted to make it work to improve things for children. Gloria and Peter Dennis, the Minister of Social Welfare, both attended as well as Hans from IRS, a young woman from Global Vision, Clementine, a social worker Gloria knew well, representing a number of local agencies, and Sr Margaret to speak for local church organisations. There were also supposed to be representatives from the President's office, the Ministries of Health and Education and someone from the Juvenile Court but she couldn't recall ever seeing any of these at any meeting.

IRS was housed in a block of flats in Mamba Point and the air conditioning was very welcome. They were meeting in Conference Room 3 the young man at reception told them. 'That's their smallest room so there must be even fewer people than usual.' As it turned out Gloria was wrong. They weren't fewer than usual; they were just crammed into a smaller space. Hans opened the meeting promptly and dealt with all the reading of the minutes and matters arising in quick time – almost. Just when Gloria thought it was safe to raise her head again she saw the young woman from Global Vision – her name was Brigitta she had discovered – raise her hand.

Gloria sensed that Brigitta was a PPP, a professional persistent participant. The name had been coined during the war by the American director of an international agency who insisted there was a particular breed of development worker – young, confident and inexperienced – who roamed disaster zones around the world, insisted on attending meetings and, because they knew nothing about the crisis or the country it was happening in, made their presence felt by filling meetings with technical points of order or references to obscure UN documents. Brigitta, with her pale skin which looked as if it had never been exposed to the African sun and her earnest expression, had been trying to speak for the last ten minutes.

Hans finally acknowledged her and Brigitta began a long and rambling introduction. Gloria heard 'interface,' 'disaster modelling' and 'broad-spectrum interventions' in the first two sentences and then her mind switched off. It took Brigitta another ten minutes to get to her main point. 'So in conclusion I feel it is very important that we establish the parameters of responsibility for this committee by developing a proper constitution with the requisite working terms of reference and roles and responsibilities in order to maximise our impact.' Hans was looking nervously at Gloria. It wouldn't be the first time she had lost her temper at the seemingly endless jargon-filled speeches, but she was smiling and when she saw Hans looking at her she jumped in.

'Well eh, thanks Brigitta, for sharing your eh, sharing your experience. I'm afraid I lost the flow a bit when you mentioned disaster modelling, I had a vision of my mother taking to the catwalk.' There was a loud laugh, especially from those who had met Gloria's mother. 'Perhaps you would write up your suggestion and e-mail it to us to give us a chance to think about it and we can have a further discussion.' Brigitta beamed. She would most certainly do that.

'Do you even have an e-mail address Gloria?' It was Clementine whispering in her ear. Gloria shrugged. 'I might have, but as there is barely enough electricity to work the fans in our offices it doesn't really matter does it.'

Hans had seized on the suggestion though and was passing around a sheet of paper for everyone to put their e-mail address on. He signalled Gloria to give her update and she gave a brief description of what she was working on, and then a description of her trip down Gurley Street the previous Saturday, and what the girls had told her about the lives they were forced to live and the dangers they faced. 'So, I think one of our priorities as a committee, should be those girls. It is a shame on all of us and we need to do something urgently.' She sat back. Hans paused and then said.

'Thank you, Inspector. I think we all agree on the urgency of doing something for these girls but we have to recognise that our time and resources are limited.' He shifted some papers in front of him. 'We are still working on some strategies based on your previous recommendations.' Gloria looked up at him as he read from the notes in front of him. 'Children from rural communities who are vulnerable to exploitation,' Gloria nodded, 'and children who are victims of domestic abuse,' she nodded again, 'and street children,' she stopped nodding, 'and the impact of HIV/AIDS on children and now girls working on the streets.' Gloria smiled.

'Ok Hans I hear what you are saying, but there are a lot of bad things happening to children and this committee should at least be doing something.'

'I agree, I think we all agree but we can't take on everything and we have to remember that we all represent agencies or organisations which have their own priorities. It's not easy.'

'And being a child in this city is not easy either Hans,' it was Peter Dennis this time, 'and Gloria is right, we have to do something otherwise this committee is a waste of time. My Ministry is drawing up a list of priorities which I will send around. One of our biggest concerns is that agency interventions are completely unregulated, what you call 'having their own priorities,' which can be very confusing and a waste of money and even, potentially, very damaging. Look at that trafficking ring your organisation and that South African crowd ended up helping or shielding, just because you were working on your own and wouldn't consult with us. We…'

There was an exasperated sigh from Hans. International agencies did not like to be reminded of their failures. 'With respect Minister, that is history and without our money the government…'

It was Sr Margaret who interrupted this time. 'Why don't we see what we are already doing and then the gaps will be more obvious. The Missing and Abused Children Helpline Organisation, for example,' – Sr Margaret had vowed never to use the acronym MACHO when talking about the citywide network of free phone lines and operators which had very recently been set up to give children the opportunity to make complaints of abuse and get help – 'is a great idea. Is it working?'

The rest of the committee looked at Gloria for a response but she felt her phone vibrating and when she looked at the screen she saw it was Barnyou calling. She signalled to them apologetically and left the room. His 'Hello Inspector' was low and serious. Not good news then, she thought.

'You need to come down to Carey Street right away.' There was a slight pause before he continued. 'There's another child's body.' That was all he said before he rang off. Gloria went back into the meeting. 'I am very sorry but Moses and I will have to go.' She wrote a short note for Peter Dennis and passed it to him. He needed to know what was going on. They got in the car and Moses asked.

'Carey Street?'

'That's what he said. Another busy place like the stadium. If it's the same person or persons they like attention, as Ambrose said.'

They saw Barnyou about half way down the street. 'It's here,' he pointed to an Indian jewellery shop. The steel shutters on the windows were still down and the shop had a 'closed' sign in the window. 'The owner, a Mr Ramesh, came here an hour ago to open up. While his assistant was opening the shutters he found this.' Barnyou raised the shutters enough so they could see inside. It was another body alright, lying spread-eagled among a few gold chains and rings. This time it was a boy.

Gloria and Moses examined the body from inside the shop to avoid attracting unwanted attention. The boy was older than the girl; he looked to be about fifteen. He was dressed in good clothes and he was wearing make-up too. It was a lot lighter than the girl but it was definitely there. His cause of death was straightforward. It looked like he had been shot once in the head. It was only when they moved him that Moses noticed the long reddish rope underneath the body.

'Wait, hold him there.' Moses crouched down and saw the rope was actually a tail, a real animal tail and it was attached to the boy. Gloria heard him groan. 'It's been sewn on, right onto his lower back. That is... grotesque.' He stood up and looked at Barnyou and Gloria. His face was thunder. 'So, another crazy on the loose in Monrovia. Jeez,' he shook his head, 'where do these people come from?'

Gloria looked at the tail and its attachment. To kill a child was terrible but this deliberate insult somehow made it so much worse. 'This is so,' Gloria searched for a word, 'so disrespectful. So completely disrespectful.' It was inadequate, to say the least, but she was struggling to put words on her feelings.

Barnyou called the shop owner over. Mr Ramesh was a middle aged man who looked very anxious. 'I have never come across anything like this before, a dead body right in my shop window.'

'Mr Ramesh has anything been stolen from your shop?'

Ramesh stopped and then shook his head. 'No, nothing. Most of the merchandise is locked in the safe at night. We only leave a few pieces in the window, cheaper pieces, but they haven't been stolen either and the safe has not been touched.'

'Do you have an alarm system?'

Ramesh raised an eyebrow. 'An alarm system? To raise who? No, most of us rely on steel doors, safes and iron bars.'

'Do you not even have a watchman Mr Ramesh?'

'No, they are usually in league with the rogues.'

'So how did the body get into the window?'

'I don't know Inspector. The doors were all locked, nothing was disturbed and nothing is missing.'

'Who has the keys?'

'Me. I have all the keys. No-one else has a key.'

'So a dead child is dumped inside your heavily fortified shop without anything being disturbed?' Barnyou was staring at Ramesh.

Gloria wandered outside. Carey Street was busy but a few police officers inside a shop was not an uncommon sight so no-one was paying much attention. A few doors up Gloria spotted Hassan her Lebanese friend, standing outside his jewellery shop. He waved to her and strolled down.

'Inspector Gloria, how are you? I haven't seen you since the riots.' He was looking at her quizzically.

'Yes the riots, that seems like a while ago.'

'You promised to come and eat with my wife and I.'

'Sorry Hassan, it has been busy.'

'And getting busier?' He looked at Ramesh's shop. 'Are you handling robberies now too?'

'It's not a robbery Hassan.'

'Well it's something big if you are here.'

'Nothing for you to worry about at the moment. Do you know Ramesh well?'

Hassan gave a non-committal shrug. 'He has his own way of doing things.'

'What do you mean?'

Hassan hesitated.

'Let's just say that I trust the people who work in my shop, all of them, even the boy who cleans and makes the coffee. They have all been with me for a long time and nothing has ever been stolen, I never have to shout and I am happy to leave them running the shop if I have to go somewhere else. Ramesh and his friends…' he shrugged again.

'They don't treat their employees the same way?'

Hassan made a face. 'In my experience people react to you the way you expect them to.'

Gloria agreed. 'I better get back in. I will see you later Hassan. I promise.'

'Drop in for a coffee Inspector, any time.'

It was a few hours before they all met back at headquarters. They had decided that for the moment they would work on the theory that the murders were connected; children with make-up on, brutally killed and left in strange places – that seemed like a fairly obvious connection. But that was as far as they had got.

Gloria had assembled her team and filled them in on the latest death. She could see the shock on their faces which was hardly surprising; children murdered and their bodies desecrated was not news anyone could digest easily.

Young Alfred had spoken to Paul who was going to research the Leopard Cults for them, but he hadn't come up with very much. 'He says he tried really hard to get some first-hand accounts of the cults when he was doing his original research but people either claimed they had never heard of them or said they no longer existed. There was only one old chief in Cape Mount who spoke to him and told him to go home and read his books unless he wanted to meet the Leopard Men himself. The chief obviously did not mean meet the Leopard Men in an informal group discussion but something a lot more threatening. Paul decided to go home. But he will get back to me tomorrow if he can think of anything else.'

'Ma'am,' Izena was waving a newspaper at her, 'just an idea. Eh, there's a story in the paper about an old lady being shot by her family because she used to change into a bat at night and go out flying around.' She held up the paper but it was a fairly common story so no-one reacted much. 'I was just thinking, the little girl was killed by the Leopard Cult except we don't really think they are the real thing, the boy was killed and then has an animal tail sewn onto him as if he was maybe changing into a bush pig except he wasn't.' She ran out of words. 'I'm not quite sure what I'm saying but the murders could be connected by our superstitions, eh traditions I mean, in some way.

Gloria thought about that and nodded. 'You might have something there Izena. Maybe some person or group who thinks they have a mission to punish us for our bad ways. I mean it's quite twisted but then the person is probably crazy. What about the Never-Die Church Christian? Did Babygirl tell you much?'

Christian was slouched against the wall as usual but straightened up. 'She was very scared, but she told me she lived in the church until she was old enough to run away. Their prophet has told them they will never die if they stay in the church but they are not allowed to go out of that small community. Actually, she thinks the prophet died, he disappeared anyway, but the elders said he had gone into the forest to pray.' That got a laugh. 'But the way they treated the children was terrible. No child lived with their own parents, they were not allowed to go to school or to play, and they just worked all the time. And as soon as the girls reached puberty any of the men could have sex with them. She says they were very cruel and she believes if they catch her they will kill her.' He looked angry. 'Anyway I showed her the picture but she wasn't sure, she doesn't think she knows the girl but,' he looked up at Gloria, 'I don't think she would even recognise her own family, she's so scared. I think she's traumatised.' Christian pronounced the word carefully, as if trying it out. When nobody laughed, he repeated it. 'Yes, I think she's traumatised so she won't be good at remembering.'

Gloria nodded. 'So we need to go and visit this church, that's for sure. They sound like fun. Ok, anything else?' There wasn't, so she again left Moses to organise the team for the next day. She would go and have a look at the Never-Die Church with Christian.

Chapter Five

The clouds hung heavily over a grey sea the next morning. Gloria hated the time between the end of the rainy season and the start of the dry season. Everything was wet all the time and the humidity was oppressive. It was only six in the morning and she was staring gloomily at her collection of rumpled uniforms. Abu was generally acknowledged by friends and family to be more domesticated than she was but even he had never managed to keep her uniforms from shrinking, crumpling or creasing after a few wears. She would have to send for the tailor again but that thought filled her with some dread as well. Richard was a young man and an excellent tailor but he considered his tailoring to be more art than craft and there were no short sessions when he came for a fitting. Gloria had tried on at least two occasions to just ask for a repeat order of previous uniforms, it was a black skirt or trousers and a black jacket for goodness sake, but Richard wouldn't have it. He had to come and sit down while they discussed materials, styles and shades of colour before they settled on the same style of jacket and trousers in the same material and the same shade of black. It was exhausting, but she put up with it because the clothes were well made, reasonably priced and usually delivered the next day – and she liked Richard.

She settled for jeans and a shirt as she was going out of town and went into the kitchen. Abu was staring at the open fridge as if willing something to appear. When he saw her clothes he just said. 'Should I tell Richard to pass around this evening then?' Gloria nodded glumly. 'But make it late, I am going to the Never-Die Church today.' Abu rolled his eyes but said nothing.

Christian was waiting for her downstairs as instructed. He was in uniform and Gloria almost tried explaining why she was dressed the way she was but gave up. 'Do you know where these people are?'

'I think they all moved to Bensonville now, they are going to stay there until the prophet comes out of the forest again.' Gloria thought Christian was making a joke but when she looked over at him he wasn't smiling. She gave up on conversation and settled back in her seat. It was going to be a long day, she thought.

The journey at least gave her the chance to make some calls and by the time they were on the outskirts of the town she had spoken to Barnyou, Moses and Lawrence.

Bensonville was a strange place. It had been intended to be the first of Liberia's modern cities but was abandoned at the start of the war before anyone could move in. It had six-lane highways, elaborate junctions and the skeletons of some very grandiose buildings. A large signpost in the town centre pointed the way to the zoo, the children's playground and the golf course. But it was like a neglected film set; grass and weeds were waist high in the roads, the buildings were either empty or home to groups of displaced families. If the zoo had ever had any animals they were long gone and the only sign of a golf course was a rusty iron pin with a faded number 6 on it sticking out of the ground through the remains of an iron fence.

A rough, hand-painted sign said Never-Die Church in black letters and pointed to a compound whose grand arched entrance still had the words National Museum carved into it. The grass was even wilder here and Christian parked the car as close to the ornately carved wooden doors as he could to avoid disturbing any snakes hiding in the undergrowth. There was no noise of any kind. Gloria pushed the door and it swung open into a large bare room. They followed a corridor to the right which took them past lots of rooms with no doors. A baby slept on a mat in one room, two goats stared at them silently from another and a large lady sat on the floor of a third room eating from a tray of mangoes. She barely looked at them.

'Maybe they have all died,' Christian whispered in her ear and this time he did smile.

'What you people looking for?' The voice seemed to come from nowhere and made them both jump. 'How come you just walking around private property with no permission?' Gloria turned and looked into the face of tall thin man with bad teeth and watery eyes.

'I think you mean government property don't you?' she said. 'And we are walking around because there doesn't seem to be anyone to talk to. I am Inspector Gloria Sirleaf and we are making some enquiries about a child who was found murdered on Saturday.' The man stared back at her before finally commenting that she didn't look very much like an inspector. He introduced himself as Prophet Wolo, assistant to their founder Prophet Daniel who had gone to spend some time alone in prayer and meditation. 'So what goes on here?'

Prophet Wolo thought for a moment and then launched into a long explanation of their philosophy and beliefs. He was clearly repeating something he had learnt by heart. The church had been founded by this man Daniel and most of the members of the church were from the same village. Daniel must have had some charisma to get control of an entire village but Gloria suspected she would never meet him. Wolo on the other hand was struggling, that was obvious.

'The prophet Daniel revered to us that we not going to die. We in our church are creating paradise right here, so no need to die and go different place.'

'I think he means revealed ma'am.' Christian whispered helpfully in her ear.

'Yes, thanks for the clarification Christian.'

'But he told us we had to keep ourselves away from the sin and wickedness of the world.' That sounded like a direct quote from Daniel. But this man Wolo clearly had no charisma and very little education and 'moving the church away from their village to give Prophet Daniel space to pray' had obviously been his last desperate move to stop the church falling apart. But judging by the state of the place his community might be disintegrating anyway. Desperate people could do terrible things she knew, to try and hold on to power. If these children had started questioning the community leaders they may have suffered the wrath of the elders.

'Do you know these children?' She showed him the head shots of the boy and girl. He grabbed the photos, hesitated and then shook his head. 'No, I never see them before. So you can go now, you are disturbing our community.'

Gloria glared at him. 'I haven't even started disturbing anything yet Mr Wolo. I want to show these pictures around the place, maybe someone else will recognise them.'

'What, no, I say no. No.' He was shouting now and a small group had gathered. 'I tell you this place is private, you can't do it.'

Gloria looked at the group. They were a bedraggled bunch; skinny men, defeated women and lots of children of all ages. As a vision of paradise it was quite disappointing. 'Actually, as I have already pointed out, this is government property. This is the National Museum so unless you have papers for it then you are the one who is breaking the law.' Wolo sneered at her.

'Clever lady policeman, just get out of here.'

Gloria ignored that. If that was his idea of insults she had heard a lot worse. 'Christian, take the women and children out of here and show them the pictures. I'll stay with the men.' There were mutterings but Christian ignored that and led the women and children out the building. Wolo looked panicked. 'You can't do this. I will call for the lawyer.'

'Go right ahead Wolo. I am just going to sit here with you all until my officer has finished.'

'You are not going to ask us any questions?' A man with thick glasses and a woollen hat on his head peered anxiously at her.

'No. I have no questions for you. Just sit here and wait.' To her surprise they all did as she said. Gloria felt a little sorry for them. These were country people, uprooted from their own surroundings and now lost.

Time passed slowly. The room got warmer and warmer and the dim figures staring at her finally got on Gloria's nerves. 'Right I'm going to see where my officer has got to, I will be back.' Even Wolo didn't react though, the fight had gone out of them.

She followed the sounds of clapping and laughing and found herself in a large yard to the back of the house. It was mostly dust and scrub and in the middle of it Christian and a crowd of children playing kick ball. Gloria couldn't remember when she had last seen such excitement at a game. They were running, shrieking, clapping, holding each other and laughing uproariously. He had stirred up a storm here. Eventually Gloria managed to catch his eye and Christian came over. She looked at him.

'I needed to get them relaxed ma.'

Gloria nodded. 'It's good Christian but we have to get some answers. Get on with the questioning. I will be inside but we need to leave soon.'

She wandered over to an outbuilding which was obviously being used as a church of some kind. It had a few benches and some rough wooden musical instruments. A small cross had been nailed to the back wall but the main feature was a large poster with the words 'Prophet Daniel' printed on the bottom of it. Gloria didn't like the look of him. He was well fed and smug, smiling down at her with all his teeth. She looked to see where the posters had been printed and then heard Christian calling her.

'Ma, we have them.' She saw Christian with some children in tow looking very excited.

'Ok Christian, let's calm down.'

They sat on the benches and Gloria listened. It was simple. The girl was from their community. The younger children couldn't help getting excited when they saw the photo and the women had admitted it. Her name was Rose. She was thirteen and she had disappeared from the compound a few months before. They couldn't stop staring at her face with the make-up and the elaborate hair decorations.

'Which one is the mother?' No-one answered at first.

'We have no mothers; we are all one family here.'

'Sorry, I don't have time for this now. Which one of you born the girl?'

A woman finally put up her hand. 'I the one born her.'

'More when did you see her last.' The woman thought for a moment. More than three months ago. She was not happy here, always grumbling and being disobedient. Then one morning she gone.'

'Did you look for her?' No-one said anything. Obviously not.

'Christian, go and bring Wolo here, he said he had never seen the girl before, he was lying and I want to know why. Everyone else must come and sit here in the chapel.'

She called Moses and told him what had happened. 'Tell Barnyou to send some men out here to search the place, see if we can find any claw-like weapons. I'm going to phone Peter Dennis and Hans. We need to take these children out of here for their own safety.'

'What about the boy?'

'He wasn't mentioned. I will see if anyone knows him. The girl was called Rose by the way.'

By the time she had contacted Peter Dennis and Hans and got their agreement to move the children from the compound Barnyou and his people had already arrived.

'That was quick Barnyou.'

'We were in Brewerville Gloria, following up some leads.'

'Maybe you need to start the search now before anything gets lost.'

The rest of the community had assembled in the church and Gloria explained to them what was going to happen. She told them the children would be taken somewhere safe until the investigation was finished. There was no response, no crying or shouting, just a tired silence.

Wolo however knew he was in trouble. His head was down and he shuffled in front of Gloria. 'So Wolo tell me about Rose. You do know her now?'

'The girl lived here but she was too frisky, always asking questions. She didn't like to work and she was rude.'

'So you punished her, made an example of her?' Wolo looked at her slyly.

'Me? I did nothing. The girl ran away. She was to be disciplined by the elders in the morning and she ran away. That's all I know.'

That's not all you know Mr Wolo, thought Gloria.

'And the boy, was he trouble too? Was he together with Rose and you didn't like that?'

'That boy is not from here, that one I don't know. With all that stuff on his face.' He made an expression of disgust that struck Gloria as genuine.

'Ok, we will talk more in town. All the adults will come to the police station.'

The head count revealed eighteen adults and thirty two children. The search of the property by Barnyou's men revealed nothing. Two rusty machetes were the only tools they found and Gloria knew they could not possibly have made the wounds on Rose body.

Hans arrived with vehicles and, Gloria was relieved to see, Clementine. She could trust Clementine to sort the children out between the different agencies. 'They are going to be very upset Clementine; we haven't got the full story of what's been going on here. Are you going to keep them in family groups?'

'Mmm well that would be the ideal but some of them are not even sure who their brothers and sisters are. I am going to take them down to our Children's Village, it's not too far and they can all stay together. Ma Hawa is in charge there, she's very good.'

The children had almost no clothes to pack and the adults looked completely dazed so the removal of the children happened very quickly. The press had already gathered outside and Gloria knew this was going to be big news. It took another hour to get all the adults into the pickups and then escort them to the police headquarters. It was evening by the time they had all been processed.

'So what do we think then Gloria?' She and Barnyou were in her office.

'Are you asking what my feelings are about the case Barnyou?' He laughed and shook his head.

'No Inspector, I am asking for your conclusions based on the evidence we have and your experience.'

'Well, there's something rotten about that Never-Die crowd, very rotten... but not murder, I don't think so. Wolo is still not telling the truth but I don't think he killed her. If he was going to kill her it would have been brute force and he would have hidden the body.'

'I agree with you Gloria. It doesn't fit.'

'I want some of my people to question them and the children tomorrow. If we can get a real picture of what was going on out there it might help. Have you heard from the Director?' Chief Inspector Kamara had been confirmed in the post of Police Director a few weeks previous and they hadn't seen much of him since then.

'Just a memo. You'll have one as well, asking for weekly reports and a reminder that sensitive issues have to be referred to him before action is taken.'

It was already seven by the time she reached home and Abu was sitting watching the news with Richard the tailor who stood up as soon as she came in the room. 'Gloria, my dear. How are you?'

Richard was only in his early twenties and really should not be calling her by her first name but he was loud and flamboyant and he was very hard to resist. He was in an African gown of deep blue with gold braiding at the neck and the sleeves, a cap of the same colour and matching curly-toed slippers. The one large earring completed tonight's outfit. He carried on talking but as usual Gloria had lost him. He spoke so fast, laughing in between, and gesturing with his hands that she could only guess what he was talking about. She looked at Abu for help and he gestured urgently to her t-shirt and jeans. 'Oh I see, no, this is not my new uniform Richard, I need you to sew some for me.' He paused and sat back down rummaging in his bag pulling out papers and leaflets. Gloria knew she could not go through this tonight. She sat next to him and pushed the leaflets with their various designs and material on them away from her.

'Richard, I am very tired. Please I just need three new uniforms.' He looked at her. 'I think you need more than that Gloria, I've been through your cupboards and most of those uniforms are spoiled. I don't know how you do it.'

Gloria looked over at Abu who shrugged and raised his eyes as if to say there was no way he could have stopped him even if he had thought about it. 'I've pressed the best two so you have something to go to work in and I will make five more and bring them by the end of the week.' Her eyes shot over to the wall where two uniforms were hanging on the door. He really had made a good job of them. 'How do you do that?' Richard raised a hand. 'Come on Gloria, you're not really interested, it's my job, the same as you doing yours. Let's just leave it there. Now, I brought you some food and managed to stop Abu eating all of it'

Abu grinned. 'It's very good; chicken and check rice Aunt Glo. Nearly as good as my own.'

'And you need a cup of coffee,' he looked over at Abu who shook his head again but went off to the kitchen to make it, 'and to sit down.'

When he slowed down Richard was also a very good storyteller and while she ate he regaled her with stories of his customers. His gossip was always mischievous rather than nasty so it was an easy accompaniment to his food. He was telling her about the wife of the vice-president who had sent for him and produced a picture of some stick-thin Hollywood actress in a very revealing dress. 'She said to me "Richard, I want to look like that." Well Gloria I had no idea what to say to her. The material in the dress in the picture wouldn't even cover her arms. As for looking like a Hollywood actress, I told her she would need to go to a Miracle Crusade rather than a tailor if she wanted to look like that.'

Gloria almost choked on the rice she was swallowing. 'You didn't say that to her did you? Mrs Roberts takes herself too seriously Richard, you need to be careful.'

He rolled his eyes. 'Oh she didn't hear me; she says I speak too fast.'

Gloria was looking at the pile of leaflets on the table. There were flyers for crusades, healers, night clubs and restaurants. Everyone in Monrovia was advertising every form of entertainment and cure for every possible condition. She recognised the face on the top one. Bishop Matthew Asholodu had his face on every billboard in town and his Resurrection Temple was the latest religious hit in town. On radio and TV Bishop Matthew promised cures, abundance and even, apparently, raising people from the dead. So we have the Never-Die Church and now we've got the Never Stay Dead Church, she thought. It was all a bit much.

'Why all the leaflets Richard?'

'Oh they give me ideas for designs and possible customers.'

'So the famous Bishop Asholodu is a customer of yours is he?'

Richard sniffed. 'Mmm, he sent for me to make him suits but then started asking all kinds of questions about my personal life, said he didn't like the way I dress and told me earrings were only for ladies. Then he tells me I need deliverance from some kind of demon.' The eyebrows went up again. 'A demon! Then I will be able to marry and have a proper family life.' He didn't look delighted at the thought.

Gloria felt her hackles going up. She knew how much Richard had suffered to be himself and Monrovia could be a very harsh place. He was incredibly determined but she was sure he had faced some rough treatment over the years. Not that you would know by looking at him. 'A demon eh. This town is full of religion, a lot of it not very good either. What did you say to him?'

'Oh I just nodded and looked grateful and said I would get back to him on the whole demon thing. Then I charged him double for the suits and used some material I had left over from dressing a body for a funeral last week.' Gloria and Abu both laughed, Gloria a little nervously. 'Don't worry my dear,' he said as if reading her thoughts, 'I wouldn't do anything to you Gloria, you are one of my best customers after all.'

Chapter Six

Gloria woke up remembering she had promised to visit Richard Varley that morning to discuss his progress. Richard was the grandson Africanus had almost framed for a murder he himself had committed. The memory of that still shocked her. Gloria had arranged for him stay with Lawrence's mother but part of the deal with the Ministry of Social Welfare was that Gloria would keep an eye on him. Peter Dennis had insisted that she do it herself and not one of her team.

'Morning Aunt Glo. I didn't get a chance to ask you last night. Did you catch anyone for killing that girl?'

'Caught a whole lot of them out at that Never-Die Church.'

Abu looked at her over his bread and fried egg. He had a healthy scepticism for all things political and religious and Liberia certainly gave him a wide canvas for that.

'Never-Die?'

Gloria explained to him what she knew of them and his head shaking got more and more vigorous.

'And you think they are involved in the death of that girl?'

'Her name is Rose. I don't know how exactly but they are involved in some way. And I'm not supposed to be discussing this with you.' Abu grinned.

'Hey it's me, Aunt Glo and anyway I have to know these things so I can be ready when they try and do something to us.'

'Not this time Abu,' her last two cases had brought trouble into the apartment, 'this is not going to be personal.'

Abu looked at her again over his bread. 'Aunt Glo you put the president's Head of Protocol in prison along with the Minister of Defence and Africanus Varley's son. Jeez. And then there's Africanus himself and Judge Weah. They're still free and they know you are still after them. That's a lot of powerful enemies. Plus you never found snake-girl.' Gloria shuddered. A girl had been sent to leave a Green Mamba in her room. Neither she nor Abu could look at snakeskin belts without remembering.

'Yes, but a girl who can do that trick will turn up again. Anyway, it's a reminder to you not to let strange girls into the apartment. How is Fatu anyway?'

Abu got up then. He didn't know himself how he felt about Fatu, Lawrence's younger sister, and he certainly wasn't discussing it with her.

Gloria got up as well, satisfied she had got the last word. That didn't happen very often these days.

It was still early when she got to Lawrence's house but the household was busy. The house was down a track and faced onto the ocean. This morning the breeze coming off the sea was strong and cool. Gloria stood for a moment with her eyes closed and enjoyed the sensation of the sun on her face and shoulders while the cool air brushed about her hair.

'Glad to see you are back in uniform.' She turned to see Lawrence in his shorts and t-shirt.

'You waiting for your ma to press yours?' Even as she said it she felt that surge of affection for him. She missed not having him around all the time, not that she would ever admit to that, or to her feelings for him. Not yet anyway.

'Come in and see her, the cup and saucer are ready with your coffee in them.'

Lawrence's mum did not use mugs, she said they were not for educated people. Gloria found the whole cup and saucer, special knives, small plates, paper doilies paraphernalia quite intimidating but there was no escaping it here. On the plus side Mrs Boakai made very good coffee.

Edith Boakai was bustling around when Gloria went in. She was always busy. She ran the house, had a thriving vegetable garden, chaired the Retired Ladies Book Club and looked after her children. She sometimes forgot that Fatu, the 'surprise' child of her fifties was so much younger than Lawrence and scolded Lawrence as if he was a schoolboy. The newest addition to her house, Richard Varley, was washing dishes when Gloria went in. He had changed, she thought, even in a few months. When she met him for the first time Richard had been a skinny boy with bad skin and an even worse attitude. After a few short months with Edith his skin was clear and the bad attitude had gone.

'It's Richard's birthday Gloria, he is fourteen today. Sit down and drink your coffee.' Gloria sat at the table. She sensed Edith was building up to something.

'Many happy returns Richard.'

'Well he received a card yesterday; it was left at the gate. We thought you should know.' They looked so serious Gloria began to get worried.

'Not from his grandfather was it? Africanus? Don't tell me he wants the boy back.'

'No,' Edith shook her head as if dismissing Africans as an afterthought, 'of course he sent a card and money, his pride will not allow him not to do that but that's not what we're talking about. This one was from Richard's mother.'

'Oh. Gloria couldn't think of what else to say to that. A few weeks ago his mother had come back, with a gun, and tried to take Richard away but he had refused to go and she had run off. 'A card is better than a gun I suppose.'

'Ah Gloria, be serious. She says she is sorry, that she understands how Richard feels and she wants to meet him. That's all.'

Gloria shrugged. She didn't have a lot of time for Nessee Varley. 'If she had turned up when I asked her we could have put Africanus in jail. We needed her testimony that Africanus was involved in killing that boy Kwame, the one she was supposed to be so fond of. Now he's still free.' She shrugged again. 'If she wants to meet him, and you agree Richard, I will ask the people at the Ministry.'

'The Ministry? What have they got to do with it?' Edith looked puzzled.

'Richard is a ward of the State now Edith. Any big decisions about his future have to be cleared with the Ministry of Social Welfare. Do you want to meet her Richard?'

He looked confused. 'I like living here.' He looked at Edith.

'No-one's taking you from here. But do you want to meet your mother?'

He shrugged and stared at the floor. 'Yeah, suppose.' Ah, the charming American boy was back, Gloria thought.

'Speak up child and look at the Inspector.'

Edith's words had the desired effect and Richard looked at her. She saw he was on the verge of tears.

'Look, I will talk to the people at the Ministry first and then you can decide. How about that?' He nodded, grateful for the reprieve. 'Now, any cake Ma Edith? I know you will have some somewhere.'

Edith smiled and brought in a large brightly coloured confection, muttering about bad habits and eating cake at breakfast but cut it anyway.

It was ten before she reached the office and Moses would have been pacing up and down her office except there was no space for that.

'Morning ma'am.' Moses was always more formal in the mornings she noticed.

'Morning Moses. You are looking very anxious.'

'Not anxious ma'am. We have started questioning those people from the church.' She nodded. 'And some woman called Marcia Reynolds has called here five times this morning. She was very persistent. Something about a chat show?'

'Yes, Marcia. She's an old friend of mine.' She caught the look on Moses face. 'I do have some friends who are not male police officers Moses. Marcia and I were at school together. She went to the States and worked in broadcasting. She's back now working at that new private TV station.'

'Oh, I see. But I think she wants to talk to you about a programme she is producing. So is she the one doing that new programme *Marcia!* the programme they are advertising all over town?'

'Yes, that's her face up alongside that Bishop Asholodu. I hope she gets a bigger audience than him.'

'When it says chat show, do you mean like those American ones?'

Moses had been subjected to hours and hours of American TV when on holiday. He was still recovering. Gloria nodded, 'Except our version will have real bullets for the cheating husband or boyfriend.' They both laughed. Reality TV Liberia-style would be worth watching.

They sat at her desk to review progress. There wasn't much. Two deaths, some links to obscure traditional beliefs or practices and the arrest of an entire church congregation.

'Paul has declared he knows nothing more about Leopard Men and he is too busy to do any more research for us.'

Gloria frowned. 'He got his transfer to CID even after the mess he made in the last case and he still acts as if we are beneath him. Anyway, I was thinking we should go and talk to Colonel Toweh.' Toweh was still the Head of Presidential Security. Moses looked puzzled. 'Why Toweh?'

'When Barnyou mistakenly tried to arrest him during the last case they discovered he has piles of archive documents in his office – I think he's writing a book about Liberia.' Moses looked a bit lost. 'Well, I'm pretty sure he won't talk to Barnyou but he might talk to me and he could have some stuff on Leopard Cults. Actually I might call round this evening after work. I did promise to go back and visit his son after we scared them half to death the last time, and Toweh might be a bit friendlier in front of his family.'

'On your own again then?'

'Yes, I'll go myself. Today we need to talk to the Never-Die people. You and I will talk with Wolo again. Get Izena to talk to the women, maybe Ambrose and her, they must know more. And send Christian and Alfred out to the Children's Village again.'

At the general meeting Gloria raised the question that was troubling her the most. 'We have no motive. Why were these children killed?'

Young Alfred jumped straight in. 'It must be to stop them talking, they must have seen or heard something.'

Izena was shaking her head. 'Not necessarily. If it was to stop them talking then why put make-up on them and then leave the bodies in very public places.'

'To make a statement or leave us a message, or just because they enjoy the attention.' Ambrose sounded disgusted.

'Or maybe a mix of all those things. But we won't know properly until we work out the connection between the children. Wolo certainly knows a lot more about Rose's disappearance and he is definitely hiding something but I'm pretty sure he'd never seen the boy before and no-one on the compound knew him did they Christian?' Christian opened his eyes long enough to shake his head. 'So we have no leads on him.'

'Did Wolo kill the girl do we think?'

'Her name is Rose, Lamine, not 'the girl' and no, I don't think he did. If he killed her he would have tried to hide the body. He's not smart enough to do stunts.'

'What about us ma'am? Is there any danger for us this time?' Gloria thought it was quite brave of Alfred to raise that. 'I was thinking more about Izena?' Judging by Izena's scowl it was even braver of him to push his concern onto his future wife.'

'Well, there's always danger Alfred, for all of us. That's why it's better to work in twos, not to discuss our findings outside the office and to keep in contact.' They all nodded solemnly and Gloria knew they would be teasing Alfred as soon as she left the room.

'Oh and ma'am could I just tell everyone that our engagement party was postponed and is now happening next Sunday and everyone is invited.' Alfred was beaming. 'It's at the Cooper residence starting at midday.'

Gloria wondered why rich people lived in residences and everyone else lived in a house. 'Well, you've a lot of work to do before that.'

'Oh and ma'am,' it was Izena now, 'I just want to say that there are to be no gifts, we just want everyone to come and enjoy themselves.' There was a cheer in the room. Most of the team struggled to pay their rent and meet whatever family commitments they had, buying a worthy gift for the daughter of the wealthy Cooper family would have been difficult.

Gloria left them to their discussion and called Barnyou. Dr Armah wanted to meet them and they agreed to meet at the hospital at two. Her phone rang again and a lively voice with a faint American twang shouted down the phone. 'Gloria! Finally. You are so hard to contact girl, how you doin?'

'Hi Marcia. I heard you were trying to get in touch, it's been very busy here.'

'Trying to get in touch? It would be easier to contact my mother,' Marcia's mother had been dead for years. 'I had spoken to the President and the Vice-President before anyone would even give me your number. Are you like the lady Robocop around here or something? Police royalty? Cop Celebrity? Top Cop, mmm, I like that, yes, I think I might go with Top Cop.'

Gloria coughed, 'Eh Marcia, I'm still here.'

'Sorry Glo, just thinking aloud, for my new show. Have you heard about it?'

'Marcia, you are on as many billboards as Bishop Asholodu and he's next to God in this town at the moment. So yes, I have heard of the show. When does it start?'

'Oh soon, emm,' she had gone a bit cagey now, 'that's one of the reasons I wanted to call you girl, so we can catch up, have lunch or something.' She paused but Gloria just waited, with Marcia there was always something else. 'And talk to you about a special show I want to put together for the opener.'

'Right, so you need help with information or finding some interesting people? I can do that.'

'Actually Glo,' Marcia hesitated slightly, 'I want you on the show, you and a few other powerful Liberian women, you know the kind of thing; Women of Power or Liberia's Leading Lights or Amazons of the...' Her voice trailed off. 'You don't like the titles do you?'

'I don't like the titles and I don't like the idea. Why would you want me on a chat show?'

'Well you are famous, and you are interesting, I read about one of your cases in the States you know. You've got a reputation.' She paused. 'Oh come on Glo, otherwise the famous women are going to be one politician who will talk about the difference she's making to the lives of women and children, two businesswomen who import used clothes from Guinea or somewhere, and some interfering old busybody who has opened a school for poor girls. It's such a stereotype of famous women.'

'Oh I see, so I get to be the novelty act.' But she relented. She was sure Marcia was finding it a lot more difficult to get a chat show up and running than she had anticipated. People always thought they knew what Liberia was like, what the problems were and that they could deal with them, but even a few years living outside changed your perception and your memories. Although people talked about corruption and war, lack of education and poor services and so on, they mostly remembered Liberia through a soft focus lens; warm days, cold beer, family and friends. As soon as they touched down on home soil the reality kicked in. 'Ok ok Marcia, you always could get your own way so there's no point in resisting but I want to be prepared.'

'Sure, can you meet for lunch today? It would be good to catch up.'

'Ok. Say around three-thirty?' They agreed to meet at Pizza Heaven off Tubman Boulevard.

Gloria knew she would regret agreeing to this but Marcia was one of her oldest friends.

Moses, on the other hand, thought it was funny, very funny, and threatened to let everyone know when the show was on.

They went down to the interview room where Wolo was waiting for them. He looked even more dejected than yesterday but despite his looks he stuck to his story. Rose had always been a difficult girl and when the church moved from Nimba to Bensonville she had got worse; she was lazy, she lied and she was disobedient.

Gloria produced the paper Moses had given her that morning. 'A few facts we need to check Mr Wolo. This is a statement from the Superintendent of Nimba County. He says that your church was closed down there because of your activities, especially for the way you treat the children. The Superintendent says that's the reason you all moved to Bensonville.'

Wolo shook his head. 'It not true. The Prophet told us we mun come here because the people in Nimba were too hard headed and they wan plesecoot us.'

'Do you mean persecute you?' Wolo nodded. 'That what I say.'

'So do the children go to school?'

'We have our own school and our own teachers. I am the Principal.'

Gloria rolled her eyes. 'We'll be coming back to look at your school Mr Wolo but for now I want to know what happened to Rose. Why did you say you didn't know her when we asked you?'

'She looked too different and my eyes are not strong.'

'Ok, so what happened to her, the truth this time?'

But Wolo just repeated his previous statement that she had run away because she was going to be punished.

'I hope the others have better luck. He is hiding something but I am even surer now he didn't kill her like that, he's just not smart enough. But he is very worried about something.' They were on their way downstairs to her car when she saw Rufus Sarpoh loitering with intent. Rufus was the most persistent journalist in Monrovia and he had a formidable nose for a story. He had, however unwittingly, provided a vital clue in their last case and had been instrumental in saving the life of the President's grandson.

He was never going to let her to forget that.

'Inspector, how are you. Have you got a minute?'

'I told you before Rufus to stop waiting for me here, make an appointment, come to my office. If you see me here then I am heading out somewhere.'

'Is it to look at the bodies of those children?' She wasn't surprised he knew.

'Look Rufus, as before. If you cooperate with me then…' she let it hang. Rufus nodded. Gloria had always been as good as her word. He had been given access to some great information because he had behaved decently.

'Just give me something Inspector. Was the dead girl a girlfriend of Abraham Kanneh?'

'What? No! She was a child Rufus. You start printing that nonsense and you will be in big trouble.'

'What about the boy. Is it true he had horns?'

Gloria laughed in spite of herself. 'Your sources have let you down this time Rufus or are you just fishing? Meet me here tomorrow morning and I will tell you what I can tell you. Agreed?' Rufus nodded, satisfied. 'And Inspector Boakai asked me to tell you that if you keep calling him Glamour Cop in your column you are going to be in trouble.' Rufus weekly column reviewed the political and civic life of the fictional town of Bigmanville. Everyone was referred to by a pseudonym but there was never any doubt who or what Rufus was talking about. It was hugely popular with ordinary Monrovians and had broken some big stories that otherwise would not have seen the light of day.

'Ah, tell him to forget it, I haven't mentioned him for weeks.' There was no love lost between Lawrence and Rufus. 'Anyway, I have a new character this week. I think you'll like it Inspector. Make sure you read it tomorrow.' He was already walking away having spotted the Director of the new Anti-Corruption squad making her way downstairs.

'He needs to be careful, he is going to get into big trouble one day.'

Moses nodded. 'I wonder who the new character is. Anyway we are going to be very late if we don't move.'

Twenty minutes later they were at the new morgue facilities. Gloria hadn't been here before and she remarked how shiny everything was.

'Let's see how long it lasts,' Moses said gruffly.

Dr Armah and Barnyou were already sitting at a gleaming steel table and Gloria was relieved to see there wasn't a body in sight. Armah waved vaguely in her direction and carried on talking. 'First of all I think these children came from quite different backgrounds. The girl was undernourished and, although carefully made up to look very pretty, was not healthy. The boy on the other hand was healthy and, prior to being shot anyway, looked as if he had been well looked after. Additionally, I believe the boy was not Liberian. Markings and the nature of his circumcision would tell me he is Nigerian, probably northern Nigerian.' Gloria could see Moses making notes.

'These killings in my opinion were carried out by the same person or persons. The strange killings and disfiguration of the bodies is something I haven't come across before. The wounds on the girl's body were deep and violent. They caused massive rupture and damage to her internal organs. The pain would have been awful,' he shook his head, 'but she would have died very quickly. In contrast the boy was shot execution style with a single bullet, instant death. Rose's attack was made to look superficially like an animal attack and the boy had a real animal tail, it's actually the tail of a Red River Hog, sewn on expertly to his lower back. They were both put on public display with make-up carefully applied after death. Now Inspectors, I have been doing forensic pathology for many years so I have seen a great deal of death and violence but there is something different about these cases. In West Africa our violence can be extreme, as you will know, but is usually opportunistic, accidental or fuelled by anger, drugs etc. This looks different to me. These deaths were staged. I use that word carefully. I have never seen anyone kill and then apply makeup and fix the dead person's hair. The wounds made to look like claw marks and the tail of an animal sewn on to a body. These killings were carefully thought through and expertly carried out from start to finish. And the make-up, by the way, and the hair decorations are not local. They are imported, perhaps from Asia.'

'Thanks doctor.' Barnyou looked at Gloria as he spoke 'This is very useful. The main question for us is 'why'. Why were these children killed and in this way?'

Gloria butted in. 'I think the main question is 'who' not 'why'. We need to find this person and stop them.'

Armah paused and then carried on as if Gloria hadn't spoken. 'Exactly Inspector. The staging of these murders suggests that this is more than just getting rid of people who know or have seen too much. Have you discovered any more about them?'

'Rose came from a group called the Never-Die Church and we are still questioning them but we have found nothing about the boy yet.'

'So they are not related to each other?'

'Well, we haven't found a connection yet.'

They left again and Gloria wondered how useful that had been.

'We need to find out something about the boy Moses, I feel we have neglected him. If he is Nigerian we can start there. It is terrible we don't even have a name.'

'I can start that now. I know the chair of the local Nigerian Community Association.'

'Good idea, but be careful, we don't want to give the feeling there is an anti-Nigerian campaign and start a panic. How well do you know him?'

'It's a 'her,' Madam Phyllis Adebayo, and she is a big friend of Hawa. They work together at the airport.'

'Ok, well I am going to lunch with Marcia and then I'll go to see Toweh. Call me if anything comes up.'

Chapter Seven

Gloria had been to Pizza Heaven several times – too many times she thought patting her waist, but it was the best pizza in town. The place itself was smart and well run by a young local couple, John and Sarah Kabah, who greeted her as soon as she entered.

'Hi Gloria, how are you? Long time-o.' Both of them had studied abroad and come back originally to work in agriculture. They had soon retreated to Monrovia and opened the hotel and restaurant instead. Gloria had heard snippets of their venture into agriculture and it sounded as if local wildlife in the form of ex-rebels and enormous pythons had done for them.

'Hi Sarah, I'm meeting someone for lunch.'

'Marcia? She told us. She's out in the garden.'

The 'garden' was a paved area at the back of the restaurant with some potted plants and plenty of shade from large striped umbrellas. Marcia was sitting in the farthest corner. She was wearing a headscarf and very large sunglasses. They hugged and Gloria looked at her closely. 'Are you hiding from someone?'

Marcia nodded. 'This town is too small. Everywhere I go people keep talking to me and asking me if they can be on my show, or their son or daughter or cousin… It's driving me mad.'

'Oh you'll get used to it Marcia. Everything is a five-minute wonder in this town.'

'Marcia laughed. 'Thanks Glo. I mean I want some peace but I don't want to disappear completely. And of course I enjoy the attention too. I lived in North Carolina for five years, produced and then hosted the most popular radio phone-in programme there and still the only people who ever talked to me in the street were other Liberians who usually wanted me to sponsor something. So I am quite enjoying this, as well as finding it a bit tiresome.'

Gloria remembered Marcia as the girl who won Miss JJ Fellowes Beauty Pageant three years in a row. That took dedication. She had been pretty then but now she was beautiful and Gloria was sure she was enjoying the attention. 'So tell me everything Marcia. I mean you left for the States straight after graduation, that's a lot of years of news.'

'Don't exaggerate Glo. You know we used to write all the time, in the days when people still sent letters. It was just the war. Almost five years before I even heard you were still alive. That was terrible.'

'True, but we don't want to talk about that now. And I loved those parcels you used to send; coffee, books…'

'And clothes.'

'Oh yes the clothes as well.' Gloria would actually have preferred more coffee or more books. Marcia laughed again, loudly this time.

'Come on Glo, I'm one of your oldest friends. I know you were not the least bit interested in those clothes but there was a lot of pressure in making up those parcels you know. If I had only sent coffee and books the Liberians would have said I was just being cheap or lazy, or both. So yes I had to put some clothes in, for the sake of my own reputation.' They both laughed then. Gloria was surprised how easy it was to reconnect with her long-time best friend. There was no awkwardness at all. It was a cliché but the years did fall away and they very quickly moved from all the serious stuff of surviving war in Liberia and adapting to life in the States to memories from school. Marcia produced the JJ Fellowes Yearbook and they had a good laugh at the clothes and the hairstyles, and a few tears at how many of their class had died.

Marcia pointed to a faded photo in the top right-hand corner. 'Wasn't that your first boyfriend? What was his name again?'

Gloria rolled her eyes. 'Patrick Adolphus Kambah III. And before you ask, no I never saw him after we left school. Hmm, he liked himself too much that boy.'

Marcia laughed. 'And you were always so secretive about your love life. We were never totally sure you were together until you turned up with him to the Prom.'

'And that's how I like it.'

'Oh, come on Glo we're not in school now.' She gave Gloria a look. 'What about this Lawrence I'm hearing about?'

Gloria sighed. 'Hearing about? Che, Liberian people are too nosy.' She looked at her friend. 'Lawrence and I have been friends for years, and we are still friends, ok?'

'Close friends?' Marcia had leaned in as if she was interviewing someone on her chat show.

Gloria started laughing. Only Marcia could keep digging like this. She stood up. 'Yes, me and Lawrence are very close friends Marcia, very close friends.' She emphasised each word and then as if to end the conversation Gloria looked at her watch. It was almost five.

'Sorry Marcia I have to go, something to do with a case I'm on at the moment.'

'But we haven't even talked about the show yet.' Gloria sat back down reluctantly.

'Ok, I will do the show. You can give me the details later though.'

'Thanks Glo, it will be great. Oh no,' she was looking across the garden, 'sorry Glo, I am going to get another unwanted visitor I think. They can't leave me alone.' But the voice behind her called out Gloria's name instead.

'Inspector Gloria, I didn't think you took any time off.'

It was Abraham Kanneh and this time he had a whole gang with him. They were all dressed in black t-shirts, gold chains and jeans.

'And I didn't think footballers ate pizza or are you just feeding the flock?' she gestured to the group who were milling around, most of them with a phone to their ear.

Kanneh laughed again. 'You didn't get back to me about my offer Inspector.'

'I will, don't you worry. This is my friend Marcia Reynolds. Marcia this is Abraham Kanneh.'

Marcia recovered quickly from her surprise at not being the centre of attention. 'Oh I know AK. I'm hoping to get you on my new chat show.'

Kanneh kept smiling but clearly didn't recognise Marcia. Gloria excused herself and left them talking. If Kanneh didn't know Marcia at the moment he certainly would by the time she had finished.

The evening was clear and pleasantly warm as Gloria forced the Polo into the busy traffic. Yellow taxis, NGO jeeps and land rovers and a few battered private cars all jostled the narrow Boulevard. At the busy Coleman Street junction she was surprised to see Captain Luseni directing traffic. Luseni had been a member of her unit until he transferred out. He must have done something very wrong to be out on the road now. He caught sight of her but didn't acknowledge her. She drove to the end of the road and turned into Colonel Amos Toweh's house. The gates were open and she saw the family were sitting on the veranda. Mercy and Amos didn't look surprised to see her but neither did they look particularly welcoming and she noticed that DG had retreated to hide behind his mother's chair. She took a deep breath and got out the car.

Mercy came down the steps to welcome her and Gloria thought she was very gracious. 'Nice to see you again Inspector. Come and have a drink.' Amos looked less formidable than when he was in his Head-of-Security persona and offered her his hand.

'Inspector Gloria, it's good to see you. Before you tell us what your business is, I presume there is some business, let me assure you there are no hard feelings about that raid on our house.' He held up his hand. 'Let me finish. I have my sources as you know and I have it on good authority that you thought the raid was a wrong move but you were manipulated into it. Let's not talk of it again.'

'That is good of you Amos. I hope Mercy and DG feel the same.' Mercy smiled at her and pointed at DG. 'You will need to ask him yourself Inspector.'

'Ok, and please call me Gloria.' She looked over at DG who was staring at her. DG had been born with a severe physical deformity and rarely went outside his garden. She held out her hand. 'Eh, come shake my hand DG.' He moved over to her very slowly, dragging his left leg behind him. His head was misshapen and swollen but his eyes were bright and intelligent. He held out his hand and Gloria took it. 'Now, I have to ask you if you can forgive me for bursting into your house DG.'

DG looked at her and then, in a surprisingly clear voice, said. 'I'm not sure. You had a gun. You came into my room waving a gun. I am only nine years old.' His tone was exasperated rather than angry and very grown up. He raised an eyebrow and then he laughed. 'Ok, I forgive you Inspector.' He lifted his hand and high-fived her.

'Quite a character you've got there, Mercy.' Mercy and Amos were laughing.

'Oh he can be frisky once he gets to know you.'

They moved to the back veranda which looked onto a beautiful garden while DG was taken by his nurse for his bath.

'Now Gloria I know you have this case you're working on. I see you found another child murdered which is terrible. So if there's some way I can help let me know, don't think you have to make conversation with us first. Come on, what's the deal here?'

Gloria explained everything Dr Armah had told them about the murdered children. Mercy shook her head. 'Such terrible things we do to children.'

'So how can we help Gloria?'

'Well we are still looking for connections between the murders, and Rose's murder was made to look like an attack by Leopard Men. We need more information about these Leopard Men, apart from a few of old Alfred's memories no-one seems to know much, and I was told you had a sizeable archive collection which might have some details about them.'

'Oh the archives, thought they might come in useful one day. Yes, I have come across some stuff but none of it very recent. Let me get it, it's not much more than a few references.' He left and Gloria turned to Mercy. 'Does DG ever go outside Mercy?' Mercy shook her head. 'When he was smaller we took him out and even abroad but since the war he hates to go anywhere. It's a big worry for us.'

'Wouldn't he even consider going to school or to make some friends?' Mercy was shaking her head. 'He says everyone will laugh at him, which is true, or do worse things to him. He's smart Gloria; he knows what it's like here.'

'But you know how it is Mercy, people will notice for a while and then they'll get used to him, give him some nickname and then forget what he looks like. He could have a fairly normal life.'

Mercy clearly wasn't sure. 'He's been through a lot, I don't know if he could take it.'

Amos was already back with a pile of papers before they could discuss it any further. He put them in front of Gloria. 'Let me summarise for you Gloria. There are accounts of a Leopard Society in Sierra Leone as far back as 1607, even an Alligator Society but let's leave that one. The Leopard Cult seems to have been mainly about the making of some powerful medicine that would give the person power and money. Apparently to join the Cult the person would have to give a member of their own family as a sacrifice – usually a girl over the age of fourteen. The British outlawed it and brought in European judges to try anyone accused of being involved. Now here it seems to have been different. The Leopard Cult, from the reports I have read, is mainly about terror and revenge. A person would be killed if they refused to obey or didn't hand over what these people wanted: money, land or their daughters! Here look at these' he handed her printed copies of old newspapers 'This is *The Milwaukee Sentinel* from December 1936.' Gloria scanned it. It was a report of men dressed in leopard skins and with blades in each hand like claws, attacking villagers in Cape Mount and robbing and killing whole families. 'There's a similar report in *Life* magazine from 1937, so clearly there was some kind of Leopard Cult activities going on but as I say they were about terror and robbery. The wounds you have described sound like a classic Leopard Men attack. But the placing of the body on the roof at the stadium, that is not typical. These are a secret society; they thrive on fear and ignorance. They wouldn't go in for this. This is just someone using Leopard Men as a gimmick.'

'It's what we were thinking Amos but it's good to know you agree.'

'What about the second child, I hear there were some strange circumstances there as well?'

Gloria told them about the tail sewn onto the boy. Well, she thought, he's Head of Presidential Security and probably knows everything already. And he might be able to help. Mercy looked upset again but Amos's face clouded over at the description. Now he looked like the man a lot of other men were scared of. 'They sewed a tail onto him? I would love to get my hands on them first.'

'I am sure.'

'What kind of tail was it?' Gloria was surprised Mercy was asking for details.

'It was a thin reddish tail, from a Red River Hog, according to Armah. I think that's what we call a bush pig, isn't it? Why?'

'I don't know Gloria but all the stories you read in the papers about people who can turn into animals, it always seems to be a bush pig they turn into. It's never a cow or an elephant.' Gloria nodded.

'One of my team suggested there might be a connection with the false Leopard Men attack, maybe a false shape-shifting thing. We are looking into it.'

'Let me know if there is any other way I can help Gloria. I mean it.' Amos was looking at her very intently.

'I will. Thank you. Now I better go home myself.'

She was on the front steps when DG appeared again. 'Inspector I want to ride in your car, please.' Gloria smiled. 'Ok DG I will come back and we will go for a ride. You like my Polo then?'

DG's face changed. 'Not that one! A real police car with the siren and the lights.'

'Right, ok, well I won't promise DG but I will do my best.' He folded his arms and said that was good enough.

The traffic on the Boulevard was in chaos when she got back near the road. It was getting dark and the air was filled with endless horns and shouts. Gloria edged forward. Luseni was still there but he was looking more than a little flustered. He saw her and this time he came straight over. 'Inspector you need to help, there's been an accident.'

Gloria rolled her eyes. 'Come on Luseni traffic accidents are not my responsibility. I am on my way home.'

'No seriously Inspector you need to come. This is very serious. It's Alfred.'

Gloria's heart was suddenly thumping against her chest. 'Alfred? How serious is it?'

'It is very very serious ma'am.' She knew what that tone meant. Alfred was dead.

'Oh god,' she was out her car and following behind Luseni, 'was he alone? Was Izena in the car with him?'

Luseni stopped. 'Not young Alfred ma'am, old Alfred. Looks like he was driving home when a tanker came out the garage and went straight across the road into his car. It's a mess.'

It really was a mess. In the fast falling darkness Gloria could see the tangle of metal and glass. The tanker appeared to have careered into the side of Alfred's car and driven it off the road into the embankment. It was crushed beyond recognition with the tanker upended in the ditch on top of it. There was already a crowd milling around and crazy tangled lines of vehicles.

'Are you sure it's him Luseni?'

'Yes, I spoke to him just seconds before; he pulled in to tell me about your latest cases. We spoke for a few moments but I had to get back on the road and I had just walked away from him when that thing smashed into him. I actually saw his face as it hit. I will never forget that look on his face.'

'Ok, ok Luseni,' Gloria could see he was going into shock, 'have you called for help?' But she could already hear sirens approaching. There was nothing she could do for Alfred but she could help contain the situation. 'Where is the tanker driver?'

'I don't know. People said he jumped out and ran that way,' he pointed towards the beach, 'but I couldn't go after him.'

'Of course not, come, sit down here.' She pulled him over to a bench outside a small shop and told the young girl to give him a drink. 'Stay here, I will come back.'

By the time she got back Lawrence was already in full command. He had arrived with a pick-up full of officers who seemed to know exactly what to do. The crash was cordoned off and everyone was being moved away and traffic was being diverted down into Jallah Town on one side and the back roads on the beach side.

'Hi Lawrence, this is awful.'

'Gloria, what are you doing here?'

'I was visiting Toweh. I just passed when it happened and Luseni stopped me. It was old Alfred in the car you know.' Lawrence made a face.

'Right, I have to get on here Gloria; we need to make sure there's no fire danger before we do anything else. A fire here with two garages and all those people selling gas out of the jars would be disastrous.'

'You look as if you've got that bit under control Lawrence. I'm impressed.'

'You can tell me that in an hour. Look, better go, there's the ambulance.'

He went off shouting orders and she saw him banging the side of an IRS vehicle which was trying to squeeze past the accident. Gloria rolled her eyes. Honestly who did these people think they were? She walked over. 'Do you want me to do this bit Lawrence? You've got enough on your hands.'

'Thanks Gloria, I really need to check that tanker but these idiots keep trying to get by.' Gloria looked at the driver. He was a young man with short spiky hair and a few days stubble. His accent, she thought, was French, or maybe Spanish.

'Look madam I need to get into town. If I go down that way,' he pointed at the lines of vehicles jostling for space on the narrow Jallah Town road, 'It's going to take me all night. Just let me through, please.' He gave her what he clearly imagined was a disarming smile. She saw his hand hover around his shirt pocket, where, she presumed, he kept his 'cold water' money but luckily for him he didn't offer her a bribe.

Gloria smiled back at him and leaned into the cab. 'Listen you fool, there has been a serious accident here. We don't know yet if the tanker is full so there is also a fire risk. So now you will turn the car around and join everyone else through Jallah Town. And for your information unless you have a pregnant woman or a sick mammy in your car,' she looked at the empty interior, 'I don't care how long it takes you to get into town.'

The man looked shocked. He spluttered something about calling his office and reached for the radio. Lawrence was already back. He whispered. 'The tanker is empty Gloria we are going to open the road now. Do you want to let him through?'

'I might have done if he hadn't tried the old 'I'm going to call the office' routine. Just leave him to me.'

She leaned back in the window. 'Any luck calling your office Jean?' she could see his id card. He must be French. He looked sheepish.

'Non, eh no, there is no answer.'

'Well I'll be seeing Hans this week. I'll tell him we spoke. Now if you could turn the car around.'

Jean smashed the gears and angrily turned the car into the Jallah Town traffic. Gloria waited until he was fully absorbed into the lines of vehicles and then opened the main road and started to allow the other cars through the main road again. It was petty, she knew that, but nonetheless satisfying.

It was another few hours before everything was finished. Gloria hadn't gone to look as they cut old Alfred's remains out the car. The equipment was poor and the smash had been severe. It was not a pleasant operation but eventually his body was loaded into a police pick up and taken to the morgue. The wrecks had been moved off the road completely and the traffic was running freely. Apart from old Alfred there had not been any other injuries. By the time they had finished, all her team had arrived on the scene. Young Alfred and Izena had got drinks for everyone and Ambrose had volunteered to go with Moses to tell old Alfred's wife what had happened. Gloria was happy to let them go and do that. Even Christian and Lamine had turned up. They all looked shocked. Old Alfred had been a constant presence for all of them. It was Izena who voiced what they were all thinking.

'Ma'am. They didn't catch the driver?'

'Not yet. He was out the tanker before it had even crashed and he disappeared.'

'What about the tanker?'

'Nothing. It's not registered; it doesn't belong to any of the big companies. It has almost no fuel in it. The garage manager said it drove in and the driver put in a 'dribble' of gas and then sat and waited.'

'So, it could have been deliberate. Someone murdered old Alfred.'

Gloria put up her hand. 'Whoa Izena, we are getting ahead of ourselves here. Why would anyone want to kill Alfred? He's been in the police for years, why kill him now and like this?'

'You mean since he started talking about Leopard Men? Well that might be why. If Leopard Men are still operating they might not like people talking about them.' There was general agreement in the dark that Gloria could feel.

'Let's not get too worried yet. Right, there's nothing else we can do here tonight, let's go home.' There was muttered shuffling and people stretched and drifted away.

Outside Gloria could see Lawrence still directing his operation.

'Are you packing up now Lawrence?'

'Yes, the road is open, there's no danger of fire and we have all the statements we need I think.' He looked tired and his normally immaculate uniform was streaked with dust and sweat.

'Your buttons will need a lot of polishing tomorrow.' He smiled. It was their running joke. 'Come on I'll give you a lift home Lawrence, let Barclay finish up here.' Barclay was Lawrence's deputy and very efficient.

They drove most of the way in silence. 'The team are worried again Lawrence. They think this was no accident, that Alfred was killed.'

'Of course they do. Why would anyone kill Alfred though?' She told him about the Leopard Men. Lawrence had closed his eyes briefly but opened them again as Gloria expertly swerved to avoid an old lady crossing the road with her market stall on her back.

'Well the circumstances are strange, no doubt about that, but Leopard Men organising the assassination of police officers! That will have the sociologists flooding in.'

Gloria smiled too. 'Poor old Alfred, he was a decent man. Not a nice way for it to finish. Moses says his wife is just as quiet, there was no screaming and shouting when he broke the news, just a few tears.'

'You did well Lawrence, your people are really well trained. A few years ago an accident like that would have brought the traffic to a complete standstill for half the night and there would have been a whole series of random arrests.'

'Well, thanks for that Gloria. We do our best. Oh listen, I got a message from the Director's office today. They are giving me some kind of commendation.'

'Commendation? Really. Well congratulations. What's it for?'

'Eh, it's for saving your life actually.' He looked at her sideways. 'You remember in the tower when that big army man was going to shoot you?'

'Of course, I remember Lawrence. It was very accurate shooting and very fast reflexes. I'm not sure you exactly saved my life though. I mean, I could have done something.'

'Really Gloria, you could have done something? You were on the floor as I remember.'

She was quiet for a while. 'Well, I did say thank you Lawrence and I did take you all out to dinner as a thank you.'

'You said that was to thank my mother for taking young Richard in and looking after him.' He was laughing out loud now. 'Eh Gloria, and you know what. If it's a medal I'm going to wear it on my uniform next to all the shiny buttons so every time you see it you can remember how much you owe me.'

Gloria frowned.

'I'm surprised you're not getting something. You did save the President's grandson.'

'Yes and the entire country if you can believe what they were saying at the time. Do you remember? But no, apparently I was just doing my job and the President feels it would be wrong to give out awards or commendations just because it was her grandson.'

'Oh, bad luck on that one. Still I'll take you up on that offer of dinner sometime.'

She dropped him at his mother's house and then drove home. She found Rohit waiting on the stairs.

'Inspector ma'am, are you ok?'

Gloria leaned wearily against the wall. 'I'm fine Rohit just another late night. There's no problem here is there?'

'No don't worry everything is fine. I think Abu was a bit worried about you though. As long as you are alright. Go sleep.'

Chapter Eight

Gloria wandered into the living room the next morning to find Abu again sitting at his breakfast. 'Aunt Glo, I will start leaving you notes. The only time I see you is for about five minutes in the morning.' Gloria was touched that Abu was worried about her but it didn't last long. 'There was no money for food again. I can't eat with Rahul every day it makes me to look cheap.'

'Ok Abu sorry. There was a big accident on Tubman Boulevard last night, that's why I was late.'

Abu muttered grumpily about her being the only policeman in the whole town.

'Not the only one Abu. It was Uncle Lawrence who was in charge actually, I was just helping.'

'He is not my uncle, Aunt Glo, he is your friend.' He stood up and walked into the kitchen.

Gloria smiled to herself at his tone. 'Ok, Abu. Anyway I will be in tonight. There was a message on my phone from your principal by the way, she wants to see me. You're not in trouble are you?'

Abu shrugged. 'Who knows, that school is so strict.'

'Well, you should know for a start.'

He shrugged again 'I'll see you tonight Aunt Glo.' He was already heading for the door. 'Just leave the money on the table please, so I can cook something. Oh and Rohit sent up today's paper, he says you will really want to read Rufus Sarpoh's piece.'

Gloria looked at her watch. How early was he going to school these days? It had better be school he was going to she thought. She opened the newspaper hoping that Rufus hadn't taken against her. Although she was tough with him she knew he would be a fearsome enemy to have. She turned to his column and couldn't believe what she was reading.

Her first reaction was to laugh. It wasn't sophisticated by any stretch of the imagination, but it made the point. How would Africanus Varley react though? Rufus was well known and that would give him some protection but Africanus was very powerful. She had had him in her grasp, literally with dead bodies at his feet, and he had still managed to evade arrest. To say he was well connected was a major understatement. Although she had never discovered the names of his influential friends they were definitely people to be reckoned with. Rufus was playing with fire here.

News From The Sidelines

Spotted at Bigmanville's football competition on Saturday: it was interesting to see the Chief back in circulation. The Chief has had a difficult few weeks but as usual he has survived. We knew he must have a few skeletons in his closet but we didn't realise he actually had them in his foundations as well. His extended family came to his rescue however and as a result his family is now extended even further - all over town; one in jail and one living with strangers. Talk about the 'sins of the fathers being visited upon the children'... in the Chief's case it is literally true.

The office was subdued that morning. Someone had already pinned a photo of old Alfred to the notice board with a message of condolence underneath. There would be a collection, of course, and a memorial service but she noticed that someone had also asked everyone to pray for 'whoever was responsible for this killing' so the murder theory was taking root.

She called Moses into her office. 'I'm not having a team meeting today, they need to be out doing not sitting around wondering if Alfred was murdered and whether they will be next.'

'That's good ma'am but they do have a point. The tanker can't be traced to anyone. It looks as if the driver sat and waited for Alfred to drive by and then aimed for him. And then, by all accounts, the driver was out and running before the tanker was even halfway across the road. It does sound as if it was planned.'

'Yes it's quite a show Moses. All that to kill one old police officer. It would have been a lot easier just to put something in his drink.'

'But if it is the same people, they like to 'stage' things don't they. Isn't that the word you used? Maybe setting up these elaborate murders is part of the fun for them.'

Gloria wasn't so sure. 'I suppose it could be. Lawrence will do a full report anyway so we have to wait for that. If any of the team are worried they can take precautions.'

'And it also means we are now three people down; Luseni and Paul transferred and Alfred dead. The chief has to give us some more people now surely.'

'Yes,' she paused and looked at him, 'I want to see the Director myself and explain to him face to face, otherwise he'll just transfer some old pappay from Traffic division to us or one of those ferocious women from Immigration.'

'True, although we do need some more women in the unit, one is not enough for the kind of cases we are getting.'

'One?'

'Yes, Izena. I mean she's good but not exactly down to earth. Someone like Clementine from St Lukes would be good.'

'For starters Moses we have two women in the unit; I am actually a woman you know.'

Moses didn't look embarrassed. 'I know, but you don't count, I mean you're the boss.'

'But still a woman Moses. And the truth is that Ambrose and Christian are better at all the empathy, winning trust and putting people at ease stuff than me or Izena. So it's not a case of needing more women, we need to make sure we have the right skills.' Moses nodded slowly in agreement. 'And secondly, we can't go around poaching social workers from local agencies and asking them to join the police.'

He looked up then. 'But we don't need them to join the police Gloria. A unit like ours should have a social worker; I mean we are always asking Clementine to handle things for us. You could talk to her boss and get them to second her to our unit. She gets an interesting job and we get a good social worker.'

Gloria thought about that. It wasn't a bad idea actually. They had needed Clementine's help in every case they had handled so far. 'That's good Moses. And we could move Izena to the office where she might feel safer but also, let's be honest; her skills are with systems not with people. She could take on Alfred's work and finally put some order in the office.' Gloria thought about all the unfinished reports on her desk alone and the nightmare that was their filing system. 'Well, I'll talk to Izena today and see if I can see the

Director as well. We still need another officer though.'

'Definitely, and preferably one we don't have to train.'

'Now, give me the feedback on yesterday. How was Madam Adebayo?'

'She didn't recognise the picture but she will ask around and she's sensible, she will do it without causing a panic. I told her it was urgent so she was going to discuss it at their meeting last night. As for the Never-Die people; the men would say nothing and the women are just saying they want to go home, that the prophet fooled them, but they are still very afraid. I don't know what hold that old man had over them but it is strong. But the children talked a lot more.' He opened his notebook, a shiny new leather affair Gloria noticed, and found the page he was looking for. 'They said that Rose was kind of their leader. She organised games for them, you know they are not allowed to play, and she protected them, though they couldn't really say what they meant by that. Her big enemy was Pastor Wolo's son, Victory. He is fourteen but a true believer apparently. He used to beat Rose and call her all kinds of things. He is still causing trouble over there now, trying to control the other children.'

'That's interesting. Father-and-son cults are always more dangerous I would think. Better move Victory in with the men then.'

'But he's only fourteen Gloria. The Child Safety Committee will have a field day with that.'

'I know but we need to think of the others, we could be putting the other children at risk and according to his religious beliefs he is actually an adult. Let him go and join the men.'

'I'll tell Clementine. She will be relieved; I think the boy is spoiled already. The children said he was always trying to force Rose to have sex with him, when he wasn't beating her that is.'

'He sounds delightful, what happened?'

'The children said Rose refused to give in to him, said it was her decision who she slept with.'

Which made Victory mad no doubt? Mad enough to kill her?'

'And that's not all. Victory wasn't the only one after Rose, his father wanted her too, according to the children, but she refused him as well.'

Gloria screwed up her face. 'Are they animals or what? That girl must have been strong. So, they had a motive and they clearly had the opportunity.'

'But the method doesn't fit does it. Those two would not go to all those lengths. I bet they don't even know where the Antoinette Tubman Stadium is.'

'No, I bet they don't. But we need to keep them behind bars for now, the women as well.'

'And about that Gloria, they have a lawyer now and he is accusing us of kidnap.'

'Kidnap? And where did they get a lawyer from?'

'They do have money, don't be fooled by appearances. We need to get our report together quickly.'

'Right, I better have that chat with Izena right away then. Let her come in now and you keep on following up what we have. You need to go back and talk to Mr Ramesh.'

Gloria called through to the Director's office and got his secretary who arranged a meeting for that morning. 'He is keen to speak to you too Inspector.' Gloria wasn't sure she liked the sound of that.

Izena was already knocking on her door as she put the phone down.

'You wanted to see me ma'am?'

'Come in Izena. Have a seat, eh just move some of that stuff.' She and Moses did most of their discussions standing up.

'I don't want to offend anyone Izena but Alfred's death leaves a big gap in our team.' Izena looked at her impassively. 'We will need to reorganise and that will take some time but I am thinking of changing your role.' She explained what her ideas were and for the first time Izena looked enthusiastic.

'So I will do the team coordination, case updates, follow up on reports, prepare scripts for court, develop a database and also do some analysis on our crime statistics?' She leaned forward as she said this, as if poised to spring into action immediately.

Gloria nodded hesitantly. 'Yes, that all sounds great but maybe it would be wise to start with the basics.' She looked at the piles of paper and files covering her desk. 'A bit of tidying up to begin with?'

Izena sat back in her chair again, a flicker of disapproval crossing her face. 'Of course ma'am. A bit of tidying up to begin with. When can I start the real work?'

Gloria sighed knowing she had lost this battle before the war had even started. 'Straight away.' She explained about the Never-Die Church taking them to court. 'We need all the documentation about the conditions at the compound, our fears for the children's safety, their possible involvement in a murder case, everything.'

Izena was already standing up. 'And what will my new title be?'

'Your new title? We don't really do titles other than your rank Izena.'

'Yes ma'am but if I have to put some order on things I will need some authority. I don't want extra money or anything, except for the new equipment of course, just a working title so the others know I can force them to write reports, you know the kind of thing.'

'I'll have a think. And there won't be any extra money either for equipment. You know how things are around here.'

Izena was too excited at the thought of all the organising she was going to be doing to let anything dampen her enthusiasm and she almost danced out the room.

Wow, thought Gloria, that is either going to work out so well or I have just created a monster.

She looked at her watch. It was time to see the boss.

Police Director Kamara looked very smart in his uniform. He welcomed Gloria and even offered her coffee which she gratefully accepted. 'How are things Gloria? I hear you have another tough case, and please accept my condolences for Alfred.'

'Thank you sir. That's part of what I want to talk to you about. With Alfred gone we are now very short of people. I need at least two more people.' She explained Moses idea about seconding a social worker from an agency. To her surprise the Director agreed immediately. 'Why don't you advertise internally for someone to join your unit? Then you can decide who is the most suitable. Draft a memo and I will send it round. And you have my backing to approach St Luke's about their social worker working with us.'

Gloria leaned back. It was all good so far.

'Now you know how much respect I have for you Gloria. You have solved some very big cases in the past months.' He paused. 'And I have always supported your efforts,' Gloria raised an eyebrow but said nothing, 'but you have managed to upset some quite powerful people and' – the Director looked at her full in the face now – 'we have a problem Gloria.' He picked up a thin file which was lying on his desk. 'I have a letter from the Ministry of Justice informing me that you are being investigated for corruption and misuse of your authority as a police officer.' He dropped the file on the desk and opened his hands in a gesture of helplessness. Gloria leaned back in her chair.

'Wait a minute sir, I am being investigated for corruption.' She spoke quietly although she could feel the small core of molten anger forcing itself up through her stomach. 'By the Ministry of Justice?'

'Gloria, Gloria, don't let this get to you. You must have known these people would come after you. If you upset wealthy, influential people in this town you know what happens. We have to fight this the best way we can. By you doing your job and letting your record speak for itself.'

She gripped the arms of the chair and managed to contain herself although part of her said that was the worst possible advice. She needed to fight back.

'There's just one other thing you need to know Gloria. The investigation is being led by Martha Dunmore.' He looked at her anxiously.

Martha Dunmore was the Chief Investigator of the Ministry of Justice's anti- corruption department. It wasn't her ruthlessness that upset Gloria but the fact that Martha Dunmore enjoyed the administration of power for its own sake – and hated when anyone crossed her. And Gloria had crossed her several times. If they were coming after her then Martha Dunmore was the ideal person to lead the charge. She shrugged.

'Look, I just want to tell you that you need to be careful. Try to keep away from eh, from controversy this time. Focus on the job.' He spread out the newspaper in front of her and pointed to Rufus's piece on Africanus Varley. 'Did you have anything to do with this for example?'

'Me? No, that's all Rufus's own work and I wouldn't try warning him sir or you will probably find yourself featuring in his next piece. He's kind of fearless.'

'Well he better be careful too.' Gloria had no idea what the Director meant when he said that so said nothing. It was clear he was finished with her though and she had to leave her half-drunk coffee and go. All the way downstairs she wondered about Kamara. He had been very supportive when she started the job but people changed and people in high office sometimes changed completely, in her experience. What kind of support would he give her and even if he did what could they do against people with that kind of influence? She shook her head as if to get them out of it and got out her phone.

'Moses, did you see Mr Ramesh yet?'

'No boss, I'm still in the office.'

'No problem, just leave him to me, I need to be busy right now. I have to go to Abu's school so I will call and see Ramesh and then I'm back down Gurley Street. I will call you later.'

Although it was only midday the mass of dark clouds hanging over the city meant she had to switch her lights on. There was going to be another storm that was sure. The tension in the air from the storm was reflected in the school. She felt it as soon as she arrived. Holy Redeemer was a good school but the noise bellowing from every classroom was a clear sign everyone was getting restless. The heavy heat which preceded the storm didn't help either. As she walked to the principal's office, past classrooms too dark now to see in and with a wet heat rolling out of them from the crammed bodies inside, Gloria wondered what kind of learning could possibly be going on. They should let them all just go to sleep, she thought, until the storm passes.

Mrs Harris looked a bit nervous. She had been school principal for a long time, before and since the end of the war, but she wasn't carrying the years well, if the dark circles under her eyes were anything to go by. Her office was as dark as the classrooms, although a lot cooler, and she indicated for Gloria to join her near the window where the pre-rain winds were blowing strongly.

'Inspector Gloria, thank you for coming down to see me.' Gloria sat down uncomfortably in the school chair. 'Now, let me say first of all that there is no trouble Inspector. Abu is doing well in his studies.' Gloria nodded. That was good news although she sensed a 'but' coming. 'But I did want to talk to you about one thing. As you know he is now in eighth grade and doing well but he is still well behind for his age. He really should be in tenth grade and getting ready for exams.' She put up her hand to counter Gloria's interruption. 'I know it's a common story but Abu is really very smart Inspector and he is never going to catch up completely here. We try our best but resources are scarce, trained teachers are even more scarce and, I hesitate to say it, our standards are not very high. That really hurts me but it is the reality. It is going to be years before the system really works. Added to that Inspector, I get the impression that Abu has been through a lot of difficult times recently.' Mrs Harris paused and looked at her.

'Can I just stop you a minute Mrs Harris. Has Abu said something to someone or is this just your own observation?'

'Well no, he hasn't said anything, but your cases are well publicised, and he does talk about his adventures; being attacked in your house and fending off the attackers with his martial arts…'

Gloria couldn't believe it. She was the head of the Family and Child Protection Unit and she was being told she didn't know how to take care of her nephew. It was just the undercurrent of guilt and that nagging sense that she didn't know how to take care of him that stopped her from telling Mrs Harris she had overstepped the line.

'And tell me Mrs Harris do you keep all your students under this close a scrutiny? Because if you are going to give out advice you need to check out your facts first…' She stood up.

But Mrs Harris was babbling on nervously. 'I just think that it might be better for your nephew to go abroad Inspector, you could send him to the States where I'm sure he could get a good education and be safe.'

But Gloria had heard enough. She left the office furious at Mrs Harris, and herself and Abu and everything. She had to walk past the classrooms again and stopped to look in at an eighth-grade lesson. With the massed storm clouds rolling in, the room was in almost complete darkness. The students, who were packed together so tightly the teacher couldn't even walk between rows, were talking and laughing and the heat was unbearable. She stared for a few moments. Was this really helping anyone? Was she really being neglectful? She remembered the conversation with Abu this morning and his attitude, maybe she wasn't doing enough or maybe she was asking him to do too much.

She reached her car just as the storm crashed into the city. The clouds opened and a wall of water descended. Huddled in her car Gloria could see and hear nothing but the rain pounding on the roof and running in waves down the windows. It was as if she was sinking into the sea and there was nothing to do but sit in the muggy damp interior and wait. She was in her own world for a few moments at least. She thought about the things Mrs Harris said to her. Of course she had considered sending Abu abroad but was reluctant to do it, telling herself people needed to stay and make things better. But was she being selfish? Was she sacrificing Abu's future? And, as he had pointed out, she had plenty of powerful enemies, so was it even safe for him to stay?

By the time she had gone full circle in her head several times the rain had eased enough for Gloria to see the road. It was swimming with water and a small torrent carrying all the detritus from Snapper Hill was running down the centre. The storm drains had overflowed as well, making it less than ideal for her small Polo, but action was preferable to this endless questioning in her own head. Those thoughts would have to wait. She set off cautiously down the hill and by using the side roads avoided the mini lake which had formed in the dip at the bottom of the hill. Carey Street, where some of the storm drains had collapsed in previous rains, was relatively free of surface water. Gloria was uncomfortably aware, though, of the vast amounts of water which must be rushing underneath the street. It's going to collapse one day, she thought, but hopefully not today.

Ramesh and Sons was open for business again although the shop was empty of customers when Gloria went in. She waited for a moment. It looked just like all the other jewellery shops on the street; glass cabinets filled with glittering rings and necklaces although, if Hassan was to be believed, a lot of the items in Ramesh's shop were fake. She had worked out he meant costume jewellery. Ramesh catered to a less wealthy clientele, people who needed or wanted the appearance of finery but without paying the prices for it. The rain had obviously kept any customers away, or even the hope of any customers, and Ramesh and his staff seemed to have gone into hiding. She wandered around. The cabinets ran on three sides of the shop. There was a cash register at the top and a set of tiny cups for coffee.

On the wall behind a stick of pungent incense burned in front of a shrine to Lord Ganesh. The smell reminded Gloria of the old-fashioned mosquito coils her mother had burnt at night; thick, heavy and unpleasant.

She knocked on the door at the side then turned the handle and went in. It was a photo studio, camera on a tripod, different coloured drapes on the walls and very bright overhead lights.

'Can I help you Inspector?' She turned and saw Ramesh coming out of another room.

'Just a few more questions Mr Ramesh.' She came back into the shop. 'So you also have a photo studio here? That's quite an unusual mix.'

Ramesh nodded. 'It's a hobby of mine Inspector. I won first prize in the Bombay, eh Mumbai I mean, under fourteen category of the 'Why I Love My City' competition. He pointed to a faded black and white photo of a woman and three children sitting in what looked like a large cardboard box with two dogs stretched in front of them. 'I called it 'Domestic Bliss' Inspector. But that was many years and many lives ago.' He rubbed his hands. 'Nowadays it's mostly passport photos and the occasional family photo. So tell me, have you found out anything more about that poor child?'

'Well, we know the boy was Nigerian, well we are almost sure. But not much else at the moment. Do you know any Nigerians Mr Ramesh?'

He shrugged as if the world outside his shop was not really his concern. 'I live very quietly Inspector.'

'Where are your family?'

'My wife is back in India, she could not take the stress of living here.' He pointed to another photo of two very serious boys. 'My boys are grown up and live in America,' he rolled his eyes, 'so I don't see much of them. As I say, I live here very quietly.'

'And you checked your stock again?'

'Yes, there's nothing missing. I'm sure the other owners have told you my stock is not worth stealing Inspector.' He smiled then as if answering his own question. 'But everyone should be able to wear nice things, even poor people. I help them to do that.'

Gloria smiled back in spite of herself. Mr Ramesh clearly didn't take himself too seriously which she liked. 'So lots of the girls from Gurley Street perhaps?'

'Not lots of them Inspector, a few of them. You might be surprised the kind of people who are wearing my jewellery.'

'I might be, then again I might not be. But that's a good idea. Why don't you get me a list of your customers and what they bought here? Maybe someone has a grudge against you.'

Ramesh nodded. 'I don't think I have any enemies like that but I will get you the list. Maybe you can see something.'

'And have you thought any more about how someone could get into your shop to leave a body in the window.'

'I have Inspector. I think it must have been my assistant. I am vigilant but you know these people…' He let the sentence trail away and Gloria wasn't sure whether that was in deference to her or because he thought his meaning so obvious there was no need to complete it. 'Anyway I let him go, I can't prove anything but it would be easy for him to make duplicate keys and sell them to someone.'

Gloria frowned. 'You think it was him and you let him go… now how does that make sense? We will decide that. Get me his name and address. If he is involved we need to speak to him.'

Ramesh was unruffled. 'Of course, Inspector. But I thought the other inspector took all those details in the first investigation. I just did not want to have someone I can't trust in my shop.'

Gloria stopped. Of course Barnyou had the man's details; in fact he had probably investigated by now. She grunted that it didn't matter and she would wait for his customer list and left to pay another visit to Doreen Walker.

The rain had slowed to a drizzle by the time she got back out but the alleyways off Gurley Street were still treacherous; mud, stones and rubbish were the least of it, it was the pools of dank muddy water Gloria was most wary of. She had no idea how deep the pools were and was anxious not to break a bone or lose her dignity. Doreen Walker's yard, on the other hand, looked clean and dry. The madam herself was nowhere to be seen and Gloria knocked the door loudly. She knew she was being watched, well she could feel it, but when she looked around she noticed for the first time that even in this backstreet of crowded houses, huts and booths not a single window overlooked Doreen Walker's house. Gloria had wondered why she still lived here when she could afford to live anywhere but perhaps this place, carefully arranged, made her feel safe, hidden from view. She knocked again. Finally, and with the utmost reluctance, the door opened and a young girl looked out.

'I need to speak to madam, can you please tell her?' The girl closed the door again and there was silence. Just when she was wondering whether to knock again the girl came back and wordlessly invited her in.

A long dark corridor led into the interior of the house past closed doors. At the end the girl opened a door into a room which was a cross between a throne room and a shrine. Heavy wooden furniture upholstered in red and with elaborately carved arms and back sat around the walls facing a large TV screen above which hung a huge painting of Christ on the Cross and an only slightly smaller painting of Doreen Walker staring sombrely into space as if receiving a vision. Gloria stood with her back to the paintings. Everyone she met in this case seemed to have some kind of religious thing going on. It was all a bit creepy.

Doreen entered and greeted Gloria like an old friend. 'Nice to see you again Inspector.'

'Hello Doreen, I'm glad I was able to catch you in, the rain isn't good for business then?'

Doreen ignored that. If the war had only inconvenienced her business, as Gloria had heard, then a few storms were not even worth her consideration. 'How can I help you again?'

'I was wondering if you knew a jewellery shop on Carey Street, Ramesh and Sons.'

'I know a lot of jewellery shops Inspector.'

'Well, this particular one, do you know it?'

'I have seen it and I know some of the girls buy their jewellery from there, I buy my jewellery in Ghana and Nigeria.'

'Do you know this boy?' She showed him the picture of the boy sprawled in the jewellery shop window.

'Why do you keep showing me pictures of children? And this is a boy; I have nothing to do with boys Inspector.'

'Doreen, I am asking for your help that is all. You are a woman who hears a lot of things. Please just look at the picture again. I accept you don't know the boy but see if there is anything about the picture that strikes you.'

Doreen reluctantly bent to look at the photo again. Gloria could see she was studying it. She was counting on the fact that Doreen thought herself very clever. 'Mmm well, it is Ramesh's shop.' She looked up. 'His jewellery is quite eh, how shall I say, distinctive.'

'Do you mean that in a good way?'

Doreen laughed. 'To be fair Inspector, he doesn't pretend to sell the most expensive items. His business is good quality costume jewellery; some of it is still fairly pricey, it's just not what I would buy.'

Gloria shrugged. 'Right, so you recognise his shop. Anything else?'

'The make-up. It is exactly the same brand as on the girl you showed me.'

'You can see that from a photo?'

Doreen laughed self importantly. 'Oh yes, and I can tell you it was applied by the same person. No, honestly,' she put her hand up to stop Gloria interrupting, 'most people have no idea how to put on make up.

It's smeared on, slapped on, caked on but when it is done by a professional you can see it immediately. This is professional. And each professional's style is as distinctive as a signature. The make-up on both these children was applied by the same professional.' She sat back, pleased with herself.

'Thank you Doreen, that is interesting. And how many professional make-up people do you know?'

Doreen's face closed down immediately. 'I don't know any Inspector. I am running a business. Half the beauty saloons in town also run classes in hair and beauty, and make-up. Maybe,' she emphasised this last word 'you'll find a professional there.' She didn't sound too hopeful.

Gloria stood up. 'Thank you Doreen, you've been really helpful.'

'I have Inspector, haven't I. I'm sure you'll be able to help me in the future sometime too.'

Gloria smiled at her. 'Why not just think of it as your civic duty Doreen, or as a help to get you into that heaven you were worried about the other day.'

Out on the street small children were shrieking naked under the water which was still gushing out of broken pipes and gutters while the adults lifted in buckets they had filled from the overflow. Rainwater was pure, they had always been told, a valuable resource. The air was filled with the pungent smells that always came after the rains, not exactly fresh but different and invigorating. Gloria went into Honeys. She could smell something cooking. I may as well get some food here she thought, rather than rely on the nephew I've apparently turned into a domestic drudge. Cassava with gravy was on the menu and it was delicious. She chewed away thinking about what she had heard today. The world of professional make-up was about as far as you could get from the Never-Die Church and it was obvious they did not know the boy. So there was a link between Rose and the boy separate from the church. But she knew Wolo was not telling everything he knew. Gloria thought she had rather under-estimated pastor Wolo; the shabby clothes and watery eyes were obviously hiding a man who knew how to manipulate people. She wondered if he really believed any of the stuff he had told her. That's when it struck her; when they searched the church compound they hadn't found a single file, document or piece of paper. The whole place had looked like a refugee camp; thin mattresses on the floor, battered cooking utensils and some old clothes. That's why she had been surprised to hear they had hired a lawyer. Wolo had to have some other place he kept official documents, account information and files, but obviously not on the compound with everyone else. She got up, re-energised and got out her phone.

'Moses, listen I am going back out to Bensonville,' she explained her reasoning, 'there has to be more out there and we need to find it.'

'Do you want me to join you; I am just leaving the airport so it will be at least forty minutes before I can get there.'

'More like an hour and a half Moses, no, don't worry I will call in at the Children's Village on the way and I can take Clementine with me, I'm sure she'll be there. That will give me chance to talk with her about coming to work with us.'

There was a silence. Moses did not like the idea of the two women going out to Bensonville on their own but he had no idea how to say that to Gloria without getting his head bitten off.

'Moses, I think we will be fine. It's Bensonville, not a war zone we're going to. My phone is on. Now get Izena to collect the names of all the establishments which teach make-up, or whatever it's called, we need to start looking at them quickly, and ask Barnyou if he had any luck with Ramesh's assistant.' She was back at her car and waved to a small boy who was coming down the hill.

'Boss, I talked to Mrs Adebayo. No-one could put a name to the photograph but some people recognised him, they are a group and are all from the same...'

'Church?' she finished his sentence.

'Yes, another church again. They all attend the Resurrection Temple.'

Gloria's heart sank. 'Ok, you will have to go and talk to the famous bishop then. No, better wait for me and we will go first thing in the morning. Bishop Asholodu is very well connected, we better handle him carefully.'

She rang off and looked at Pascal who was waiting patiently for her. He had been one of the first street boys she had got to know and she was still close to him.

'How are ma Anderson and the family?' Pascal had been taken in by the Anderson family and had settled in with them well but hadn't lost his connections on the streets.

'They are all good, old ma. I am going to see her now, she's just finishing work at the Chinese Clinic and then we are going to talk to those children.' Gloria nodded. She knew Pascal and Mrs Anderson spent time with the street kids, doing some basic health education work with them. 'How are you? No good cases this time?'

Pascal also considered himself a bit of an ad hoc consultant to the police after his involvement in previous investigations.

'Nothing for you to worry about Pascal, I'll let you know if I need any help. Maybe you should just focus on trying to grow, even small. I know you are eating plenty with the Andersons but you're still too short man.'

Pascal laughed. It was their standing joke.

He stood beside her, shoulder to shoulder, and indicated that he thought he was closing the gap on her. 'I will soon reach, old ma.' It was her turn to laugh now. They parted ways with Pascal promising to look for her soon.

Chapter Nine

The drive out to the Children's Village was easy enough until she reached the track leading off the main road. It was muddy, very muddy, and eventually Gloria abandoned the Polo and walked in.

The Children's Village was a collection of small houses built around an open patch of grass and a communal palava hut. It was quiet and Gloria saw Clementine sitting with a group of women over near the kitchen area. She waved and walked towards her. Clementine was about the same age as Gloria and was the epitome of calm and good sense. She understood how things worked in Liberia and she knew what to do to get things done, whether that was negotiating with the police to get a child released from the cells, discussing with a family to take their daughter back or working with a community to make sure their children were safe.

'Hi Clementine, how are you, it's very quiet here.'

Clementine smiled. 'Most of the children are sleeping Gloria, they just finished eating. They will be up later. Did you want to see them?'

'No, actually it's you I wanted to see. I am going to Bensonville and I wondered if you could come along.'

Clementine nodded vigorously. 'Oh yes, I can certainly come with you and I need to get away from these people.' She indicated the three women sitting around the coal pot.

'Trouble?'

'Oh yes, trouble for them.' They started to walk back to the car. 'Do you have any idea how much time I spend training these people and even just talking to them about how they are supposed to care for these children. Ma Hawa is great, but she can't do everything and the others, I don't know, sometimes it's as if they don't like the children, or are jealous of them or something.'

'So, what's happened?'

'Ah, all the usual stuff, you know, punishing the children by taking their food away or even hitting them for the smallest things, or calling them very rude names. But last week was the worst.' They were on the mud track now and it was quite slippery. 'We had a boy, about eight years old, Old Pa they called him. Well, he came to us from that settlement out at Chocolate City, you know mostly people from Lofa who have not gone back yet.' Gloria nodded. She knew the place well. Despite its picturesque name life out there was no box of chocolates.

'So what did they do?'

'Old pa was brought to us because his behaviour was, well, quite disturbed; rolling around, hallucinating, screaming.'

'Epilepsy?'

'We thought so, maybe made worse by some kind of trauma. We don't have a lot of specialist help available, as you know. Anyway we did everything we could, we even sent a worker out just to be with him all the time, until he settled down. I'm sure he was getting better, and he was happy. But those women, they were scared. You know, maybe the other children would 'catch the spell' from him, or maybe he was possessed.' They had reached the car.

'All the usual stuff, it's going to take time to change those ideas Clementine.'

'Yes, I know, but what did they do? Ma Hawa was in town visiting her own children and Old Pa had a really severe fit. They all got scared, said he must have a really bad spirit in him and took him to some prophet church down the road and left him there to get prayed over. When they went back in the evening the church people said the spirit in him was too powerful so one of them had carried him to town to a more powerful healer.'

Gloria stopped walking and made a face. 'That is crazy. So he has just disappeared?'

'Yes, and no-one seems to know who the person was who carried him or where they've gone. They just left a vague address. And of course now the Ministry of Social Welfare wants to know where the child is and why we just gave him away.'

'Eh yah, you must be so worried. Poor child could be anywhere and...'

'... with these very strange killings going on I am more than worried Glo. This town gets crazier and crazier.'

'So what are you actually doing?'

'Well I've sent Moko, the worker who was looking after him, to go find him. And told him not to come back until he has. The two carers will have to go though, fired I mean, I can't keep them. I just need to persuade my boss about that, he doesn't like trouble of any kind. And both those women,' she flipped her head back in the direction of the Village, 'have cousins or nephews or something who work at the Ministry and who are willing to fight for them!'

Gloria saw her opportunity. 'Well, there's something I wanted to ask you about Clementine. I know you will be looking for this child for now but we are looking for a social worker to join our team.' She ran through the recent events down to her conversation with the Police Director. 'So, we have permission to ask for a social worker from the Ministry and I wanted to ask you. We have worked so closely recently... would you be interested?'

She saw her hesitate. 'Wow, well I never saw that coming Gloria. Join the police though, no offence but you guys are half the problem in a lot of these cases. Well, your colleagues are Gloria. But it would still be the police.'

'You wouldn't be joining the police Clementine. You would still be a social worker but based in the Unit, that's all.'

'Thanks for asking Gloria. I need to think about it though. It's great working with you; I am just not sure about working for you.'

It wasn't quite the response Gloria had expected but she just shrugged. 'Of course you need some time. Let me know soon eh.'

'Why are we going to Bensonville anyway?' Clementine broke the silence after Gloria had negotiated the car back onto the tar road.

Gloria explained her idea and Clementine agreed, there must be more documents around. Gloria filled her in on Dr Armah's findings, the theories about Leopard Men and fancy make-up and could see that in spite of what she had said Clementine was fascinated and horrified by the case. By the time she had finished they were already at the Never-Die compound. They both looked at the deserted building.

'Well, the whole place was searched so I don't think there's anything here to interest us.' Gloria looked around the area. 'Did we search the administration block?' She pointed to a group of half-finished buildings away to the left of the compound.

Clementine shook her head. 'I don't know Gloria, I think they concentrated the search on this compound. The whole church seemed to be living here.'

'Let's have a look then.' They followed a paved path through the trees and into the administration area. A large rusty sign warned it was private and off-limits to visitors. There was still no-one around and they pushed open the glass doors and went in. Most of the interior was bare cement and empty spaces waiting for doors or windows. Down a short corridor one door was closed and padlocked. They headed for that and examined the padlock, it was not a standard market lock, this was a solid, heavy-duty padlock, the kind that cost a lot of money. Gloria examined the door and the hasp for the padlock, both had been fixed in such a way that there were no exposed screws. The only way into this room was with a key or a sledgehammer. Or so she thought.

Clementine had also been looking at the padlock very closely; she looked as if she was weighing it in her hand. She looked at Gloria, shrugged and then produced a pin out of her bag and put in the lock.

'I had to get one of the kids from the Benson Street night shelter to open my door one time when I lost the key. I learnt a few things that day. Firstly, I can open most padlocks now with a pin and secondly, the security on my house is an illusion, any of those babies off the street could get in.' She twisted the pin carefully, all the time holding the padlock. 'It's the weight and the angle with these padlocks, you have to use the weight of the padlock itself and at the right angle it takes only a slight touch of the pin,' Gloria heard a loud click, 'and it opens.' She took the padlock off and held it up with a grin. 'Are you sure you still want me to work for you Gloria?'

'Oh yes, even more now.' She pushed on the door and went in. It was a very comfortably furnished apartment, very different from the rest of the compound. But the room was stale, and the smell of unwashed clothes and rotting food hung heavy in the air. 'Looks like our friend Wolo lived a bit differently from the rest of his people, let's just look for anything that might tell us a bit more about him.'

'Is this legal Gloria?'

'Well, a grey area maybe. We should have searched it the other day but it got overlooked in the walahala. Let's just see what we find. But open a window first before we pass out.' They couldn't, the windows were all padlocked closed. 'We'll have to be quick then.'

It didn't take long. Wolo had obviously not been expecting to be searched and nothing was locked. There were piles of paper everywhere, drawers stuffed with notes and receipts. After ten minutes Clementine stopped, sweat was running off her and she had a handkerchief to her mouth. 'What exactly are we looking for Gloria? There is a ton of stuff here.'

Gloria stopped. 'Ok Clementine, I have a theory. Wolo and his church are from a small village in Nimba. They have nothing; no-one in Nimba has anything right – there's no gold or diamonds there just a bit of scratch farming. But this church has money.' She held up a sheaf of bank statements. 'So what do they have that's worth money?'

Clementine only had to think for a moment. 'Children!'

'Exactly. Children who are separated from their parents, parents who are too scared to question their leaders. It's ideal. I think that's why Wolo moved the church down here, not to give Prophet Daniel space but so that he could sell the children easier. In fact, I wouldn't be surprised if he knew the church wasn't going to last very long and he was getting rid of all the children.'

'That old man? You think he's smart enough to plan all that Gloria.'

'Well he didn't have to plan very much, it was all set up already, maybe they were even selling children before prophet Daniel died. All he had to do was keep it going.'

Gloria was putting papers in a bag. 'And we would have known this earlier if we had asked the children. We only asked them about Rose, so they only told us about Rose.' She took her phone out and called Moses. 'Get someone to go back and ask the children if any of their other friends has disappeared. We're on our way back now.'

There was just one large cupboard in the corner they hadn't investigated. Gloria hesitated; it was padlocked as well and they already had piles of documents. Maybe they should leave this one for CID to complete. The oppressive atmosphere in the room was weighing on her. It was her instinct that propelled her, that uneasy feeling she got in her stomach. 'We may as well look Clementine; can you open this lock?'

It was easy, according to Clementine, and she had the lock off in seconds. They were both hit by a wave of even staler air as Gloria pulled the doors wide open. Instead of finding shelves or more files they saw the cupboard was actually the entrance to a small room. Gloria went in and her stomach lurched. It was a cell, windowless and airless except for two small vents at the top of the wall. A mat was rolled up in the corner with a dirty lappa cloth beside it, swarms of ants were crawling over the bones in a tin dish and several large cockroaches were crawling into even darker corners.

Behind her Clementine gasped. 'So this is how he kept them under control.'

Gloria was out the room calling Moses again by the time Clementine reached her.

'I will take photos but I need Izena to come out and go through this stuff carefully, and tell Ambrose to come out with her. This is not just some crazy church, this is organised crime against children.'

'It's going to be too late for that now boss, it will have to be in the morning.' Moses was trying to calm her, she could tell by his tone of voice. Gloria looked at her watch but the late afternoon haze outside told her that Moses was right. It would be dark soon.

'You need to send Lamine out here now then, with someone else, just to secure the place. I don't want anything to go missing in the night.'

Suddenly they were both anxious to leave. The place was oppressive.

The drive back to town was quiet and Gloria dropped Clementine in town before driving wearily home. Now she had to face Abu and she had no idea what to say to him; it had been a long day but she had to find out what he was thinking. His mood that morning had been resentful. Again the thought came to her that maybe she was being selfish by keeping him with her.

The smell of cooking hit her as soon as she opened the apartment door. Her delight was tempered by this new evidence that Abu did all the work around the apartment. Gloria entered the kitchen cautiously but Abu's good humour seemed to have been restored to him. The sting of the peppers hit her in the eyes but through her tears she could see he was happy.

'The food will be ready in half an hour Aunt Glo.'

They sat down to eat and Gloria looked at him as he wolfed down his rice. Abu had come to live with her when he was only eight years old after his parents were killed in a car accident. They had stayed together during and after the war and it had always been a fairly uncomplicated arrangement. But Mrs Harris's words and Abu's attitude over the past few days were niggling at her. She couldn't just let this pass.

'I spoke with Mrs Harris today at the school.'

'Mmm.' Abu didn't even look up.

'Abu, she is worried about you. She doesn't think you're making enough progress, you're still at least two grades behind.'

Abu put down his spoon. 'I was three grades behind Aunt Glo, or four I think, so if I am only two grades behind now then I am making progress. And you knew that already, you're always behind me to study.' He looked at her with a mock puzzled look.

'Well, she kind of gave me the idea that you were not happy, or that maybe I'm not taking care of you, you know, maybe putting you in danger.' Abu was still looking at her with a slightly bemused expression on his face. 'Look, she thinks I should send you out the country to go to school, so you can catch up and where you will be safe.'

'Eh Aunt Glo I swear, how you manage to let that woman get to you so. I don't believe it.' He sucked his teeth. 'Send me out the country! Yeah, she would like that. You even know that woman Aunt Glo?' He put the spoon down and spoke in a slow voice you might use on a child. 'That old ma there, she jus worry that I spying on her. Tha the whole story there.'

'Spying?'

'Uh huh. She wants me out the school but not because she is worried about me, she thinks I'm spying for you.'

'Spying? Why? What is she up to?'

'Only the usual things; small bribes, money to pass exams… but it doesn't matter because I am not spying for you.'

Gloria sat back. Mrs Harris had really got to her.

'You have plenty enemies Aunt Glo; teachers, judges, politicians…'

'Yes, alright.'

'So you can't send me away. Who would protect you?' Abu was laughing; he didn't often see his aunt so unsure of herself.

'The way you've been looking these few days Abu, I thought maybe she was right. You didn't look happy today at all.'

Abu's face fell. 'No, that was something different. The scout I told you about, the one who came to the game on Saturday, he is gone.' Gloria remembered his excitement about the scout coming to the games. 'He says Liberia is too dangerous and he can't stay. So we lost a good chance.'

It didn't sound that serious to Gloria but she knew better than to say that out loud. 'So what is the chance you've missed?'

'We need someone who can connect us with some big teams, some proper teams outside the country.'

'I could talk to Abraham Kanneh if you like, I'm sure he knows people.' She said this casually and was startled when Abu leapt up.

'You mean it Aunt Glo, you could talk to him?'

'Yes,' she shrugged, 'why not. He came to my office and offered to help and I don't need any more people helping me to solve murders, so maybe he could 'make some connections' for you.'

Abu was so excited he couldn't sit back down. He was babbling about times and places.

'But Abu you invited him on Saturday, I thought you knew him.'

'Me? No, we got the Minister of Youth and Sports to invite him. He won't speak to me.'

'Well I'm glad I can be useful.' She said it jokingly but inside a wave of relief was unknotting her stomach. For the first time that day she relaxed a little. Maybe being around so much cruelty had made her too sensitive to Mrs Harris criticism. She looked at Abu who had gone back to his food and marvelled again at how much he and his friends knew. They seemed to know everything, maybe because adults still overlooked them, unaware that the children were watching, listening and talking to each other. She realised Abu was asking her something.

'Aunt Glo, after practice on Sunday I want to go on the beach with some friends, is that ok?' Abu always knew when to make a request.

'Mmm, what friends would that be?' He would never normally bother to ask her about going on the beach.

'Well just one friend,' he was staring at his plate, 'and just for a few hours.'

'Do you mean Fatu?' It had to be her. Abu nodded. 'Abu she is too young to be your girlfriend.'

'She is nearly fifteen.'

'Yes, which means she is actually fourteen. And you can't go anyway. We have to go to Alfred's engagement party remember.'

Abu scowled. He had forgotten. Alfred still played on his team sometimes so he couldn't miss the party.

'We'll talk about this, if you really like Fatu but she is too young.'

'She is fifteen next week, for here that makes her a woman Aunt Glo.'

He was hating this discussion. Gloria let him off. She nodded.

'Ok, but why did you even ask me.'

'Come on Aunt Glo. I'm your nephew and Fatu is Lawrence's sister. You don't think someone is going to see us and then run to tell you or him?' Gloria laughed. She wasn't sure about that but if Abu thought so that wasn't a bad thing.

As they were clearing up Gloria remembered all the things she hadn't got round to doing that day.

'So Abu if I speak to Mr AK for you' – he laughed at her using his street name – 'and talk to Lawrence about you and Fatu, will you do something for me?'

He looked at her suspiciously. Aunt Glo did not usually request his help; it was usually taken for granted.

Gloria explained about DG and how he never went outside his yard. 'I'm going to ask Lawrence to give him a ride in a patrol car on Saturday but I wondered if after that he could join you for football practice, with your junior team. He is scared that people will laugh at him but...'

But Abu interrupted her, relieved at her request. 'It's fine Aunt Glo, don't worry. Let him come down, no-one will bother him.'

He said this with such assurance that Gloria knew it was true.

She made two calls that evening over her last coffee of the day. A short one to Peter Dennis telling him that Richard Varley's mother was back on the scene and wanted to see him and a much longer one to Moses.

'I tried calling you three times boss but your phone was busy. Lamine is out at the Never-Die compound now and Izena is going first thing in the morning. And you were right, when we went back to the children, they said that children can disappear all the time. Wolo tells them the children have run away or have gone to school somewhere or moved to live with other family, but they didn't believe it. That's why they were all so terrified. Ambrose is still out at the Children's Village with Christian talking to them to see how many names they can get.'

'And we charge Wolo in the morning with trafficking, kidnapping and torture,' she thought again about the tiny cell, 'and get an accountant to go over all his records, he must have been making money out of this.'

Chapter Ten

A trip to another church was the last thing Gloria would have asked for but there she was, at seven in the morning, on the airport road halfway to the place where Bishop Asholodu had his church. She looked at Moses who was whistling to himself.

'You look happy Moses.'

'Just happy to be on the job, boss.'

Just past the Baptist seminary there was a large sign for the Resurrection Temple and they turned off the road. In the early morning sunshine the burnt orange of the dusty track and the green of the trees stood out vividly against the sparkling blue of the distant ocean. They both were quiet for a few moments taking in the scene.

'Our country is so fine eh.'

Gloria nodded. 'It's too bad for us we are usually looking at bodies on the ground or staring into the eyes of some killer isn't it? I can't remember the last time I went on the beach.'

'Well it won't be anytime soon, boss.' He pointed to the horizon where the rainclouds were already gathering. It would rain again today. 'Maybe by Christmas you'll get back on the beach.'

Gloria shrugged. 'If we ever finish this case.' Her natural impatience was beginning to boil up. That and the heavy feeling that had settled in her stomach. 'Right. So tell me what everyone's doing today.'

'Izena has gone out to Bensonville and Lamine will stay out there and help her. Alfred is questioning Wolo again and Christian has the list of beauty saloons.'

Gloria laughed. In Liberia a salon was always a saloon, just as a carton was always a cartoon. 'He will be delighted with that assignment. And he's the right one for the job Moses, some of those places on Gurley street are definitely more saloon than salon. There were fights in three of them last week alone, I mean real fights.'

Moses laughed. 'I know, Barnyou was called out for one of them and he wasn't very happy about that. Yes, you can get your hair fixed and your face rearranged all for the same price.'

Barnyou's name reminded Gloria. 'Has Barnyou found out any more about Alfred's death? Was it an accident?'

Earlier that morning they had driven past the gas station where old Alfred had been killed. The wreck of his vehicle was still there, looking as if it had taken its rightful place with all the other vehicle skeletons.

'They don't know, they can't find the driver. I don't think he's giving it too much time though.'

'Oh I'm sure he isn't, he's got better things to do.' She rolled her eyes. 'What about Ramesh's assistant, has he interviewed him yet?'

'Well I don't know boss, I really can't just interrogate a senior officer about his investigation can I?'

Gloria nodded and waited a moment. 'So has he interviewed the assistant or not?'

Moses laughed again. 'Yes, but my sources tell me he drew a blank, the guy lives with his wife and child in Westpoint in a shack and just wants his job back. There's nothing to suggest he was selling copies of the shop keys.'

'So we are no further forward on that either. Ah, I hope Bishop whatever can tell us something.'

'Asholodu.'

'What?'

'It's Bishop Asholodu.'

'Oh I know Moses but I am so tired of all these religious people.'

'Well restrain yourself boss, this man is very important and we have enough enemies at the moment.'

'You sound like Abu now. Ok, I will be quiet and respectful.'

'Well I wouldn't go that far, but at least don't go for his throat.'

They were turning down a smooth tarmac road off the dusty track, following an enormous neon sign flashing out the words 'Resurrection Temple' in vivid yellow and red. Next to a portrait of the smiling bishop a painted slogan proclaimed their mission as 'Bringing the Dead To Life.'

The compound of the Resurrection Temple was as different from the Never-Die compound as you could imagine. The entrance was via large iron gates manned by uniformed security who waved them through. The centre of the compound was dominated by a huge church building which was still being finished and around it were offices, a meeting hall, a school and a large house.

'Wow, there's money in religion Moses. This is quite a set up.'

They stopped in front of a single storey building and entered a large reception area. With its air conditioning, imported furniture and marble tiles the place spoke more of corporate enterprise than soul saving. A very pretty girl at the front desk asked them to have a seat while the morning service was finishing.

'We'll go and meet him then,' Gloria signalled to Moses, 'I'm afraid I will get cold sitting in your air cool.' The girl looked as if she was going to protest but changed her mind when she saw the expression on Gloria's face. She pointed to a colourful tent beside the church.

'He's in the Resurrection Garden.'

Gloria rolled her eyes again and started walking towards the tent.

The sound of singing and clapping reached them before they got to the tent. Inside, a small group of mostly women were swaying and singing while a tall woman in front held her hands in the air and with her eyes closed was encouraging them to sing louder and louder. The famous bishop was nowhere to be seen at first until Moses nudged Gloria and pointed to a small knot of women who were standing in a circle around a prostrate figure on the floor. They were poor, that was obvious from their faded lappa skirts, worn t-shirts and old cloths tied around their heads, and they were probably desperate too, thought Gloria. Suddenly out of the circle of women a deep powerful voice carried across the garden. It was a voice with authority and absolute assurance and just for a moment even Gloria felt herself moved. The words he was saying were indistinct but both groups of women were swaying with him and working themselves up into a frenzy. Suddenly the woman on the ground sat up, threw her arms in the air and shouted a great 'hallelujah' and all the others started clapping and dancing.

'Do you think she was dead?' Moses whispered in her ear.

Gloria glared at him. 'I don't think so Moses, but I'm sure we'll hear all about it now.' She indicated a large man who was striding towards them with a beaming smile and an outstretched hand.

'Inspector, peace be on you.' He turned the full power of his smile onto her and despite herself Gloria felt an electric thrill run down her back and the small hairs on her neck stand up. This man certainly had charisma, very different from Abraham Kanneh's easy charm and, she suspected, a lot more dangerous.

Gloria and Moses shook the outstretched hand and again Gloria felt a small current run through her. She looked at Moses but he seemed unaffected.

'Ok reverend, thank you for seeing us, you are obviously very busy.' She looked over at the groups of women who were still dancing and singing.

They went over to a small palaver hut at the side of the garden and sat down. 'You will have heard about the murders that have taken place, the two children.'

Asholodu's smile never wavered but Gloria felt the energy he was giving off suddenly fade away. She gave herself a mental shake; however fanciful, it felt very real to her. Maybe this was how charisma really worked. And if so, why had it suddenly faded away when she mentioned the two murders.

'Of course I've heard Inspector, it is a terrible thing... but not so very unusual here unfortunately. I come up against demonic forces every day here. I see with different eyes Inspector, I see what others don't see.' So does the crazy old man who stands begging at the bridge every day, thought Gloria wryly. 'We are at war with evil and my church is leading the battle, with prayer and power.'

Gloria let him talk. The energy force or whatever that current of charisma was, had not come back. These were just words, a set script like Wolo explaining the work of the Never-Die Church. This spiritual warrior, or whatever he was, was hiding a secret, exactly like Wolo. Gloria was sure of it. And he was scared. She brought out the photo and showed it to Asholodu. The smile disappeared and a look of appropriate concern replaced it. Gloria sensed he was going to deny any knowledge of the boy and headed him off.

'Several members of your congregation have already identified him as someone who attended your church here, he is Nigerian.'

Asholodu nodded slowly. 'Oh yes, I believe he was a member here, I'm not sure how frequent he was but I think I recognise him. How terrible. Have you any idea who did this Inspector?'

'Can you give us a name reverend?'

'A name? I'm sorry, I don't think so. We have over four thousand members Inspector, I can't remember them all.'

Especially not the poor unimportant one, Gloria said to herself. 'Well, can we show the photo around, ask some of your members?' Gloria was uncomfortably aware that she was treating Asholodu with a deference she hadn't shown to Wolo but her instincts and the slight pressure of Moses elbow in her side convinced her it was the right approach.'

Asholodu was standing up. 'Leave the photo with me and I will make sure I ask people. If I get any information I will get straight back to you Inspector.'

For a pastor who had lost a member of his flock under horrible circumstances Asholodu was remarkable unruffled. Gloria could see Moses shifting uncomfortably in his seat out of the corner of her eye. He was standing too.

'Sorry boss, I don't think my system has readjusted to the water or the heat after America. I really need to use the rest room.'

Like a switch being flicked Asholodu was suddenly all charm and consideration again, illuminated by the dazzling smile. 'Please go over to reception captain and my assistant will show you where to go.' When Moses hesitated Asholodu continued. 'Don't worry, it's very civilised, there's running water there.'

Gloria stared at Moses as he muttered about not being used to Liberia's primitive hygiene and sanitation facilities and went off at great speed to the reception area. With Moses gone and the subject of the dead boy dealt with, Asholodu's charisma returned at full force. The current of energy hit her like a bolt in the stomach and for a moment again, Gloria felt herself being drawn in. But only for a moment. She listened as Asholodu talked about his work and his plans and wondered if the fact of him mentioning the names of almost every prominent politician in the country was a not-very-subtle warning to her. Thankfully Moses was back before she could analyse it too much and they left.

They were on the dusty road again before Moses said, 'Peter Wajira.'

'What?'

'The dead boy's name is Peter Wajira.'

'How did…'

'The receptionist was very chatty. As soon as I showed her the photo she gave me the name. She seemed to know him very well.'

'And yet the bishop couldn't recall him?'

'Yes, strange that. Especially since the receptionist told me that Peter was one of Asholodu's success stories.'

Gloria slowed the car and stopped before they joined the main road again. 'Ok Moses, tell me the whole story. I take it the whole rest room thing was just an excuse.'

Moses grinned. 'Come on boss, you didn't really think I was worried about the toilet facilities did you? Since the reverend didn't want to talk to us, I thought someone else would, and who better than a receptionist. They see everything, hear everything and are usually overlooked. She was dying to talk.'

'And Peter was a regular church member?'

'A member? He was part of the show. When Asholodu opened his church here last year there was too much competition, too many other churches. His attendances were small until…'

'He performed a miracle?'

'Got it in one. Two people claiming to be Peter's parents turned up in the middle of a service last year bringing what they said was the dead body of their son, wrapped in a shroud, the complete works. She said Asholodu gave a great speech and then sweated and prayed and danced around that body until they all thought he had gone mad. Then the shroud moved, a leg came out, then an arm and within half an hour the shroud was off and the dead boy was dancing around the altar.'

Gloria looked at Moses. 'Really? It sounds like a very bad Nigerian movie plot.'

'She did say you had to be there, the atmosphere was electric, the spirit was moving and they were all caught up in it.'

Gloria thought of Asholodu's strange magnetism. In the right atmosphere he could probably influence a whole crowd. 'It's funny that Asholodu didn't even remember him then. I mean, you'd hardly forget someone you raised from the dead, would you?'

'Even more so someone you raised from the dead more than once.'

Gloria shook her head. 'All right Moses, give me the rest of the story.'

'Well after the first miracle the church started growing very quickly, money was pouring in and they started all this building work. But Asholodu kept talking about all the other places they had to go to carry the message; so he started going to other parts of Monrovia and further afield and holding these revival services. The odd thing was he would not allow anyone from the church to go with him; said God wanted him to go alone. But one day the receptionist was over in Buzzy Quarters and heard his voice through the loudspeakers and went in to listen. She said she was just in time to witness another miracle but she was surprised when the shroud fell away and it was Peter again!'

They both laughed. 'But why is she still working there then?'

'When she confronted him he told her it was based on the biblical principle of substitution. The first miracle was the real one but biblically it was acceptable to 're-enact' it, or substitute their little drama for an actual miracle as a way of promoting faith.'

'And she accepted that?'

'She said she wasn't sure but after he prayed with her she was convinced.'

They had started driving again. 'Wow, what a great story. Asholodu does have some power you know. Some ability to influence people, I could feel it.'

One look at Moses blank face told her he had felt nothing. Well that was good to know. She had better make sure Moses came to their next interview as well.

'So he works the scam with this boy for months, to promote himself and his new church and then tells us he just about recognises him. Should we go back and confront him?'

'I don't think so boss. We definitely know he is involved in some way now but if we go in too quickly we might never get the real story. He thinks he has fooled us; the receptionist is not going to say anything to him, she's too scared. So, let's leave him for a little while.'

'And he apparently knows everyone in the government, he made a point of letting me know that.'

'Right. We need to know why the boy was killed and what his connection to Rose is. I don't think it's through the church. Wolo and Asholodu are crooks and abusers but there's something or someone apart from them that connects the children.'

Gloria wasn't so sure. 'Maybe it is simpler than that Moses. Peter knew all the bishop's secrets for a start. Maybe he was blackmailing him or maybe Asholodu just wanted him out of the way, you know, he felt his reputation is big enough now to stand on its own.'

'But to kill someone boss? It just seems like a big step for someone who is basically a con artist.'

'Except if his whole career was being threatened?'

'Well if that was the case why not do it quietly, just make the boy disappear instead of going for that elaborate show.'

Just like Wolo, thought Gloria. Both children had put themselves beyond the power of their abusers, so they had the motive to kill them, or want them dead, but the method was just wrong.

They were back at the office by now and at least, thought Gloria, armed with a bit more information. Maybe they could now make some progress on catching the people responsible for the killings.

The office was empty except for Ambrose who got the job of writing up their information.

'There was a call for you ma'am, a Marcia Reynolds. She asked if you could call her back urgently.'

Gloria frowned and Moses laughed. 'You're turning into a celebrity boss. You had better be careful. That show is starting next week so she probably needs you for a rehearsal.'

Gloria snorted. It wasn't ladylike but it summed up her feelings exactly. 'If she calls again tell her I will be in touch.' But as she finished the office phone rang again. Ambrose answered and started to pass on that message but even across the office Gloria could hear Marcia insisting that she speak to Gloria now. Ambrose hesitated and the battle was lost. Gloria snatched the phone and started to speak but Marcia kept talking in a low urgent voice.

'Gloria, listen please. I know you are very busy but this is important. It's not just the show.' Gloria stopped trying to speak then. 'Well it is the show, but it concerns you. It's the other guests.' She stopped.

'Marcia, you had better just tell me what's bothering you, the show is on next week isn't it?'

'That's part of the problem. The producer has lined up the other guests and one of them is a judge, Dorothy Weah.' She paused. 'It's just that one of my team told me today that you and her don't see eye to eye on a lot of things.'

Gloria shook her head. 'You know that song we loved when we were at school Marcia' – she dropped her voice and gave a tuneless staccato version of "This town ain't big enough for the both of us" – 'well that's kind of how it is between me and the judge.'

Marcia laughed, sensing a breakthrough. 'Look Gloria I know you don't like her and you've had your differences but she is a woman and a judge, she's got a great profile for the show. Are you sure this is not just some creative tension between two strong women?' Gloria could hear the anxious hopefulness in her voice.

'There is that Marcia,' Gloria paused briefly, 'plus the fact she is corrupt and directly responsible for the trafficking of numerous children into slave labour and death.' There was silence then from the other end of the line.

'Wow, okaaay, so not much room for compromise there.' Marcia was clearly at a loss. She paused as if waiting for Gloria to contradict her, which she didn't. 'I thought she was some kind of hero. Didn't she help you in your last case, signing the search warrant for big man Varley's house?'

'Yes, with a little pressure from me. And I gave her the credit for that. I didn't say I would not pursue the other case against her though, which I am doing.' Gloria didn't add that the case against Judge Weah was not going well because her chief witness, Richard Varley's mother, had disappeared. She knew Weah was guilty because she had caved in as soon as Gloria put the information under her nose but without any witnesses or documentation the case was going nowhere.

'But you haven't formally charged her with anything Gloria, are you allowed to go around making these accusations?'

'They are facts Marcia, but no, she hasn't been formally charged. Neither has she taken me to court for defamation which speaks for itself too.'

Marcia sighed and then groaned. 'Ah, Gloria you are infuriating. So, you won't appear on the same show as her because you suspect her of a crime for which you have no evidence. Oh, this country is going to kill me!'

Gloria laughed then. Marcia had always been able to make every situation about herself. 'Marcia, I didn't say I wouldn't go on the same show as her, I'm just telling you what I think, no, what I know about her. Actually, Judge Weah, me and another person might be a far more interesting show than three worthy women talking about all the good they do for poor people.'

'What, so you will still come on the show?'

'Oh yes, any chance to have a chat with the judge is useful, and in public too. Count me in.'

'Great.' Marcia's voice betrayed how unsure she was. 'Well thanks Gloria, that's good news, I think. I will be in touch soon with all the details.'

She rang off and the two men who had been listening in suddenly bent their heads over their desks. Ambrose looked up as she went past. 'Was that a real song ma'am?'

'It certainly was Ambrose, but before your time probably. And the original version is much better than mine, believe me.'

She went into her office followed by Moses. 'So you and Judge Weah on the same show, that will be interesting boss.'

'Not really. I can't accuse her of anything on TV. But it might just remind her that I am still watching her.'

'Her and Africanus Varley. You don't go for anyone small, do you?'

Gloria sat down heavily on her chair. 'You know Moses, sometimes I think it's good that we remind ourselves we are the Family and Child Protection Unit. For every person we've caught and put in prison there's a trail of children's bodies leading to them. We are not doing a lot of protecting at the moment and while people like Weah and Varley get away with anything they want we will always be playing catch up.' She drummed the desk. 'It's not good enough, simple as that. So I am not giving up on those two. We will get them eventually and then perhaps we can say we are protecting children.'

Moses nodded but didn't say anything. He pointed instead to a pile of papers on her desk. 'Well these might help boss. These are the people who have applied to join our unit. We could take a look at them while we wait for the others to get back.'

Gloria looked at the pile of papers. 'All these in such a short time? We must have the cream of the crop here then.' She made a face indicating the opposite.

They sorted them into two piles and settled down to read them. It was as she feared. There were applications from junior clerks in the administration department, officers who had only been working for a couple of months, others who were on the brink of retirement and some completely inappropriate ones like the lady in charge of the police canteen. As the afternoon heat seeped further and further into the room Gloria's spirits sank lower and lower. So far she had three possibles: a graduate from the School of Criminology, a young woman who had studied psychology in the University of North Carolina – and the woman in charge of the police canteen – well she at least had spent three years at the Police Academy although the only 'passing out' ceremony she had attended had been the entire student body passing out the back windows of the dormitory and running into the bush when the rebels had attacked one night.

Moses had two possibles: a young woman who claimed to have been a rebel commander in charge of 'policing' the town of Tubmanburg at the height of the war. Gloria shuddered at the memories that conjured up. 'Really Moses? Another rebel, and one who clearly thinks police work is all about instilling fear through violence?'

'There wasn't a lot to choose from boss. You got the best ones I think. What about the other one?

Gloria read through the remaining application form. It was written in neat handwriting with correct spelling which was a good start, she thought. The short letter listed three reasons why the person wanted to join her team; she was a trained police officer, she knew the system was corrupt but felt she had a better chance of fixing it from the inside than from out, she was unhappy with her current position in the anti-corruption squad. Gloria looked up at Moses. 'You knew this was a good one, why keep it till last.'

Moses laughed. 'It looks even better after you've read the others boss.'

'She writes good English, she is a trained officer, she seems to be straightforward and she hasn't mentioned how she thinks the children are the future and she wants to spend the rest of her life saving them. She' – she looked at the name on the letter –'Mardea Jackson is our best bet so far. Fix up some interviews for early next week then and include the others.'

The office was thick with the late afternoon heat and it was with a huge effort that Gloria gathered the team together; well the ones who had managed to get back. Izena looked unusually dishevelled and reported that it would take at least another two days to go through everything from the Never-Die compound but that they had at least managed to collect all the financial papers. Lamine was staying out at the compound for another night to keep an eye on things. Christian had called to say he was just leaving from the Vatican Beauty Saloon on Ashmun Street but he had nothing to report except a few bruises.

Moses continued reporting his conversation with Christian. 'The proprietor of a place on Snapper Hill attacked him with a broom he says, and when he tried to break up a fight between two customers in another place they threw hair dye over him.' They were all laughing.

'If the government had deployed all the women of this country during the War, the rebels would not have got near the city,' Alfred blurted out before seeing Izena's face. She didn't like this characterisation of Liberian women as some kind of modern-day Amazons. In her family women were expected to be educated, graceful and assertive but definitely not tough, loud or aggressive.

'All right, let's get on with the rest. Alfred what happened with Wolo and company?'

Alfred looked totally disgusted with what he had heard that day. 'He wasn't going to say anything ma'am, just sat there with his arms folded until we charged him with aggravated child abuse. He sent for his lawyer. He is denying everything of course except that the small room off his office was a punishment cell but that the rest of the community knew everything he did and he had their permission so we would have to charge everyone. There was nothing illegal in what he was doing, he claims. In fact if more Liberian parents took their responsibilities seriously there would be less violence in the country.'

Gloria shook her head. Wolo was a lot cleverer than she had given him credit for. If he was going to use a lack of discipline among children as his defence, he would find a lot of popular support in the country.

'But one thing was different ma'am. I asked him why he hadn't reported Rose missing when she ran away. If he was proud of his discipline methods and was really concerned for the child there was nothing to stop him going to the police and getting help or even just calling MACHO. There's a MACHO phone line in Bensonville and a billboard the size of an elephant advertising it, right next to his compound.'

Gloria nodded. 'Another question is why none of the children rang it either, did they not understand what it's for or how to use it? But it's a good point about Wolo Alfred, makes his story even more unlikely.'

'But ma'am, the point is he got worried then. He says now that Rose did not run away, he says he put her into domestic service so that she could be independent and earn some money.'

'Domestic service? Well it should be easy to trace her last movements then. Where did she go? Don't tell me, he sent her back up country and he lost contact with her.'

'No, he handed her over to an agency called Domestic Angels, after their representative called to see them. He doesn't know what happened to her then but he claims to have a signed agreement with the agency which proves it.'

Moses looked around the office and stopped at Izena as the only one in the room who was likely to have professional domestic help at home. 'Anyone ever hear of Domestic Angels?'

There was a snigger from Alfred and a surprised look from Izena who nodded. 'Yes ma'am, there should be something here.' She started shuffling through a huge pile of papers she had in front of her and after a very long minute she pulled one out and waved it at them. 'Domestic Angels, here it is. It's a receipt.' She read out. 'For services rendered to Domestic Angels, the sum of one thousand United States dollars paid to Isaac Wolo.'

Gloria hit the table. 'Yes! Now we've got him. He sold the child and we've got the proof. No-one pays money to take a girl into domestic service. And Wolo will know that. Right. So maybe he didn't kill the girl but he basically sold her, that's trafficking. Let's get back to him now.' She hesitated, looking at Moses and then Alfred. 'Ok, you two go and interview him again. Find out everything you can about this agent and the agency. It's probably a briefcase agency, you know, just someone travelling around collecting children for…' She trailed off. For what?

'And let me know what happens,' she called to their departing backs as they headed for the door.

'Well done Izena, paperwork is important.' Izena wasn't exactly beaming, that wasn't her style, but she looked very pleased. 'Shouldn't you be at home now getting ready for Sunday?'

'Getting ready? No, I just have to be there, that's all. There are people doing everything.' She sounded a little vague. Setting up and clearing away were not things she ever had to bother about obviously.

Gloria stood up. 'Well I am going home. If you're finished for the day, you all should go too.'

Chapter Eleven

The muggy darkness fell on Gloria like an old blanket as soon as she stepped out of her car. The lights were off in the apartment building and the whole area was lit only by passing headlights and the kerosene lanterns on the market tables at the side of the road. Gloria stretched and breathed in deeply, the smell of frying meat and salt from the sea filling her nostrils. There was peace here, a sense that all was well with the world, even when it clearly was not. Although it was dark there was no menace; the street and the yard around the apartment block were bustling with people and the noise from inside was just as loud. The instinctive reaction of most people in the block when the lights went off was to open their doors, light lanterns and candles and for adults to stand in doorways talking while the children played on the stairs or went back outside.

Gloria said hello to groups of people on the stairs as she squeezed her way up to her apartment. Her door was open too and inside was lit by just a few candles – they had obviously run out of kerosene again. But it was also unusually quiet; no music, no noise from the kitchen and no-one around. She went over to the door leading out to the porch and out of the corner of her eye saw a tall figure rising silently and quickly out of the rattan chair by the window. She dived for the kitchen, cursing herself that she hadn't brought a weapon with her. She grabbed the heavy flashlight that sat on the cupboard and spun round fumbling with the switch. In the few seconds it took her to abandon the switch and raise the flashlight over her head she heard a familiar voice.

'Gloria, my dear, what are you doing?'

It was Richard the tailor.

She lowered the flashlight, feeling the weakness wash over her. 'Richard, what are you doing here in the dark? Lord, this is Liberia my man, you don't sit in the dark in someone else's house and then make a dramatic arrival. Eh you are lucky I don't have no gun with me.'

'So tense Gloria, you really need to relax a little.'

The combination of Richard's complete unconcern at his near miss and her relief that she was not being attacked in her own house again gave her a fit of giggles and when Abu came in from buying more kerosene for the lanterns he found her sitting on the floor, clutching the flashlight and rocking with laughter, with Richard standing over her shaking his head. And then the power came back on.

They blinked in the glare of the lights and Gloria scrambled to her feet and went off to her room to change. When she got back Richard had again organised a reluctant Abu and there was food and beer on the table.

'No more coffee today Gloria. You need a beer to calm down a little.'

'That's true.' She accepted the cold beer gratefully and there was silence as she and Abu ate the greens and rice Richard had brought. He wouldn't eat with them but he sat and chatted about the goings on in the world of tailoring, or as Richard always called it, the Liberian fashion world. He was plainly dressed tonight in a t-shirt and jeans, no jewellery or extravagant shoes. Apparently the Liberian fashion world had been rocked by a huge scandal involving two rival fashion houses, Divine Designs and The Palace of Fashion had been rivals in a bid to win a contract to design dress uniforms for the newly-constituted national army. Richard shook his head dramatically. 'It all got very messy.'

Abu and Gloria exchanged looks. From his tone and his look it was easy to imagine there had been running battles and bloodshed in Congo Town where the rival designers operated in shops opposite each other. 'Was anyone hurt then?' Abu enquired.

'A lot of people were hurt Abu, I was hurt myself. When designers steal each other's ideas and pass them off as their own it is very hurtful.'

Gloria could feel the giggles coming back. 'Yes, but was anyone actually injured Richard?'

'Injured? Oh my god, no Gloria. We are designers not rebels.'

'So what happened then?'

'Divine Designs were awarded the contract but when they revealed their design Palace of Fashion claimed they had stolen their ideas.'

'And…'

'Oh, nothing much really, lots of talking, and now lots of not talking.' He launched into a detailed description of who was doing what but Gloria's 'Sweet Liberia' ringtone started and she retreated to the porch to take the call.

'Are you busy boss?'

Gloria looked at Abu who was trapped listening to Richard's story and shook her head. 'No Moses, go ahead.'

'Wolo is sticking to his story that he believed he was giving Rose an opportunity and says the money he received was for the upkeep of the church because they would be losing the services of one of their members. But he wasn't as sure boss, he is wavering. We told him he had to produce the contract and the details of the agency or he would be charged with trafficking.'

Gloria nodded. 'We need to keep the pressure on him Moses. First thing tomorrow, I know its Saturday but we need to keep going, get back on him. What about Christian?'

'No luck. He visited every saloon on the list and a few more besides and no-one could tell him anything about styles of make-up.'

'Ok, although I wonder if he really knew what he was looking for? I mean make-up is a bit of a specialised subject. We need someone who really knows about the subject.' Her eyes wandered back to the table where Richard was still holding forth despite the empty look on Abu's face.

'Listen Moses, I will call you back. I've got an idea.'

She went back in. 'Richard, let me ask you something please.' She indicated to Abu who made his escape. She explained the whole story of the two children and the make-up and Christian's lack of success. 'Where do professional designers go if they are putting on a show and they want the best hair and make-up?'

'Monte Carlo.'

'Monte Carlo?' And then it dawned on her. 'Oh, Monte Carlo, at the top of Broad Street?'

'Yes, that's the place to go.'

'But I thought that was a training centre for girls, and a rough kind of place too?'

'Yes, to both of those Gloria. Myself, I would never go there but they do have the best teachers.'

Gloria nodded. 'That is very helpful Richard, and there's nowhere else?'

Richard shook his head emphatically. 'No, they are the experts that I know.' He stood up and stretched. 'I have to go Gloria, here's your new uniforms.' He pulled them out of the bag he always carried, a bag with seemingly endless capacity. 'Now take care of them, well not too much care or you won't need my services for a while.'

She let him out and called to Abu. 'It's safe now, you can come out.' He appeared grinning.

'Che, Aunt Glo, please take care of those uniforms. I need to rest from Richard for some time now. The man can talk.'

'True, but he does a good job. And he knows a lot. Now, tomorrow, don't forget I'm bringing DG down to the football training.'

Abu shrugged. 'Anytime, did you speak to AK yet?'

'No, I will see him on Sunday though. That reminds me.' She got out the phone again. 'I left three messages for your uncl… for Lawrence today. Let me try again.' This time her call was answered. 'You having a busy day Lawrence?'

'Just a bit. I'll tell you about it tomorrow. I'll pick you up at nine and we'll go for DG and give him that ride.'

She heard the banging on the door as she finished the call. 'Wait Abu,' she looked at her watch, it was after nine. Abu hesitated by the door. He looked at her. 'Do you need your flashlight Aunt Glo?'

Gloria frowned. She wasn't going to live that down for a while. 'No, let's just see who it is first.' She went to the door and opened it a little. Through the crack she saw the battered face of Rufus Sarpoh. She opened the door and the man half stumbled and half fell into the room. He was covered in blood and his shirt and trousers were both torn. Abu helped him up off the floor and they got him into a chair. He tried to speak but Gloria stopped him. He wasn't bleeding now and didn't appear to have any broken bones. 'Let's get you cleaned up first Rufus and then you can tell me what happened, although I think I can guess.' Rufus smiled through broken teeth and nodded. 'Thanks Inspector, I can't go home, not tonight anyway.'

'I'll help him Aunt Glo, leave him with me.' Abu helped him up and Gloria let him get on with it. Rufus looked grateful that it was Abu and not Gloria who was going to clean him up.

It was an hour later that Rufus emerged looking much better in a t-shirt and pair of Abu's shorts. With the blood cleaned off him and in new clothes Gloria could see the wounds were only superficial. Nonetheless painful but not life-threatening.

'Ok Rufus, so you finally upset someone powerful enough to try and kill you. Anyone I might know?'

Rufus laughed. 'Kill me? Nah, it was a warning, you know, a good beating but no bones broken and no lasting injuries. And only one tooth missing.' He pointed to the gap in his top row. 'It's not the first time Inspector and it won't be the last. I like to think of it as a critical review of my journalism.'

Gloria started laughing. 'This has to be good Rufus, go on.'

'Look, I have upset someone enough to want to warn me off – that's good, my writing is having the desired effect. But they don't want to kill me, or even put me in hospital, that's also good because it means I am famous enough that if I just disappeared there would be a big investigation, which they don't want. A beating like this,' he pointed to the huge bruises appearing on his upper arms and thighs, 'means that people in power are taking me very seriously indeed.'

'Mmm, as awards go it's not the most comfortable one. Most people would prefer a plaque or a certificate, maybe even some money, but you like a beating in recognition for your excellence in journalism? Some people would think that's a bit strange.'

Rufus laughed out loud. 'A lot of people already think I am a bit strange Inspector, including you I suspect. That doesn't bother me in the least.' He stopped and sipped the hot tea Abu had brought in, swallowed the paracetamol and closed his eyes for a moment. When he opened them again he looked relaxed and calm. 'Now, do you want a description of the attackers or shall I do that in the morning?'

'No, let's do it now, if you feel up to it.' Rufus had a photographic memory which was one of the reasons he was such a formidable journalist, but Gloria was interested to see if it extended to details about the people who had attacked him.

'Two men, one short and one tall, in dark clothes, both wearing cloths around their faces. They didn't speak and they were very professional about what they were doing – maximum pain, minimum damage. All finished in five minutes.' He stopped and Gloria looked up from her notebook. 'That's it Inspector. They knew exactly what they were doing so there's no point in even trying to find them. Don't waste your time.'

Gloria looked at him. 'What about your family? Do you think they might target them next?'

Rufus laughed again. 'I have no family Inspector, no wife, no children, just a casual girlfriend when I need some company and an uncle who lives up country. That's how it has to be. I don't even have a place of my own, just some rooms here and there. It all makes it harder for anyone to get at me.'

Gloria looked at him with new eyes. Possibly a bit mad but Rufus was clearly someone who was absolutely dedicated to his work. The people who had attacked him did not understand who they were dealing with. 'So why did you come here Rufus. You are not really looking for my help to find whoever did this.'

'We already know who did it Inspector, and I came here because we have a common enemy. Did you read my last report from Bigmanville?'

'Africanus. Yes, you were not very subtle Rufus. Everyone knew who you were talking about.'

Rufus sucked his teeth contemptuously and shook his head. 'Subtle! I think we are a long way down the road past subtle Inspector. People like Africanus only understand one thing – power.'

Gloria agreed. She thought about pastor Wolo and Asholodu. They were like Africanus. Any threat to their power and they became absolutely ruthless. 'So you think we should join forces or something.'

'We're already on the same side Inspector. I just think you need to be more careful.' He looked round the room at Abu. 'I know people have already tried to get you but your enemies are getting more and more powerful and unlike me, you do have family and friends. They can be weak spots you know.'

Gloria felt weary, just what she needed to hear. 'Well thanks for thinking about me Rufus. But I am as careful as I can be. The only thing I need now is some sleep. And I think you should get some too.'

'He can sleep in with me' Abu threw out as he went to his room. Gloria looked at his departing back and wondered again if this fragile family of hers was going to survive.

Chapter Twelve

Gloria tossed and turned all night. Garish dreams of Africanus Varley applying lipstick while inviting her to visit his cellar under the cinema room, a room which turned into the cell at pastor Wolo's office as soon as she stepped into it, were overlaid with the small figure of Rufus Sarpoh lisping through a broken tooth, 'I have no family,' his face changing to that of Rose and then Peter Wajira, all saying the same thing, 'I have no family.' They closed in on her like extras in a bad horror movie and she woke, struggling to hold them and fight them off at the same time, to find she was tangled in her mosquito net, drenched in sweat and weighed down with a feeling of helpless panic. She lay still, not even bothering to untangle herself, until the panic started to recede. It was morning but she felt more tired than she had the night before.

She searched her memory for some words of comfort that would help her face the day. All she could remember was her mother's repeated advice to her when she was growing up. 'Come on my girl, you better wash your face, get your head up and get yourself out there.' There was something else about clean underwear, she seemed to remember, but she didn't need that piece of advice now. It wasn't exactly profound wisdom but the memory made her smile. And it had stood her mother in good stead. She remembered standing next to her mother, aged thirteen, at her father's funeral. Even at that age she knew that she and her mother were expected to wail and cry during and after the funeral but her mother was having none of it and had stood tall, sung all the hymns and, to the scandalised looks from family members, had walked unaided behind the casket. Her aunties were of a similar character. As a whole, her family did not do a good line in helpless females.

Roused by the memory Gloria was up, face washed, and ready to face the world before Abu appeared in his football kit. He looked suspiciously at her efforts to boil cassava and claimed he couldn't eat anything before going for practice. 'Especially since I didn't sleep much.'

'Did Rufus keep you awake talking then?'

'Talking? No, but the man can snore like a rhino. No wonder he hasn't got a wife.'

'His snoring disturbed you?' For a boy who had shared rooms with an entire football team and still slept it meant Rufus's snoring must have been spectacular. 'Well, I will see you in an hour or so with DG. You sure you are ready?'

Abu just raised his eyebrows. 'Just bring the boy, Aunt Glo, he'll be fine.'

At nine sharp she was outside the building waiting. Rufus had walked down with her and, although he must have been finding it difficult to walk, he said he was going back to work.

Lawrence arrived on time in the lead escort car, a huge four-by-four affair with spotlights and sirens on the roof and a loudhailer through which he was calling her.

She got in with her eyebrows raised. 'You couldn't have gone for a smaller car Lawrence? This will get us both suspended, unless you got permission?' She asked this with a faint hope.

'No, no permissions. Who was I going to ask? The President? Anyway she's not at work today, it's young Prince's birthday, so if we are lucky no-one will remember us speeding down the road.'

It wasn't far to Toweh's house so Gloria didn't pursue the conversation. Young DG had been thoroughly scared by the stupidity of the police department so as far as she was concerned it was worth taking a risk to give him a treat – and besides, the thrill of breaking the rules at high speed might help to snap her out of her frustration.

DG was jumping up and down with excitement by the time they got out and his parents looked both pleased and terrified at the prospect of him getting in the car.

'He'll be fine, I promise. It's just a ride to the beach and then he can join the football practice. We'll have him back by noon at the latest or sooner,' she caught their look, 'if he's not happy.'

It had been a long time since Gloria had seen such pure excitement up close. The self-contained little boy who had spoken to her so solemnly a few days ago had been replaced by this bundle of energy who was managing to bounce up and down in spite of his seat belt and at the same time keep up a high pitched screech of joy beyond words. Mind you, Gloria had to admit, it was smooth, noisy and very exciting. Everything just moved out of their way as the noise of the sirens cut a swathe through the Saturday morning traffic and the spotlights, which Gloria thought were a bit unnecessary, bounced off windshields and mirrors. With the air conditioning on high they travelled in comfort through the morning heat. They sped down

Tubman Boulevard, past the City Hall and the University and then when they had passed the exit for the Executive Mansion Lawrence slowed down and turned off the siren and the spotlights. Going any further with all that noise would definitely get them into trouble.

'Did you enjoy that DG?' Lawrence looked at the little boy who was settling into his seat now.

'Yes I did, it was the best ride of my life!'

'Good, well now it's time for some football practice.' He turned off the main road and followed the side road down to the beach. As always on a Saturday morning it was packed with teams practicing. It was impossible to see where one practice ended and another started. Gloria wondered if this was the best place to introduce DG to public football. As it turned out, it was. The crowds of young people intent on their football had eyes for no-one else. Their arrival made no stir at all as they walked through the crowds to the far end of the beach where Abu's various teams were practicing.

Abu waved them over to a group of younger children who were practicing under the guiding eye of Alfred. 'Hi DG.' He shook the boy's hand and ignoring Gloria and Lawrence, took him over to Alfred. 'You start practicing with the under elevens. This is a new team so they are all learning.' He patted him on the head and left him with Alfred who waved at them and then spoke to DG before gently pushing him onto the field. Abu trotted back over. 'He will be fine Aunt Glo, we've got coach Black with us so I need to go. DG will be finished in an hour.'

Gloria and Lawrence looked at each other and shrugged. 'I suppose we can go for coffee then, unless you want to join in.' Gloria looked at Lawrence who had put on his most ceremonial uniform for the occasion. He shook his head. 'No, coffee will be fine.'

They finally persuaded one of the booth owners to boil some water for coffee after agreeing that nine thirty was too early for a beer and settled down under a spindly beach umbrella to wait. 'Is that Hassan Black Abu was talking about?'

Gloria nodded. 'The coach for the under 18's national team. It's a big thing apparently having him come down to watch your team.'

They chatted about everything except the case and Gloria found she was enjoying just sitting in the sun with Lawrence, drinking coffee and watching the football practice. 'We should do this more often Gloria.' He was smiling at her, coffee cup raised as if he was going to make a toast. She raised her own cup 'We really should you know,' the warmth of her reply surprising them both as they awkwardly chinked cups and then went back to being football spectators.

Twenty minutes later Lawrence could see Gloria was getting impatient. Pleasant as this was, sitting still was really not one of her strong points and the conversation had drifted back to the case. She had told him about Rufus's dramatic appearance last night. 'Two murders and Africanus Varley back on the scene and I'm sitting here on the beach.' She looked at him again questioningly.

'If you need to go somewhere, we can go now. DG looks as if he will be fine for a while yet and if not there's enough people around to get in touch with us.'

'You're right,' she had brightened up immediately, 'I want to go to Monte Carlo.'

'Don't we all, my dear, but that could be difficult to do in an hour.'

'The training centre on Broad Street.'

'Oh right, well let's go.' Lawrence was up and moving to his car.

It was a short drive up to the centre where the metal gates stood open, even though it was Saturday. A steep flight of steps took them up to the third floor where young women stood around in groups eating bread and discussing last night's adventures in very loud voices. The sight of Lawrence in full dress uniform caused a number of loud and very direct comments.

'The man fine-o, too fine.' This from a large girl in a short skirt and tight top who was wielding a teapot like a weapon.

'That one can arrest me any time.'

Lawrence seemed completely unbothered by the remarks. He approached a timid looking man in a shabby security uniform and asked where the staff were. The man pointed back to the large woman with the teapot. 'Tha one there, she the boss lady today.'

Gloria sighed to herself. When Richard said the place was rough, he really meant rough. In her experience any school or training centre where the staff could be mistaken for the people they were working with, was bound to be a tough place. But Lawrence had already engaged her in conversation and, in true Lawrence fashion, had her laughing uproariously. The other girls had drifted away, having lost interest very quickly.

'Gloria, this is Miriam, she teaches the girls Hospitality and Catering.'

Gloria raised an eyebrow slightly and looked at Lawrence. His bottom lip was quivering as he tried to suppress the smile. Hospitality and Catering at Monte Carlo. I bet that would be a curriculum worth seeing, thought Gloria.

'She is the only instructor here today; they have a special contract to prepare the food for a wedding reception this afternoon, but she knows who you are looking for. An Indian lady turned up a few months ago and volunteered her services. She said she was a beautician but her husband was in Liberia on a contract with an engineering firm and she wanted something to fill her time. Her courses are very popular and they have people coming from all over town to ask her advice or to have their make-up done.

Miriam, it turned out, did not know the mysterious Indian lady's name or her address and could only say she was expected back on Tuesday. Gloria pulled Lawrence away. 'We better let you get on with your work Miriam or this wedding will not be happy.' Miriam shrugged and pointed to a large yellow cake with red and pink icing. 'The wedding not so big and the cake is fixed, we'll make it.'

Gloria insisted and they left her and the girls to their preparations and went back down to the car. It was already after eleven. 'Was that useful Gloria?'

'It was useful small, but we need to find the woman not just know she exists somewhere. I'll send someone back on Monday to talk to the centre director, maybe they have the woman's details.'

'I wouldn't bet on it.'

'No, but she will definitely know more than Miriam, hospitality and catering expert.' They both laughed. 'I'm afraid she might be teaching those girls more than cake making.'

Lawrence shook his head. 'Nah, did you see those girls. There's not much anyone could teach them. They wouldn't have survived this long if they didn't know a thing or two about life and how to manage it. I know some of them and their stories would shock even you Gloria.'

'Yes, probably. Well, we better get young master DG back home or we'll have other worries.'

She needn't have worried. When they got back to the beach DG was sitting with a group of other children listening raptly to Alfred's analysis of the practice session. Even for these young children football was a serious business, and for Alfred who was explaining something about a four-four-two formation they would be trying out next week. The children were hanging on his every word although Gloria was pretty sure most of them had no idea what he was talking about, but he was a minor footballing celebrity in Liberia.

When they broke up, DG limped over to them, sweaty and covered in sand but beaming from ear to ear. Abu came over with Alfred and they congratulated him on trying so hard. 'You did fine DG, I hope you'll come back. We need people like you on the team.'

DG looked at Alfred and laughed. 'You don't need people like me on the team Mr Alfred,' he slapped his left leg, 'I can't even walk good, never mind kick a ball. But I enjoyed it today too bad, so yes I will ask my ma to let me come back.' The serious nine-year-old was back, thought Gloria.

The Towehs were actually waiting on their porch when they turned in to the house and looked relieved when they saw DG jump down from the car and immediately start talking about the ride and the practice and could he go back next week. Mercy was delighted and invited them in for a drink but Gloria declined. 'Thank you Mercy but I think you are going to need to give all your attention to DG for the next couple of hours.'

Colonel Toweh walked them back to the car and shook her hand. 'If you ever need anything Inspector, I mean anything at all, then just let me know.' She nodded. She needed some allies in the establishment and Toweh was still a powerful player in the shadowy world of government. 'Oh, and you can tell Inspector Barnyou to relax now, the debt's been paid,' Toweh grinned at her, 'so if I can help him with any enquiries he should come and see me.' Gloria just raised an eyebrow and nodded.

'All that because of a ride in a car and a game of football.' Lawrence was edging into the traffic again.

'No, all that because of his son. People will do anything for their children Lawrence, you know that. That's the first time DG has been out on his own, and practically the first time he has mixed with other children.'

'But he said it himself, he can't actually play Gloria. What happens when he goes week after week and never gets to play a game?'

Gloria shrugged. 'It's football Lawrence, it's a different world and not one I understand. But my bet is he will keep going and eventually they will put him in charge of the equipment and then, because he's smart, they will get him to write up the team sheets and reports or something and before you know it he will be a key member of the team even though he can't actually kick the ball. And one thing about those teams is their loyalty, once you're part of them they will stand by you.'

Lawrence looked at her quizzically. 'You do know a lot.'

'Not really, that's just years of half-listening to Abu and his endless football talk.'

Further discussion was interrupted by her phone ringing. It was Clementine's number.

'Gloria, you need to come.' Gloria's heart sank. Clementine's choked voice and urgent tone could only mean the worst possible news.

'Where are you?'

'I'm at a place called...' there was a brief muffled discussion in the background, 'the Haven of Refuge, it's on the beach, near...'

'I know where it is Clementine,' Gloria jumped in, 'unfortunately. Don't say any more, I'll see you there.'

Lawrence had already forced the car into the traffic. 'I know where it is too Gloria. More bad news, I presume?'

'Yes, I think so, she sounded very upset which is unusual for Clementine, but we'll soon know. I wonder what she was doing down at that place though. The Haven of Refuge.' She said nothing more as if the name itself was sufficient and Lawrence focussed on driving as quickly as he could but it was still twenty minutes before they had negotiated the weekend traffic and turned off the main road again.

The deserted stretch of beach near the American Embassy did not hold good memories for Gloria. She shuddered as they bumped onto the sand. Clementine was standing next to a figure she recognised as Andrew Wright, or Bishop Worthing as he liked to call himself. His Haven of Refuge was a thinly disguised brothel which had been closed down several times but somehow always managed to reopen. Gloria had dealt with him on a number of occasions and his implacable self-righteousness had almost driven her to murder a few times. But today he just looked shocked. In fact they both looked to be in shock.

Gloria jumped down and Clementine blurted out 'It's Old Pa.'

Old Pa? Gloria searched her memory until it came to her. Old Pa was the child from the Children's Village.

'He's dead Gloria.' Clementine looked as if she was going to faint. She started to cry, quietly. 'He's dead.'

Andrew Wright stepped forward. 'Inspector, this is nothing to do with me.' He was shaking.

'Show me.'

They followed Wright to a small outcrop of rocks behind his Refuge where he pointed to a small figure positioned between two of the biggest stones. At first glance under the glare of the sun he looked like a child sheltering from the heat. The little boy lay curled up in the foetal position. His legs drawn up tight to his chest and his arms crossed over them. His eyes were closed with one large tear balanced on the edge of his nose, like those sentimental African Child paintings tourists seemed to love. There was a lot of blood on his hands and around his eyes and mouth. His features were screwed up in pain. And he was wearing make-up.

Lawrence was already on the phone and Clementine had composed herself enough to explain that Wright had found the child and panicked at first. He was going to move the body, he had admitted, because 'the police always think bad things about me,' until he saw the kind of wounds the child had and he couldn't bring himself to touch the body.

'Stuck into Old Pa's hand was my card and Wright was shrewd enough to see this was no ordinary killing. He called me and...' her voice broke again,' I recognised him at once of course and called you. But Gloria, look at him,' she was crying now, letting the tears run down her face, 'they suffer that child too much, it is too terrible.'

Gloria nodded. She knelt among the rocks and looked at the body without touching it. Clementine was right. The suffering inflicted on this little one was appalling. His eyes were closed because they had been sewn shut with rough stitches, his mouth had been sewn shut as well and when she looked at his hands she saw where the blood on the sand had come from; his index fingers had been roughly cut off.

She stood back up. 'We need to wait for Dr Armah.'

Lawrence indicated his phone. 'I've called Barnyou and Moses. They are going to get Armah and bring him down.' Lawrence needed action in these situations. Gloria could see he was carefully avoiding looking at the small body lying just in front of him.

'Lawrence, could you take Mr Wright here and get a statement from him.' He nodded gratefully. 'Clementine and I will try and put up a shelter over Old Pa.' The afternoon sun was beating down on them like a physical weight trying to force them into submission.

Using the rocks and some poles and a piece of tarpaulin which Wright helpfully found for them, they put up a makeshift tent over the body and while Gloria took some photos she listened to a distraught Clementine.

'This is our fault Gloria. We gave that child to some people and he ended up here. It is, it is just terrible. I will never forgive myself for this one Gloria, never.'

Gloria looked at her. She had never seen Clementine so upset and they had seen some grotesque murders.

'Clementine, it is terrible, absolutely terrible but it's a long way from the Children's Village to this beach, I mean there's been a lot of people involved, there has to have been. So, don't be so quick to take on the blame. The main thing is to…'

'… find out who did it. I knew you would say that and I know you are right but it is not enough.'

'Well if it's not enough Clementine then you might want to think about the offer I made to you.' Across the beach she could see the figures of Barnyou and Moses with the short Dr Armah behind them, making their way over.

Clementine looked at her, her shoulders sagged and she said quietly 'Ok. I accept.' She didn't look happy about it and Gloria conceded it might have been a bit unfair to ask her now, but she really believed it was for the best and it would be good for Clementine.

There was no time for more discussion as the team was briefed and people got to work. Gloria thought it was strange that this killing, the youngest child and a savage attack, was being treated with almost complete detachment by everyone. There had been no outbursts, no comments, apart from Clementine, just the team swinging into action. Maybe it was one of those Liberian reflexes. When things got beyond words there was only action. She wasn't sure if that was healthy, but it had been her own reaction too, she recognised. Otherwise this would all be too much for anyone to cope with.

But by the time the body was being loaded into the van to go to the morgue the silence on the beach was neither detached nor thoughtful, it was just oppressive. No-one was talking, no-one was looking at anyone either. Crimes against children destroyed not just the child and their family, she thought, they ate away at the souls of everyone who had to deal with them. She was calm but she knew the night would bring the dreams again, another face to add to the ones which already haunted her sleep.

Gloria, Barnyou and Moses huddled together in what was becoming a sadly familiar routine.

'Another one?' Moses question was more of a statement.

'It looks like it. Child tortured, killed and dumped in a public place. And with make-up on. What is it about the make-up? Whoever is doing this is hiding nothing.

'One difference is we know who this child is and at least part of his history.' Barnyou was staring at his notes.

'Yes, but there's a lot we don't know. And the pattern is different. The first two children became a nuisance, a threat even, to people in power which put them in danger and, if not the direct cause of their deaths, was probably a major factor. This one is an eight-year-old boy with a serious medical condition, separated from his family. What threat could he be to anyone?' Gloria was kicking the sand with her toe. She could feel the sand in her shoes and in her clothes, mixing with the heat and the sweat, and almost relished the discomfort. The sensations at least broke through the numbness which had crept over her since she had arrived on the beach. She recognised with relief the flicker of anger in her stomach.

'We need to shake things up; you know, turn it all upside down and see what drops out. There are too many different people involved here, by the time we go around them all again and again someone else is going to be dead.' She looked at Barnyou who nodded.

'I agree Gloria. If we plod along it's going to take us months to get to the bottom of this and by that time the bottom will be so murky we will be lucky to see our own hands never mind catch a killer. What will we do?' There was no reticence now. The other three were looking at her, expecting a plan.

'We,' she indicated Moses and Lawrence, 'will find the Monte Carlo director and then look for this Indian lady. Clementine will look for the social worker and find out what happened to Old Pa when they took him to town. And you, Inspector,' she smiled for the first time in hours, 'you are going to organise a raid.' All the heads went up, a raid was proper action.

'And who do you want me to raid Gloria? I am not going to like this am I?'

'I don't know. But I think you and your team should pay a visit to Bishop Asholodu very early tomorrow morning. He is hiding something, we know that, so search for anything relating to Peter Wajira and question all the people there. Someone knows something about why Asholodu took against the boy and then what he did with him.'

'It is Sunday tomorrow, there will hundreds of people there.'

'Maximum disruption for the Bishop. That might help you. There are bound to be some people who are jealous of him or don't approve, there always are in these religious organisations, it might be just the right setting for them to talk.' She had half expected Barnyou to refuse or at least put up all the objections about Asholodu being so well connected and the difficulty of getting a search warrant, but he did none of these.

'Leave that with me Gloria. I will call you tomorrow when we are finished – if I'm not in jail myself that is.'

They split up then. Clementine, walking beside her, had regained some of her old composure. 'Does everyone take orders from you Gloria?' She was smiling.

'Not nearly enough people Clementine, in my opinion. But I'm working on that. Listen, if you want to think about your decision to come and join the team, take some time. I shouldn't have pressured you like that.

'No, I don't need any more time. Just promise me I'll get the chance to slap a few ears from time to time. That's the only thing I've missed as a social worker.'

'Oh yes, and really big ears too. Now do you need someone to go with you to find Moko?'

She shook her head. 'No, I know where he lives and we will be on this all night if we have to, until we find these people. I'll call you.' She walked off into the last of the day's light, an unexceptional-looking woman for whom darkness and the wild streets of Monrovia held no fears. Gloria was glad Clementine was now on her team.

Chapter Thirteen

It was six in the evening, it was dark, and it was very, very hot. Moses, Lawrence and Gloria sat in the Daybreak Mouth Open Food Center eating fried fish and planning their next moves. It was a simple plan. Find the Monte Carlo Director, find the mysterious Indian lady, find the killers.

'I'm not sure we will be able to do all of that tonight Gloria,' Lawrence was staring at her.

'I know, I know, I am not completely mad, but we have to set our sights high. I feel we have been relaxing too much as if we have all the time in the world. Three children have been killed in a week, three! We need to make a stir, come on guys, it's the only way things get moving here.' She finished her food and stood up. They had agreed, although reluctantly on Moses's part, that he would join Barnyou on the raid as he knew more about Asholodu that anyone else. Lawrence would come with her to find the various people. 'Let's go now, ah, you people are too slow. Moses, you better get some sleep, Barnyou is raiding at five tomorrow morning. Call me as soon as you can.' She walked over to the car with Lawrence in tow.

'We have to take this car back Gloria. I can't drive this around Monrovia all night,' he added when he saw the look on her face, 'it will only take ten minutes. Do you want to go and change your clothes?' Gloria looked at him mystified.

'Why on earth would I change my clothes now? And you can forget it too. You'll just have to wear that outfit.' Lawrence climbed in, shaking his head. He had taken off the formal jacket with the gold braiding and the epaulettes but the white shirt was sticking to him with the sweat of the day and Lawrence did not like feeling so grubby. 'It really is an ugly uniform Lawrence.'

'Well I wore it today for DG, to make his ride special. I didn't think I would still be wearing it at this time of night.'

'That is true, thank you for that, DG loved it and he loved the ride. You did well for him, for both of us.' She reached over and touched his cheek. Lawrence took her hand, looked at her and then kissed it. She smiled.

'Come on, let's go and do some work.'

The presidential motorcade was kept in the underground garage of the Executive Mansion. Lawrence had surprisingly little trouble in getting into it. 'Well it is my job, they all know me.'

'But what if I had a gun pressed to your ribs, forcing you to take me inside.'

'They know you as well Gloria,' he laughed, 'stop being so dramatic. Let's get a car and get out of here.' There were a lot to choose from. Row after row of shiny top-of-the-range vehicles of every description. Lawrence chose a small jeep, one he often used for his inspections.

It was a fifteen minute drive out of town to the home of the Monte Carlo director at Paynesville. Several wrong turnings later and they were at her house, a sprawling run-down bungalow. The gates were open and the yard was busy with people cooking, talking and laughing.

Famatta Howard was a tall elegant woman who even in an old lappa and head tie looked every inch the director. She invited them to sit on the porch and listened to their story. Gloria allowed Lawrence to do the talking. He really was better at winning people over in a short time and Famatta was already laughing at something he had said.

'Our beautician is Mrs Fernandez, a very nice, cultured lady, and very good at her work. She volunteers with us three times a week. But what do you want with her?'

Lawrence was halfway through his explanation when Mrs Howard's eyes narrowed and she began to nod angrily. 'Oh, I see what you are saying. These poor children are killed and because they have make-up on them you want to connect their deaths to my centre. Because, of course, we only have bad people at Monte Carlo so they are probably killers as well.'

'Mrs Howard, all we are saying is that the make-up on the children was done professionally and very distinctively and, as far as we can tell, your Mrs Fernandez is the most professional. We just want a word with her. There is no connection with your centre or the girls.' Lawrence was at his most persuasive and Mrs Howard thawed slightly under his charm. She gave them an address in Sinkor for Mrs Fernandez with a warning they better not upset her.

'How can it be eight already?' Gloria had just remembered to phone Abu who appeared not to have noticed she wasn't around. 'That's nice though, my nephew just says 'Oh, ok' when I tell him I'll be back late. I could disappear and no-one would notice.'

Lawrence looked at her. 'Are you feeling sorry for yourself Gloria? You know the last thing you want is people constantly checking up on you.' She snorted, partly because it summed up her feelings and partly because she knew it annoyed Lawrence. She didn't know what she was feeling today; tired, frustrated, angry.

They turned into the Sinkor beach apartments and got out. The security officer directed them to the third floor where the door was opened by a middle-aged lady who had obviously been expecting them. Mrs Howard must have phoned ahead.

'Come in Inspector.' She was looking at Lawrence and indicated some chairs in the middle of the room. As they sat down it became obvious she presumed Lawrence was the officer-in-charge, addressing all her questions and attention at him. After five minutes of this Lawrence finally interrupted her flow. 'I think there is some confusion here Mrs Fernandez, Inspector Gloria is the one leading this investigation. I am just assisting her.'

Mrs Fernandez was caught off balance. She looked between the two of them in a comical way. 'It doesn't really matter Mrs Fernandez, as long as we get some answers.' Gloria sat up in the chair she had been assigned by the window. 'So Mrs Fernandez, tell us about yourself. How long have you lived in Liberia?' Mrs Fernandez smiled and seemed to relax. 'Oh, I came here with my husband in the 80s, so I know Liberia very well Inspector.' She pointed at a faded photograph on the table. 'He was the accountant at a big import/export firm for years. When he died I decided to stay on. I like it here, I feel I have a purpose here, helping out different groups. Or at least I used to.'

Gloria took the hint. 'I'm sure you still will, we just have to ask you some questions.' She took out the photos of the first two dead children and placed them in front of the woman. 'Can you tell me anything about these children?' Mrs Fernandez flinched and covered her mouth. Gloria asked the question again but she could see the woman was confused.

'Pictures of dead children? What can I possibly tell you about these? What do you mean?' Her confusion looked genuine but Gloria pressed her to look again, carefully. Mrs Fernandez picked up the photos and looked at Peter. 'Well this boy is wearing make-up, which is very strange for here.' She looked up. 'In my culture, in certain situations, a boy may perhaps wear it. But I have never seen it here.' She examined the other picture, interested now. 'The make-up is beautifully applied, in fact,' she looked closely, 'if I didn't know better I would say it was my work.' She laughed and then stopped, staring at each of them in turn. 'Wait, you think I'm the one who did this, you think I'm involved in killing children.' She stood up. 'My friends warned me about this, they told me I shouldn't volunteer, that something would go wrong and I, the foreigner, would get the blame.

It's always the way isn't it.'

Gloria held up her hands. 'No-one is blaming you for anything but you said yourself it looks like your work. So, calm down and tell us what you know.'

Mrs Fernandez did not look at all reassured; her hand hovered over her phone as if she was thinking of calling someone.

'Mrs Fernandez you are not under arrest or even being questioned officially, we just want your help. If you want to call someone to come along, please do. We are simply asking for your assistance.' Gloria breathed deeply. She knew the stories that passed around the ex-pat community; that foreigners were always being set up to take the blame for crimes or were frequently blackmailed or even whisked off to prison and never seen again. It was part of the underlying prejudice against Liberia fuelled by sensationalist foreign journalists and silly travel writers. According to her friends there were parts of London and Los Angeles that were more 'heart of darkness' than here but Liberia was an easy target. In this case, however, her assurances seemed to work. Mrs Fernandez sat back down and gestured with her hands.

'Ok Inspector, I will trust you. What can I do?'

'Please take another look at the photographs. Tell me anything that strikes you, anything at all.' She picked the photos up and studied them closely and then gently traced her finger over one of them, seemed to compare it to the other and then put them down. 'This work is almost identical to mine except for some small details.' She pointed to the picture of Peter Wajira. 'The difficulty with make-up is not applying it, as you probably know Inspector.' She looked at Gloria who shook her head, make-up was not a big part of her daily routine. 'Oh, right,' Mrs Fernandez smiled, 'well, the technical part is to make it look as natural as possible while using it to enhance the best features of a person. So, it involves not just a good hand with the brushes and pens but an ability to 'read' the contours of another person's face, their best features, where the light will normally strike them and, of course, areas that need disguising. It is hard to see on the photographs but when I looked closely I can tell this is not my work. Whoever did this has watched me do it or been taught by me and has cleverly copied my style. And they are very good, beautiful strokes, lovely texture, no clumps or bumps.'

She looked up at Gloria again 'All harder to do than it might sound. But what they have not learnt to do is to 'read' a face. Look at this,' she pointed to a tiny bump on the side of Peter Wajira's bottom lip, 'and this,' a tiny scar below his left eye. 'I would have disguised these Inspector.' She went on then for a further ten minutes pointing out minute flaws in the children's faces which should have been disguised with make-up, particular areas of their faces where there should have been more make-up and areas where there should have been less.

Gloria was left with two convictions: that Mrs Fernandez had not been responsible for the make-up but one of her pupils almost definitely was and that she had been right to steer clear of any artificial beauty aids.

'Well that has been very instructive.' Lawrence looked genuinely interested which was a slight worry for Gloria and looked as if he had a lot of questions. She interrupted quickly.

'Can you think of anyone, in any of your classes, who had the potential to be almost as good as you?' Mrs Fernandez shook her head immediately.

'Please don't misunderstand me Inspector, I really enjoy volunteering at Monte Carlo and in many ways I really admire those young women there but there is not one of them who doesn't think the first rule of make-up is slap on as much as you can. Believe me I have spent six months trying to persuade them otherwise, with no effect. And,' she caught the look on Gloria's face, 'they are strong and smart, but they are not subtle, so no, in my opinion, they are not pretending to be rough while hiding a wonderful talent underneath.'

Gloria nodded. 'Well what about your other customers. I know you are in great demand. Can you give us a list of all the places you have been to, perhaps highlighting your regular customers? That might be a help.'

Mrs Fernandez had brightened up considerably. 'Certainly, I will bring it down to you tomorrow.'

They left her and made their way slowly back to the car. Lawrence stretched again and repeated his opinion of the meeting. 'That was interesting.'

'Interesting? I thought you were considering a career change the way you were taking it all in. It's make-up for goodness sake Lawrence, rubbing paint on your face basically.'

'Well not really, but it was the subtleties that interested me. All that stuff about reading people's faces, seeing how light affects them, highlighting positives and disguising even the smallest defects.'

But Gloria was not in the mood for this. She sensed they were heading off into one of Lawrence's monologues about the importance of observing the smallest details.

'I need to call Hans. I should have done it earlier. We need to activate the CSA.'

'What's that?'

'It's the Child Safety Alert, a system we put in place in case of an urgent and specific threat to children.'

'And… how does it work?'

'Well to be honest we have only just set it up, we've never used it. What happens is I call Hans and he calls all the international agencies, Clementine, who contacts all the local agencies, Sr Margaret likewise with the church organisations and we put everyone on alert.'

'Sounds like a recipe for panic and mob violence.'

'No, that's the whole point. With everyone giving the same message the hope is we can increase security without starting a panic. At least people will be aware and can keep an eye on their children.'

Lawrence shrugged. He wasn't convinced. And he had seen the mob at work too many times. 'Go carefully Gloria.'

They arrived back at her apartment and Gloria invited Lawrence in for a coffee. It was now after ten but the muggy heat of the night had not lessened any and Lawrence looked at his now very grubby shirt which was sticking to him with sweat and dust and then at Abu who was leaning over the balcony watching them. 'Not tonight Gloria, thanks,' he said, and as she turned away, he added 'I really need a long shower and some sleep.' He leant in and kissed her and then climbed back into his car. 'Call me tomorrow if there's any more news.'

The sound of Sweet Liberia woke her with the thought that she would really have to change her ringtone. She had fallen asleep in the chair on the porch and as she reached for her phone she could see the first light of the morning beginning to spill onto the sea but the insistent ring gave her no time for dreamy reflection. It was Barnyou.

'Morning Gloria, hope I didn't wake you,' Gloria strongly suspected that wasn't true, 'but we are at the Asholodu compound, we are just about to go in. There is already a big crowd of people here for the early service. I will keep you informed.' Barnyou sounded excited. Quite different from the unsure, depressed man she had first met a few months ago. But still, he didn't need to wake me before the raid she thought grumpily. It's not as if I will be following the operation live by video camera or something. She got up to make some coffee. The apartment was quiet and still lit only by the early dawn light and the blue gas flame under the kettle with its comforting hiss. Abu appeared in the doorway of the kitchen, eyes bleary. He looked at her.

'Have you been awake all-night Aunt Glo?' He shook his head like a despairing parent and turned back into the living room. 'I am going out training.'

To her horror Gloria felt tears welling up inside her and the effort of holding them in caused her body to tense. Too much death and too little sleep, not a good combination. She pressed her hands down hard on the kitchen table, fighting for control and then felt Abu's arm around her shoulders. 'Sorry, sorry yah.' He was comforting her as you would comfort a small child. 'Sit down Aunt Glo, sit.' He propelled her to a chair by the window and she stared out into the grey morning until she was sure there were no tears and she had control of her voice again.

'I fell asleep in the chair. I need some proper rest, that's all. I thought you were going training.'

'I am.' He gave her the coffee he had prepared. It smelt delicious. 'Was it bad yesterday Auntie?'

She looked over at her nephew, the boy-man, who was staring at her with real concern on his face.

'It was the worst Abu, and that's all I'm saying. So go and practice, I'm fine.'

He shook his head. 'No, you're not fine, you need a holiday, a proper holiday.'

'I need to find a child killer, that's what I need to do.'

'Well at least get Lawrence down, he's usually here anyway.'

She looked at him again. 'I thought you didn't like him?'

'No, I mean yes, no, I don't not like him.'

Gloria raised an eyebrow. 'So, you like him or not?'

Aunt Glo I like Lawrence, ok? He is like my uncle, although I don't want to call him that,' he added hastily. 'I mean I have known him since way back, but now, well now it's too embarrassing.'

Light finally dawned on Gloria. 'Oh, because you and Fatu are...'

'Yes, because of me and Fatu. I mean if you and Lawrence get married then my girlfriend is going to be my half-sister.'

Gloria started laughing; a laughter that shook her whole body and when she looked up Abu was smiling and shaking his finger at her. 'You, Aunt Glo. You.'

'No Abu, I'm not laughing at you, honestly. The whole thing is funny, that's all. Look, Lawrence and I are close,' Abu pursed his lips, 'but we are nowhere near getting married. And even if we got married, Fatu would not be your stepsister, she would be...' she shook her head. 'Oh by that time, if it ever happens, you'll both be off living somewhere else anyway. But at least you've solved one mystery for me today, why you suddenly seemed to dislike Lawrence.' She looked at him again, feeling that familiar surge of affection for him; this 'frisky teenager' as her mother would have said, who was always quick to defend anyone he thought was being bullied or treated badly but who couldn't keep his room clean. 'Stop worrying and go and practice, you need to be thinking of something else apart from girlfriends. And getting married is the last thing on my mind right now.'

Abu laughed and winced at the same time. He got up and for the first time in a long time gave her a full hug, not the shoulder squeeze which was their usual sign of affection. He left singing, 'Oh, my Aunt Glo, she's crazy-o, crazy-o, crazy-o' in a high pitched voice. It was a song he had made up when he was eight years old and had first come to live with her. He had sung it every time she tried to get him to do some work or insisted on what he considered some crazy rule. She smiled at his departing back, he hadn't sung that song since before the war.

Chapter Fourteen

She had just turned on the water in the shower when the phone rang again. As expected it was Barnyou and he sounded very excited.

'Gloria, it's me.' The raid must have gone well, she thought. 'It was tough,' he followed up, 'that bishop has a huge congregation but Moses managed to find some people in the crowd who were not exactly happy with his leadership, you know the usual complainers. We avoided a riot but only just.' He described the huge crowd of the faithful murmuring and some 'wardens' who looked like professional wrestlers, taking up position at the doors in what he called a 'threatening' move. 'For a few minutes I thought we were going to be in real trouble but suddenly Moses's friends in the choir started singing 'I am on the battlefield for my Lord' and everyone just joined in, end of tension. We took Asholodu outside and man did he talk… the whole story about Peter and the rest. You were right, he knew a lot more than he said but he denies anything to do with the murder, says he was shocked but acted the way he did because he knows "how foreigners get treated in Liberia". Gloria snorted, were they all using the same excuse now? 'But he still denies any wrongdoing except not giving us enough information. He had nothing to do with any murders and apparently feels very badly about that, but he says he had to protect the church.'

'Are you bringing him in for a chat then?'

'We don't have to worry about that Gloria. He has volunteered to come down and give a statement, in fact he is insisting he comes with us. Are you joining us?'

Gloria hesitated. 'I don't think there's any need for me to come down. You and Moses can cover that. Moses can fill me in this afternoon at the big party. Will you be there?'

'I'll be there.' He didn't sound enthusiastic.

The rest of the morning passed quickly. Lawrence and Rohit turned up with food and for a little while she was able to forget about dead children and just relax with friends. She looked at Lawrence a few times but he seemed completely relaxed. So much so that she began to wonder if she had imagined their parting words last night. He avoided any reference to the case and was regaling Rohit with stories from his department. It was a familiar ritual. Rohit, who knew more about Liberia than anyone else, would act suitably shocked or amused by one of Lawrence's stories and then match it with a tale of how many Revenue or Immigration officials had been in his store that week looking for money or give them a snippet of news from the Indian community. It was a story he was telling about a wedding that reminded her about the case.

'Do you know a woman called Mrs Fernandez Rohit? She's a professional make-up artist and does a lot of weddings for the Indian community.'

Rohit nodded immediately. 'Oh yes, she is in great demand, lots of people use her for their weddings and other events.' He shrugged. 'I don't know much more than that. Make-up is not something I need myself.' They laughed at his understatement, but RohIt's face quickly grew serious. 'She had a hard time during the war you know. Their own houseboy, someone who had lived with them since he was a child, brought some of the fighters to their compound and when her husband tried to talk to them they just shot him, right in front of her. Very sad.'

They were all quiet for a moment then – war stories had that effect still, triggering everyone's personal memories of fear, betrayal and anger.

Rohit shook his head. 'They always kind of kept to themselves but now she doesn't mix with anyone from our community, except to do make-up. In fact, some of the aunties were wondering why she stays here on her own.'

'Well she did say she liked it here,' Lawrence jumped in, 'felt she had some purpose, could help people.'

Rohit grimaced and then spoke slowly, almost reluctantly. 'It's not quite as altruistic as that, I don't believe so anyway.' He looked at them again. 'I don't want to gossip, that woman has suffered, but there was a scandal a few years ago. Her husband was accused of serious financial misconduct, that's what we heard, and it looked like he would be fired, maybe even go to prison.' He paused again and Gloria, her mouth full of croissant, motioned with her hand for him to continue. 'Well that's it really. One minute there was all this talk of prison and investigations, and the next it was all over. The accusations just disappeared, he was back at work and everything was back to normal.'

Gloria sighed. That was such a common occurrence here it was hardly a great revelation. Rohit laughed. 'Gloria, that's not the end of the story. Mrs Fernandez let it slip a while back when some of the same aunties managed to corner her, that her late husband's pension will only keep coming to her for as long as she lives in Liberia.'

Gloria frowned. 'Is that even legal? I mean can…'

Rohit held up a hand to stop her. 'Legal? I don't know but I think that this pension deal was part of the renegotiation of the husband's contract – in return for these charges to go away and for him to get his job back. So…', he put both hands up as a sign that this was the end of this discussion, 'she might be happy to be here or she might have no choice. That's all I'm saying.'

Gloria nodded and got up. Whatever about the case, this new information was somehow just sad. And discussions of Mrs Fernandez's life and circumstances had certainly broken the spell of their relaxing Sunday morning. She might as well get back to work.

'I need to phone around the Child Safety Alert Network and see if there is any news. And,' she looked at Lawrence as if he was to blame, 'I should have heard from Clementine by now. I forgot all about her.'

'I'm sure she's fine and anyway, you're not her boss.' Lawrence's eyes narrowed when Gloria didn't look at him. 'Are you? Gloria what have you done now?'

'I haven't done anything. I simply made Clementine an offer and she agreed to join our team, as a social worker. I just haven't made it official yet.'

'So why the guilty look then? There's something else.'

Rohit stood up, excused himself and left. Gloria sat down again.

'Well I asked her first when we were going out to Wolo's compound, and she said no.'

'So? You asked her again and made her a better offer?'

'No. I did say she would get the chance to slap a few ears, something she's been itching to do for a while I think.' Lawrence started laughing. He got up.

'You phone, I'll clear this stuff away and then I'm going home. I'll call back for you later.'

Gloria felt relieved as if she had got away with something. It wasn't a very comfortable feeling. Despite herself she did feel a bit guilty about asking Clementine when she was obviously feeling responsible for a child's death. In the past, meaning yesterday, she would have justified herself to Lawrence, defended her actions and thought no more about it. Now she wanted him to understand, even approve of what she had done. That was a big change in a short time, especially considering nothing else had changed. The number she had called was ringing and then she heard Clementine's voice.

'Hello Gloria,' her voice sounded dull and Gloria's heart sank.

'Hi Clementine, how are you?'

'Moko and I talked to everyone at that church yesterday but we got nothing. Now they're denying that anyone from their church carried him to town. They say they prayed with him and when it didn't work someone who was visiting with them that day offered to take him to town to some powerful healer. But of course, no-one has any names or idea who this healer was.' Clementine had become a bit more animated as she spoke. 'I've sent Moko back out to the Children's Village to see if anyone there has any more information but I'm not hopeful.' She paused and her tone hardened. 'So, Inspector, what would the police do? A child is taken by a stranger to an unknown address and then murdered. What do you do now?'

'Come on Clementine, someone always knows something. No-one knew the child was going to be at the church that day right? I mean they hadn't planned it, had they? So we assume for the time being that, however crazy, the person who carried him had no intention to kill him.' She sensed Clementine nodding her agreement down the line. 'So it is likely that Old Pa was taken to a healer in town somewhere.'

'All we need to do is search all those places then?'

'Well if we had weeks and weeks yes, but there's more churches and healers in this town than beauty saloons, and believe me Clementine, there's a lot of beauty saloons. No, we have to narrow it down a bit.' There was something missing from this whole narrative, Gloria thought, something obvious that she should have noticed. Then the penny, almost literally, dropped.

'Clementine, did you ever hear of a healer or a pastor doing something like this for free? There is always money involved. And white chickens or goats or other things. So who paid for it all? Someone will have been asked to foot the bill for this exorcism or whatever they called it.'

She heard Clementine breathe in sharply

'I've been stupid Gloria, I've been so upset about him being killed I haven't been thinking properly... his parents.'

'His parents? I thought he was an orphan.'

'No, not Old Pa. Not all the children at the Village are orphans. Some of the children are there for other reasons and Old Pa was one of them. I told you all this the day we went out to that compound. Let me think,' she paused. 'Yes, Old Pa was brought there about six months ago. As far as I remember his parents live in the displaced camp out at Chocolate City and... Gloria, let me call you back. I'll get the real information first.' She rang off and Gloria sat down to wait. She didn't have to wait for long. In less than five minutes her phone went again. It was a slightly flustered Clementine.

'How could I have missed this. Old Pa was brought to us because his parents couldn't control him, the 'spell' you know, the fits and the odd behaviour. They told the camp doctor that the boy had some kind of spirit behind him, and they wanted to take him to the bush for treatment.

The doctor got worried because he knew the boy needed to be treated for epilepsy, so he contacted us. I'll get the details and go look for them today, they need to be told anyway.'

'Well I'll see you at the party then, or just call me if there's anything before that.' Gloria listened to the silence at the other end of the phone for a moment. 'Clementine, we have to go to this party, you know that right?'

'I know, it's Izena and Alfred, it just doesn't feel…'

'Clementine, it's got nothing to do with it being Izena and Alfred, well not much anyway. It's even more important than that. It's about remembering that, you know, that there is life, not just death. Imagine, I've got my nephew worried about me, telling me I need a holiday. This job will kill us if we are not careful-ooh. So, be at the party, and that's an order.'

Clementine snorted down the line. 'Hmm, an order eh? Well if you say it like that.'

'I do say it like that, my dear. So, see you later.' Gloria rang off. Surely they had to get some kind of breakthrough soon? They had so much information but no real leads. She checked her watch wondering how the interview with Asholodu was going.

By two they were all ready for the party. It turned out that half the residents of the apartment block were going.

'Mmm, I hope the food is plenty or some people are going to be hungry.' Gloria looked at Abu who was slouching against the wall waiting for Lawrence. 'You try and make yourself useful when we get there before you start eating, I'm sure you can help moving things or something.'

Abu gave her his that's-not-worth-a-reply look as they climbed into the minibus Lawrence had borrowed for the day. He made a beeline for the back seat where Lawrence's sister, Fatu, and Richard Varley were squeezed in next to Mrs Boakai. The seat in front had some of the members of Mrs Boakai's Retired Ladies Book Club including Mrs Gray, the bishop's mother and Mrs Kromah who were arguing about this month's book choice, and the seat in front of that had an enormous lady in yards of pink frilly chiffon, a tall thin man wearing a suit in yellow with red trimmings – and a goat.

Gloria climbed into the front seat. 'Really Lawrence, really, a goat?'

'Mum says that's what you bring to engagement parties, so that's what we're bringing.'

Gloria looked at the set of cooking pots, handles sticking out of the wrapping paper, that she was bringing as a gift and shrugged. Well, they had been told not to bring anything but she knew, as their boss, that didn't include her. There wasn't much need to make any further conversation, well actually there wasn't much chance due to the noise from behind her; three excited teenagers, three voluble old ladies and then the rather disquieting stare of the fat lady and thin man every time she turned around.

'Are those your neighbours Lawrence?' She indicated the couple with a wry expression.

'Well not exactly neighbours but my mum knows them well. Salome,' he indicated the vision in pink, 'was the Cooper's nanny for years. She was employed by Izena's grandparents initially and stayed with the family until Izena graduated from High School.'

Gloria rolled her eyes. 'We'll be lucky to get in the gates never mind get near the food table with the crowd that'll be there.'

Lawrence laughed. 'I wouldn't say that, have you met Izena's mother? She is a strong woman and is likely to have everything organised to the last degree.' They were turning into the Coopers' drive where two huge black steel gates stood open and uniformed security were checking invitations and looking under cars and in the boots of some vehicles. Others were speeding through with no checks or second glances. Their vehicle was stopped but the security turned out to be one of Lawrence's off-duty traffic cops who looked very embarrassed and waved them through while half saluting Lawrence and mumbling something about 'just helping the people'. Lawrence didn't react at all but as soon as they drew up he said to Gloria he was going to look for Barclay, his assistant, and she guessed that someone was going to be in trouble today.

Everyone was being waved past the front doors of the enormous mansion and around the side into the garden where Izena and Alfred were standing under an open-sided thatched roof structure receiving people. And people there were, hundreds of them, standing in a long straggly line talking, laughing and dancing to the deafening music of the band which had set up near the first swimming pool, an oval-shaped affair with tables and chairs set into the grass around it. There was another pool further down the sloped garden and then beyond the formal gardens Gloria could see a tennis court, a basketball court and at the far end a very impressive marquee. The place was huge, and it was heaving with people.

Gloria gave the pots to Abu. 'I'm not standing in a line to shake hands with those two, you can do it for both of us and give them our gift.' Abu scowled but brightened up when she added 'Richard, why don't you come with me,' which meant that Abu could give all his attention to Fatu. She indicated to Edith that she was taking Richard and the old lady smiled. Now the Retired Ladies Book Club could start the serious work of discussing who was there, what kind of gifts were being given and, most importantly, what everyone else was wearing.

Gloria and Richard set off down the slope towards the second pool, Gloria waving to various people she met along the way. She was half looking for Clementine and didn't see Africanus Varley until his voice boomed in her ear. 'Ah, it's Inspector Gloria. Taking some time off Inspector? Or are you pursuing criminals?'

The sound of his voice and that pompous tone just set Gloria's teeth on edge. 'Oh I don't think I would have to actually pursue criminals here, just a quick trawl around with a big net would do, don't you think?' But she could see Richard was terrified. In the presence of his grandfather he seemed to shrink. She moved to put herself between him and the boy but Africanus was too quick. He grabbed Richard's arm and pulled him towards him. 'Enjoying living with strangers are you boy? Just don't forget who you are, and anytime I want I can come for you.' Richard didn't resist and didn't look up. He looked like a rag doll in this man's grasp. Gloria moved in and jabbed Africanus right on the excruciating point of his elbow. He squealed, released Richard and turned to her snarling. God, she thought, this must be what bear baiting feels like. She took a step back into an iron table and stumbled just as Lawrence appeared out of the crowd. He righted her with his left hand while at the same time jostling Africanus backwards. The little tableau froze and just for a second Gloria thought Africanus was going to end up in the pool, but he regained his balance in time and the comic moment passed. He turned and walked away without another word.

'Richard, come here.' She pulled him over and awkwardly tried to reassure him he was safe. The boy was shaking. Gloria looked at Lawrence and shook her head, this Africanus man had to be stopped. 'You're ok, now. Calm down. Come on, we'll get some food.'

Richard didn't move. 'I want to go to the old ma.' Head down, shoulders rigid. 'I wan see the old ma.'

'Ok my man, let's go and find her, she just over here with the other ladies.' They took the boy by the shoulders and propelled him back up the slope to the queue where the ladies were still standing in line. As soon as Mrs Boakai saw them coming, half-holding, half-guiding Richard, she started down the hill and without a word took Richard from them. 'Mum, we bumped into his…' but Edith waved at Lawrence to be quiet. She put her arm around Richard and led him away talking quietly into his ear.

Lawrence looked at Gloria but she said nothing at first, her anger physically choking her. 'How is this allowed to happen Lawrence? Eh? He gets away with murder and then struts around here issuing threats to everyone. This is nonsense, absolute nonsense.'

'Come on Gloria, we've been through all this already, there is no point getting all vexed until you can do something about it, and you can't just now. Richard's safe for the moment and you have three murders to solve.' He put up his hand as she was about to interrupt. 'No, I mean it. Forget him and just focus on these murders. Do what you can do, not what you can't.'

Gloria snorted. 'Is that today's proverb then? We should be able to do more, much more.' She glared at him. 'We are a joke, you know that, a joke.' She strode off, trying to suppress the anger she could feel in her throat. She wanted to punch someone so when she felt the tap on her shoulder, she swung round with her fists already clenched, much to Clementine's surprise. 'Are you ok Gloria?'

'No I'm not, and neither is this country.' She was going to go on but Lawrence's words had stuck in her head, however reluctantly, and she took a deep breath. 'Never mind Clementine, let's just push on with this case. What did you find out?' She kept walking and Clementine fell in beside her.

'It was so easy when we started looking in the right place.' Gloria bit her tongue rather than state the obvious and let Clementine continue. 'We just looked at the referral letter and found the name of the camp doctor at Chocolate City and he took us right to Old Pa's parents.' She looked down at the ground. 'They were worried we were bringing Old Pa back to them, well they were at first until we told them the real news, that their son was dead. Gloria I couldn't do it, I mean I couldn't tell them he had been murdered. They just assumed he died from his illness and I left them at that. I couldn't go into all the details, not in that camp surrounded by so many people.'

'Ok, ok Clementine, we will sort that.' Breaking bad news in Liberia was often done in the most roundabout way anyway so this wasn't exactly unusual. 'Did you get any information from them?'

'Yes, we did. The day after Old Pa was taken to town some people turned up at their place asking for money and, wait for it, three white chickens, two new lappa cloths and a bag of rice. His parents just didn't have that but they borrowed some money and gave the people the new lappas they had collected for their daughter's wedding. They said they were from the…'

'Oh no, it's another church isn't it.' Gloria's shoulders sagged.

'Yes, the Healing Garden Ministries. They specialise in exorcism and prayer against bad spirits.'

'I bet they do, who runs it?'

'Have you not heard of this one Gloria, she's quite famous. Mother Euphemia Harris. Apparently she had a dream one night and…' Gloria jumped in, she had prayers prophets and pastors coming out of her ears. 'Just the details Clementine. Where do we find her?'

'Oh that's easy. She's right over there talking to Alfred.'

Chapter Fifteen

Mother Euphemia Harris was tall and very imposing in her white dress and head tie and gold sash.

'No, I'm not going to tackle her here,' Gloria said as if reading Clementine's mind, 'I've had enough confrontation today. But find out all you can about her and her church and we will make a visit tomorrow.' She looked at Clementine who was staring at her and in spite of the events of the last few days, smiling.

'Eh, I think you'll find Gloria that I don't work for you officially yet and that today is Sunday. So, what I'm going to do is get some food, a cold beer and somewhere cool to sit down.' She raised an eyebrow questioningly and Gloria relaxed.

'You're right Clementine.' She turned towards the tent where all the food was but saw Barnyou standing by the pool with his wife. They didn't look happy. 'But I need to have a word with Barnyou first. I'll catch you up.' Clementine just laughed and watched her stride away.

Abraham Barnyou looked extremely uncomfortable. His wife, whom Gloria had never met before, was standing apart from him and surveying the crowd. She clearly wanted to be mingling with the great and the good and not standing here with her reluctant husband on the edge of a swimming pool. She shook hands with Gloria and as soon as she and Barnyou started talking she drifted off very deliberately in the direction of a group of well-dressed and very loud men and women who had commandeered the small pavilion.

'Now she'll be happy, she can go gossip with all her "civilised" friends.' He watched her sidle into the pavilion and greet the people there, all smiles and chat now.

'Did you not tell her I can be civilised too?' Gloria asked him.

Barnyou laughed and rolled his eyes. 'She doesn't want to discuss books Gloria she wants other people...' he stopped himself and put up both his hands. 'Forget it, she's happy now, that's what matters. Did you want to talk about our bishop friend?'

'Let's hear it, did he confess to everything?'

'Not quite, in fact his story is a bit like the others I think. He admits he used Peter to build up his congregation, well he justifies it with something he calls the principle of…'

'… substitution, yes I've heard the religious jibber jabber before – what does he say happened though?'

'According to him he was very good to Peter but the boy was ungrateful and then started to threaten him.'

'So what did he do?'

'He arranged for Peter to go off and learn a trade with one organisation who came to the church one day.'

Gloria was shaking her head. 'Che, what is it with us and giving children away when they become a problem, I bet it's the same story with the pekin we found on the beach. So that's it, that's his story? So why did he lie about it?'

'Ah Gloria, the man knows he did bad, he's been lying to his church with the false miracles so when he saw the pictures he knew he was going to be in trouble over the boy as well. He just hoped it would all go away somehow!'

'Did he even show the smallest sign of being sorry?'

'Mmm, he did say he was sorry he ever met the boy, but I don't think that's what you mean is it?'

Gloria growled. 'Yes, well tell him he will be even more sorry. He needs to tell us everything now; the name of the organisation who took Peter, where the boy's parents are… I mean everything, before we charge him with kidnap and trafficking and as an accessory to murder.'

Barnyou looked at her impassively. 'In other words you believe his story and it doesn't help us solve this case?'

'Oh I believe him all right, I mean if he was going to make up a story it wouldn't be anything like that, would it. But it's another link in a chain that doesn't connect with the other parts of this story.'

'So what next?'

'Next? Next thing is we follow Clementine's example, a cold beer, some food and somewhere cool to sit down.

The rest of the afternoon passed quickly and noisily. Most of the 'celebrity' guests had left by early evening and the mostly young people who were left danced and laughed until it grew dark. In the remains of the evening Gloria managed to get a cup of coffee and wandered over to Alfred who looked exhausted. 'Well it's a bit late Alfred, but congratulations, and… good luck with the rest of your new family!' She looked over to where Izena's entire clan were sitting in a noisy group with her mother in pride of place at the centre on what looked suspiciously like a throne, her children and servants all around her.

She looked again at Alfred whose natural good nature seemed to have been exhausted. 'So how do you get on with Izena's family?'

'They look down on me. They think I am not worthy of their family, never mind their daughter. Most of the time I can put up with it but today was tough and when they act like that towards my mother,' he indicated a well-dressed handsome woman sitting at a small table at the side, 'that gets me angry.' Alfred was smart, good looking, serious about his work and usually immune to the snide comments and remarks of his new family but obviously they had managed to get to him. He was also a minor celebrity in his own right as a regular player and occasional goal scorer on the national football team. None of that mattered with families like Izena's though. There they sit, Gloria thought to herself, invincible in their arrogance and she felt her anger surge again. Alfred was worth three or four of them and she hated to see him put down like this. She walked over to his mother.

'Mammy, how did you enjoy the day?' The old lady looked at her with a twinkle in her eye.

'It was like seeing into the future Gloria. And it wasn't something that made my heart leap for joy I can tell you. But then again Alfred has to remember he's not marrying all of them, only Izena.'

Gloria nodded. 'It can't be easy though. I think I would have killed some of them by now. Mind you I feel like that about quite a lot of people at the moment.'

The old lady laughed again, an infectious sound that Gloria found very relaxing. 'They are mostly just stupid my dear, not worth going to prison for. I hear you've got some real bad characters on your books though.'

'We sure have, in fact I better get going if I'm going to have any patience with all these religious people tomorrow.' She stood and stretched. The two beers which had made her feel a bit relaxed now threatened to send her to sleep. Then out the corner of her eyes she saw Abu waving at her. He was way down on the basketball court with a group of boys but was frantically pointing at the small path which led to the pool. Abraham Kanneh was surrounded by a group hanging on his every word and Gloria remembered her promise. She wandered down to him reluctantly, she might as well try and salvage something positive from the day she thought. As soon as he saw her Kanneh turned his brilliant smile on her.

'Inspector, this is an honour.' With barely a flick of the wrist he made it clear to the group that they should leave, and they did. 'I must say I am surprised to see you at a party Inspector. Didn't really think it was your kind of thing.'

Gloria returned the smile in spite of herself. 'Oh, I can enjoy myself too, but this was a work thing as well. The happy couple both work for me, but I think you knew that already.'

Kanneh shrugged and leant in close to her. She could smell expensive aftershave. 'You never got back to me about my offer to help. The offer is still there-ooh, all left with you Inspector. But I hear you could really do with getting some assistance.'

'Look...' She hesitated.

'AK, Inspector. Just call me AK, like everyone else.'

'Ok AK. We will need your help,' her mind was whirring, trying to come up with something, 'especially if we get this campaign going but,' she pressed on before he could ask what campaign, 'before that I was wondering if you could help some of our young footballers with, well with whatever help you can.' His face fell. It was obvious he wanted the excitement of a police investigation and not more football requests but he rallied quickly.

'Of course Inspector, very happy to help. Maybe you can call me when this campaign is getting going and we can discuss both these things. I suppose you will be starting the campaign soon, if you want it to help your investigation.'

Gloria smiled to herself. He was quite good at these manoeuvrings. Not just a smiling face then.

'Agreed. I'll be in touch this week, or somebody from my department will be, maybe Alfred since you know him.' A reference to Alfred's appearance on the national football squad.

But Kanneh frowned and shook his head firmly. 'Better if you come yourself Inspector, if you can just make time for that, so we are talking on the same level.'

Gloria shrugged. The same level? Which level was that she wondered? Anyway it didn't matter. One more thing to do was not going to make much difference. 'No problem.' She stuck out her hand to signal the conversation was over and headed back up the path.

It was after midnight by the time they all got home and going to two when she finally closed her eyes. But the voices and faces of the day rolled around her head. From down the corridor she could hear Abu stumbling about looking for something and remembered she hadn't told him about her meeting with Abraham Kanneh. Well, that news could wait.

Chapter Sixteen

Abu's delight at the news about Kanneh helped Gloria to forget for a few moments about the day that lay in front of her, although much to her own surprise she was feeling fresh and sharp this morning. Action suited her better than gnawing introspection and today was going to be a day of action, and hopefully some results.

She stopped off at the convent on her way to the office. It was early but she found Sr Margaret in her office at the nursing school staring dejectedly at her laptop. 'Have you any idea what a log-frame differentiation timeline is Gloria? Project proposal writing has turned into some kind of mystery religion as far as I can tell.'

Gloria shuddered. 'No I don't, and I am off all kinds of religion as well at the moment so I can't help you on either count. I'm here about MACHO,' she couldn't help grinning as it was Margaret's turn to shudder. 'I am up to my eyes with these murders but it's vital that people start using the helpline to make sure the CSA is effective.'

'So many acronyms Gloria, you are beginning to sound like the UN!' She placed a cup and saucer in front of Gloria. The rich taste of the coffee was delicious but honestly, she thought, why don't people just use mugs instead of this doll's house crockery.

'The Child Safety Alert, Margaret. You were alerted yesterday. After the third murder in a week!'

Margaret sat back down. 'Of course, sorry Gloria. The endless quest for funds sometimes takes over my whole life. But these murders are horrible.'

'And there could be more if we are not careful, that's why I want you to coordinate the CSA for the time being. It needs more attention that I can give it, I know you are busy…' Margaret had put up her hand to interrupt Gloria.

'Of course I'll do it. I'm ashamed I haven't given it more thought. This money business…' She trailed off and for a moment looked uncharacteristically weary.

'Action, Margaret. That's what you need.' She finished the coffee and carefully placed the china cup on the saucer. 'Maybe you could call round the…'

'Just leave it with me Gloria.' Margaret was busy thumbing through a telephone list and making notes at the same time.

'Ok, then we will talk later.' But Margaret, who was already talking to someone on the phone, just gave her a wave.

The Polo was heating up by the time she got back, the early morning warmth a hint of the dry season which was on its way. She revved up the engine and for the first time in a long time she switched on the radio. Bad Boyz Beat, one of Liberia's most popular bands were blaring out a very cheery tune and Gloria was humming along to it before the words pierced her consciousness.

'We de children, battered and bruised,
We de children used and abused,
One day we'll rise up, we'll get to the top,
One day we will make this violence stop.'

She switched the radio off. One day eh? Better make it soon.

By the time she got back from the Director's office to arrange Clementine's transfer everyone else was in the office and waiting. News of Old Pa's death had seeped out and they were ready for action. Even Alfred and Izena were in the room although officially they had been given the day off to recover from the party ordeal. Moses had already given out the day's tasks but they were waiting for her to say something. She looked around the room. 'I am proud of you all.' The team looked confused. 'I know we are in the middle of a terrible case and it feels as if we are doing nothing but we are going to get the people who did this. So, let Old Pa's death be the last. Enough, enough, enough... let's get out there and stop this once and for all.'

For a moment it seemed they might start clapping, but they didn't. Instead they stood up and started heading for the door.

'One last thing, some good news. Clementine,' she indicated to the window where they could see Clementine walking down the corridor, 'has been transferred to the Family and Child Protection Unit full time, so she will be around a lot more.'

It was Christian who spoke for a lot of them. 'Thought that old ma worked here already, I can see her in this office every day.' There were nods around the room.

Gloria sighed. 'Well the point is she does now so...' she broke off, distracted by Izena's frantic waving from the back of the room. 'Oh, and one other thing. Izena is now our Information Officer so she will be bothering you for reports and information.' She could see Izena unfolding some

A4 sheets with a lot of writing on them. 'I think we'll leave the detailed explanation of your job until later Izena,' she tried for an expression of mild regret but it felt more like a frown, 'you know, let people get used to things while they get on with the investigation.'

'There's just one more thing ma'am.' It was Alfred this time. Gloria could feel her irritation and impatience beginning to boil up. 'It's about Alfred's funeral.'

'Yes, Alfred's funeral, it's on…' She hesitated.

'Tuesday ma'am, it's Tuesday afternoon.'

'Yes, tomorrow afternoon, so you better get out there and get some results today then.' They did leave this time and she turned to Moses. 'I thought that was going to go on all day. We like talking too much.'

Moses looked at his watch. 'It's only gone eight-thirty boss. I think we're doing ok. I'm off to interview Asholodu now with Barnyou. I assigned Alfred to go with you to interview that other church woman.'

'Harris, Euphemia Harris. OK, fine. No, I tell you what. Let Clementine come with me this morning and send Alfred to get those lists from Ramesh and Mrs Fernandez.'

Moses opened his expensive-looking notebook and wrote something down. 'I'd forgotten about Ramesh. What's the list from Mrs Fernandez?'

'All her customers, especially her regulars. She seemed sure that none of the girls at Monte Carlo had the skill to do all that make-up so we're going to check other people who know her work.'

'Her work?'

'Oh, skilfully applying make-up to highlight or hide certain features. It's an art apparently.' She caught the look on his face. 'Exactly, you really don't want to know any more. I had an hour of it the other day, and that was an hour too much!

The Healing Garden Ministry was situated in, appropriately enough, a very pretty garden on the edge of the beach near the Catholic Hospital. The building itself looked more like a clinic than a church with its whitewashed walls and white-coated staff walking about.

'You know Clementine, I have met more church people in the last week than in the rest of my life and it seems to me that, whatever they call themselves, most of them are more about money than religion, they are businesses basically.'

Clementine looked at her laughing. 'You just getting to know that now Gloria? Everything in our country is a business. People open schools to make money, start clinics to make money and have a vision and establish a church to make money.'

'Doesn't that bother you?'

'Why should it bother me? They can still make money and do a good job at educating children or taking care of sick people. In fact I feel better sending my children to a well-run school or clinic which I have to pay for than these so so 'free' schools or 'charity' clinics where they still take money but they provide a poor service.'

Gloria looked at her. Clementine's pragmatism in her work was obviously also her general approach to life. 'Yeah, I see what you mean but still, something about it makes me uncomfortable. And when it comes to churches...'

'Well churches are different Gloria. Their big problem is they don't want to admit they are a business. So they dress everything up with "God talk"; visions, prophecies... I mean if they were all true there would have to be a special department in heaven just dealing with Liberia.'

It was Gloria's turn to laugh now 'That's so true.' They were at the front door by this time. 'Right, well let's see what the story is at the Healing Garden.' She pushed open the glass door and strolled past the reception desk ignoring the lady who called after them to take a seat.

'Have you got an appointment Gloria?'

She shook her head. 'Nah, some days I make appointments. But this isn't one of those days.

'Do you even know where you are going?' They were in long corridor with doors on both sides.

'Don't need to, not to find the boss. If there's an upstairs the boss will be upstairs. If there isn't then they will be at the furthest distance from the main entrance. The farther people have to walk to get to you the more important you are. It's a very simple universal Liberian principle.' She walked to the end of the corridor, followed by the very irate receptionist, and threw open the door. They were in a chapel.

'Ok, when I say it's a universal principle I might have been wrong,' Clementine was grinning, 'but we've still found who we're looking for.'

At the front of the chapel Mother Euphemia Harris was towering over two hunched figures. She appeared to be lecturing them rather than doing any dramatic praying and she stopped mid-sentence when she saw Gloria and Clementine at the back. She stared, or glowered, at them.

'Who are you and what do you want? You cannot just come here and interrupt my work.' The figures in front of her didn't look up or even change position.

'And what is your work?' Gloria walked to the front of the chapel and stood looking up at Mother Harris. 'And, by the way we are police officers,' she threw Clementine an apologetic look, 'and we really really need to ask you some questions.'

Mother Harris paused and then shrugged. 'Please have a seat then and I will join you soon.' She turned back to the people in front of her. 'So, you remember all de tings I telling you yah? You mun keep your minds and your hearts clear and free.' She pointed to her head and her heart as she spoke, as if the people might not know where these parts of their bodies were. 'You getting me? Eh, you understand what I'm saying?' She spoke quickly and loud, her words shooting out like stray bullets. Gloria realised she was pressing her back into the bench, unconsciously trying to avoid being hit by them. The two people finally raised their heads under Mother Harris's verbal assault and Gloria saw their faces for the first time. They were young, hardly more than children and they looked hungry and scared. 'Now, go take your morning bath, Patrick will go with you.' The children looked even more scared as Mother Harris indicated the small fat man who had entered the chapel silently. His smile only served to accentuate the coldness in his eyes. Gloria didn't like him, not at all. The children stood up and followed him, their eyes staring only at the floor as they went.

'They look old enough to take bath by themselves.'

'Oh they are but this is a spiritual bath they are taking, they can't do that alone. Patrick will take them down to the sea.'

'To the sea?' Gloria remembered being at JFK hospital at some point during the war and helping nurses and other volunteers carry children and adults down to the ocean every morning and putting them in to wash their wounds in the hope the salt would prevent infection, gangrene and speed up the healing. But spiritual healing?

'What is the matter with them?'

'I shouldn't really discuss this with you but their parents brought them to us. One has a spirit that makes him roll around in the fire and the other is sad all the time.'

Gloria stared at the woman. 'And going into the sea is going to cure them is it?'

Clementine butted in. 'Mother Harris we are looking for a child, well we have a child's body and we need to find out what his story is.'

Gloria shook her head at the interruption but produced the photo of Old Pa. Even on the tiny screen of her camera it was still shocking. Mother Harris flinched and put her hands in the air as if she was going to pray. Before she could actually say anything Gloria continued talking. 'We know he was brought here, so don't start by denying everything. People brought him here from Brewerville to be healed. What happened to him?'

Mother Harris said nothing but her face twitched and Gloria could read her thoughts as easily as if she had been speaking out loud. She wanted to send for her lawyer and she wanted to contact some of her influential friends in government to make Gloria and all this mess go away. But she couldn't do that without appearing to be cold and calculating and that conflicted so strongly with her image of herself, as one of God's 'chosen' ones, that she was paralysed. She took a step back, then sat down and started fanning herself with some papers. Still, she said nothing.

Gloria sat down next to her. 'Look, we know you saw the boy, he came here and now he has turned up dead on the beach. This is very serious. You have to tell us what happened, just the facts, nothing else. Otherwise, as far as we can tell you were the last person to see Old Pa alive and possibly he was murdered while he was in your care.' She raised her eyebrows. 'That surely has to be worse than any embarrassment?'

Mother Harris sighed deeply. 'It's true the child was brought here by some people from Brewerville. They said they had tried to heal him in their church but that the spirit in him was too strong. So, of course, we took him in, we take in all who come here looking for help…'

'And you went straight to his family on the camp and demanded they give you money, chickens and the like…' Her statement hung heavy in the air, an almost-accusation, as Abu called Gloria's habit of sometimes leaving her sentences unfinished, inviting the other person to complete them – and incriminate themselves.

Mother Harris pursed her lips. 'We have to support our work, and these people can always find something if they really want to.'

'How did you find out where his family was?' Clementine wanted to know.

'Oh, I'm not sure. Patrick does all that. I think one of the other patients recognised him. We receive a lot of troubled souls from the camps you know.'

Clementine squeezed Gloria's arm to keep her calm. 'So what happened then?'

Harris shifted in the chair. She looked very uneasy. 'Well some of these cases are very difficult; there are some very stubborn spirits around, especially after the war, you know.'

Gloria knew her patience was running out, she had had her fill of religious talk. She stood up. 'Ok, enough. Three children are dead and all I hear is how much you people are worried about your churches. I have had it. So, get up and we will go down to the station and you can tell me exactly what you know. I don't care about all this,' she waved an arm around the silent chapel, 'so come on, let's go.' Mother Harris had recoiled from Gloria's arm and looked at her, shocked.

'Go? Go to the police station? Eh Inspector, you not serious. I can't go to the station. Me? Mother Harris?' Her indignation was almost comical in its extravagance but was nonetheless real. She stood up and took out her phone. Gloria took it from her.

'Answer the questions or we go.'

Mother Harris did not crumple in defeat, instead she seemed to make a decision and then straightened up. She stared at Gloria for a very long moment before sweeping past the two of them, barking out, all business-like now. 'We can talk in my office. Follow me please.'

Her office was a large room opposite the chapel dominated by a desk the size of a small football field with a garish portrait of herself overlooking it. She sat behind the desk and stared at them, all traces of graciousness gone. 'So? Your questions?'

'It's just one question. What happened to Old Pa?'

Mother Harris leant back in her chair, as if consulting some invisible adviser, and then started talking very quietly. 'Old Pa was brought to us by some church people from Brewerville. They said they had tried to help the child but had not been successful. We took him in of course and then we went to his parents.'

'No, I was mistaken about Patrick finding his parents. We found his family by asking him.' She smiled smugly. 'The child was not an idiot Inspector, he was sick with a bad spirit.' Clementine shifted uneasily in the chair next to Gloria.

'We know that, go on.'

'Well…'

Gloria interrupted. 'When I say "go on" I really mean get to the facts ma'am… quickly.'

Mother Harris hesitated and then obviously decided it wasn't worth her while taking on Gloria and with a 'humph' noise and a roll of her eyes she continued.

'It's like this Inspector. To heal someone they have to want to be healed, you understand that? It's not magic, ok?'

It was Gloria's turn to roll her eyes, not magic eh?

'We tried with the boy, with Old Pa, we really did but the boy was stubborn. Some people are just bad you know, even children. They like having a spirit in them, it makes them to feel special, or different or something. So all our prayers and exorci…' she caught herself almost in time, 'exercises had no effect at all. Sometimes even we…'

'Ayaya, he was epileptic, madam healer.' Clementine hissed the words through clenched teeth. She was shaking her head. 'He needed medical help and a bit of love. He wasn't possessed by a spirit, he was a frightened child who was ill.' Gloria put a hand on Clementine's arm and gently pulled her back into the chair. Mother Harris sat frozen in mid-sentence.

'Just finish your story, what happened to him?'

Mother Harris spoke slower now, choosing her words carefully, her eyes on Clementine's bowed head. 'It was our good fortune that we were visited by a very nice couple, Nigerians they were, who said they had come across this kind of spirit, eh condition, before, back home in Abuja. They asked if they could take Old Pa. They were sure they could heal him.'

Gloria was shaking her head again. 'How much did they pay you?'

'Pay? Now look Inspector...'

'How much?'

'Well they wanted to compensate us for all we had done so they did make a donation.'

'And, now think carefully before you answer this, where do this couple live?'

Mother Harris opened a book at the side of her desk and copied something out. She handed Gloria a piece of paper with an address in Congo Town on it.

'Doesn't it shock you, or even worry you, that a child in your care, that you handed over to people you didn't know, has been found murdered. Doesn't that bother you, as a human being first of all, never mind the director of a place like this?'

Mother Harris assumed a well-tried expression of regret. 'Of course it does Inspector but in this ministry I have learnt that some people are just...' she paused and looked at Clementine, 'you know, are just, not good, you know, they are going to be in trouble, attract trouble...' she petered out and made an vague gesture with her hands.

Gloria stood up. 'Enough. You'll have to come with us. Come on Clementine, let's go.'

Mother Harris stood up too. She knew she was in trouble. 'Ok Inspector, I will come to the station but let me come down on my own. I will be there in an hour.'

Gloria considered for a moment and then nodded. 'Ok, be there in an hour or I will be back.'

Clementine said nothing until they were on the main road again.

'She will turn up Clementine, don't worry.'

'Oh, I know she will. She is too well known to run away, she will turn up with lawyers and assurances from people in government and she'll be out in an hour.'

'I'm not so sure. But we'll see. Come on, we've time for a coffee before we get back.'

They were approaching Pizza Heaven and Gloria turned in and parked under a straggly tree that looked as if it was losing the battle for survival. Nine-thirty in the morning and the sun was already pressing down like a hot iron.

Pizza Heaven was empty and Gloria ordered coffee for herself, water for Clementine and pizza for both of them – well, it felt like lunchtime, and the pizza was good.

'So we have three organisations, with three children they describe as 'bad' in some way or other and hand over to complete strangers who kill them and dress their bodies to make it look as if they were ritual killings. So the main questions are still 'who' and 'why',' Gloria looked over at Clementine who was pushing a large pepper around her plate, 'don't you agree?'

Clementine looked up and smiled. 'I agree Gloria. I just can't get over how bad all these people are, using these children in the worst ways, blaming them for being bad, and then just getting rid of them without a second thought. To me, it's so bad. I not even got words for it. And we can't do nothing to stop it.'

'I know Clementine, I know but maybe we have to be a bit like them, less hand wringing and more focus, you know. Myself I feel bad too but that doesn't help so… if you're going to eat that pepper eat the thing and then let's think about this.'

Clementine shrugged, put the pepper in her mouth and opened her notebook. 'Ok, let's go.'

'The way I see it is this. These murders have been very carefully carried out, they are clever, if you can say that about a child murder. They are connected to each other in that they all point to some kind of religious organisation and the children themselves are all very vulnerable.'

'But we still have no idea why? Why they were killed and why they were killed in this very public way. If all those pastors and prophets were responsible for killing them, they would have done it secretly. There is someone else in control here.'

Gloria groaned. 'Another criminal mastermind! That's all we need. Let's get back and see if the other interviews tell us anything.'

The office was quiet when they got in.

'I need a desk Gloria. I wan start on my report right now.'

Gloria nodded and pointed her to a desk in the corner of the office. She looked at her own desk piled with several weeks worth of notes and papers waiting to be written up… and went to look for Moses instead.

Chapter Seventeen

Moses had both lists from Ramesh and Mrs Fernandez, and his conclusions from interviewing Asholodu. He didn't look delighted when Gloria explained that Mother Harris would also be coming in and needed to be interviewed, but they both agreed that the three churches, or cults or whatever they were, had, at the least, been abusive, and were guilty of profiting from the exploitation of children – and that none of those accusations would stand up in court at present. The new Children's Act, which would allow them to be prosecuted for these crimes, had been stuck in the debating chamber of the Legislature for the last three months and was making no progress at all. Under the present laws, drawn up by the Americo-Liberian settlers in the 1800s, a child was basically the property of the family, and an 'outside' child – one who was illegitimate or a distant family member you chose to bring to your house – was on a par, or slightly lower, with the family's goats or chickens.

But they also agreed that none of these church people, bad as they were, was guilty of murder. The urgent question now was, who is the killer?

Ramesh's list of customers and Mrs Fernandez's list were both long.

'Give them to Ambrose. Tell him to go through them now and see if he can spot anything. Any names that look familiar or strange. But,' she tapped the sheets, 'we also need to look at other people – what about the ones who go to that church or patients from the Healing Garden. Get somebody onto that too. You and I will go and look for the couple who took Old Pa and…'

'I have an address for the training place Asholodu claims to have sent Peter to so we can go there as well.'

'Any luck with Domestic Angels?'

'Yes, surprisingly. Izena tells me they are a real outfit too. Her aunt uses them.'

'Ok, we can go there too. I really thought that was going to turn out to be fake.'

The nearest address was the Nigerian couple in Congo Town so they decided to start there. Madison Avenue turned out to be a small dirt track which ran alongside the beach, and number 72 was a dilapidated villa with rusty gates lying open. The yard was deserted except for an old lady sitting on the porch. She stared at them without interest.

'Hello ma, how the day?' Moses went up onto the porch and crouched next to her. 'We coming from the police,' he carried on talking while the lady just stared, 'tha your one living here ma?' She continued to stare at him in silence and Moses saw nothing in her eyes, neither fear nor comprehension.

'What you come here for?' The harsh voice from behind belonged to a young man in shorts and a t-shirt. He had a machete in his hand. 'I say, what you come here for? You can't leave the old ma?' He advanced towards Moses who stepped back and put his hands in front of him.

'Eh eh eh pekin, take time now. We not come with no bad intention. I beg you now, put that thing down. We the police.' Moses somehow managed to get his ID card out his pocket. The man slowed, studied it and then threw the machete into the corner.

'Ok, so you are the police eh. What do you want? He had reverted to standard English and indicated a wooden bench for them to sit on. The old lady hadn't moved.

'We are looking for a couple, a Nigerian man and his wife. They gave this place as their address.'

The young man, who had introduced himself as Victor, sucked his teeth dismissively. 'No Nigerian people live here I can tell you. This is my auntie's house. Only she and I stay here.'

Gloria shrugged. This wasn't unexpected. 'Any of your neighbours Nigerian? Or you see any strange people in the area recently?'

Victor laughed and rolled his eyes in the direction of the huge white building they could see about 200 yards away. 'That's the Nigerian embassy right there Inspector. So, Nigerian neighbours? Yes. Strange people? Yes. This is Liberia.' He laughed and the old lady turned to him.

'What's wrong with your auntie?'

'What's wrong with all of us Inspector? The war, that's what.' He paused and stroked his aunt's arm. 'You don't recognise her?'

Gloria and Moses stared at the old lady again and noticed that she wasn't actually that old. 'No, I don't think so.'

'She is Agatha Fahnbulleh.'

'Agatha Fahnbulleh, the Voice of...'

'The Voice of Freedom, yes, that's her, or what's left of her.' His face clouded over and he patted the lady on the shoulder.

Agatha Fahnbulleh had been Liberia's most famous radio journalist before the War, articulate, controversial, funny and challenging. She had taken on politicians and businessmen, locals and foreigners, government and rebels, speaking, as she always put it, for 'ordinary people'.

Gloria stared again and asked the question although she didn't want to know the answer, not the details anyway. 'What happened?'

'I told you, the war happened. My aunt refused to leave this house when the rebels were getting nearer. She said it was her job to try and get people to talk and to listen. Right to the end she continued to believe that people were reasonable if you could just get them to talk to each other.' He shook his head and they could see the tears in his eyes. 'The savages found her here. They used her very badly and they kept her as a slave in her own house for months. When I got back here this is what I found,' he stroked his aunt's hair, 'this old lady who doesn't speak, doesn't move. But anyway,' he straightened up briskly, as if to avoid their pity, 'there is only me and my aunt here, no Nigerians, no nobody actually.'

'Thank you.' It was Moses who found the words. 'It's all we can do, take care of each other.' He got up and shook Victor's hand.

They both sat in silence in the car for a few moments. Liberia was going to be like this for a long time thought Gloria, the thin veneer of the ordinary suddenly cracked open to reveal the wounds of the war and the pain it had left behind.

'Let's go Moses. Where is that training centre?'

'It's out at Seventy Second.

They drove onto Tubman Boulevard which was unusually quiet and neither of them spoke for a while. Eventually Gloria broke the silence.

'So what did Asholodu say exactly?'

Moses shrugged. 'He stuck to his story is all. He thought it best for Peter to learn a trade and get working so he sent him to this place for training. As you said boss, we can't hold him on anything the way the law stands at the moment. I checked with Counsellor Baysah,' the department's newly appointed legal advisor, 'we have to let him go. And his powerful friends are making noises too.'

'You mean our powerful enemies!'

'Exactly, and you know what they can do when they want to.'

Gloria thought for a moment about Abu's words. Pastors, judges, politicians and businessmen… she really knew how to make enemies. She wondered how long it could be until the wealth and influence of her enemies outweighed the protection her very public successes had gained for her.

They turned off the Boulevard and then after fifteen more minutes took a left turn at the Victory Clinic and headed down a rough track towards

Muscle Arm Vocational Skills Training Centre. The logo of a flexed arm with superhuman muscles made them both laugh. 'One for your book boss?' Gloria nodded. Her 'book' was a collection of funny sayings on the back of taxis, shop names and logos which she and Lawrence had been collecting for years.

'One day we might even write them down instead of just having them in our heads. Could be a project for my retirement.'

From the outside the Muscle Arm Vocational Skills Training Centre looked like most of the other training centres Gloria had visited – a roughly whitewashed wall, with rusty gates, surrounding what had obviously been an upmarket home before the war. Hundreds of these places had sprung up after the war with varying levels of professionalism. It was true there were computer schools which had no electricity never mind any computers, places teaching agriculture in the middle of the town where there were no tillable fields for miles around and others teaching skills with no practical application whatsoever – like the School of Aeronautics on Gurley Street. But there were also a lot of centres like this one, which had given hope and practical skills to teenagers who considered themselves too old to go back to school and wanted to start earning money. Gloria had a lot of time for them and the people who ran them.

The centre was buzzing with activity. They waded through hordes of teenagers with welding torches and planks of wood, skeletons of cars, half-finished chairs and beds and tried to make themselves heard over the shriek of electric saws and the whirr of what looked like hundreds of sewing machines. The office was a little calmer and Fenton Anderson, the centre director, gave them seats. He listened intently to their story but was shaking his head before they had finished.

'Inspector, I'm sure the place looks completely chaotic to you,' he gave a loud belly laugh at their expressions, 'but I know every one of these young people and where they came from. This particular group all came to us through the UNICEF demobilisation project, all of them, the boys and the girls. We have a contract with them you see. So, no, there is no 'Peter,' no Nigerian boy here, no-one who came to us just off the street or from some personal recommendation. I assure you.' He smiled. 'Your story is not unusual Inspector. I had a lady from the American Embassy in here last week asking about a boy she had been sponsoring to attend here through his uncle – we had never heard of the boy or his uncle, and had never seen any of the sponsor money. And the old ma out there,' he pointed to the dark corridor where a frail-looking woman was sitting, 'came to thank us for her daughters who learned sewing here and are supporting the family.' He raised an eyebrow and shrugged slightly. 'Again, what those girls learned and how they are earning money is nothing to do with us, they were never here. So, when I say there is no Nigerian Peter here, I really am sure about that.'

Gloria didn't argue with him. 'Well thank you anyway Mr Anderson and thanks for the work you do here with your actual students. Your centre looks really well equipped and well organised. Which NGO is supporting you?'

Anderson sat back in his chair, proudly pointing to a photo behind him on the wall. 'We are entirely locally supported, no foreigners, no big NGOs, no embassy people – just Liberians. Our friends at LUTC supply us with everything, we only have to ask.'

Gloria was impressed, I mean it was rare to find a Liberian initiative entirely supported by Liberians. These LUTC people certainly seemed to be very generous.

They were out and back in the car again. 'We don't have time to go to Domestic Angels Moses eh? It'll probably be the same story anyway, but I'll get somebody to call round there, maybe Izena. Whoever these people are they were clever enough to pick real places but, of course, the children were never near any of them. My big question is how they knew where to find these really vulnerable children? Where do they get the information?'

'That's true boss, they must have some system, it can't just be random.'

'I'll check with Sr Margaret, I asked her to keep an eye on the CSA for the time being,' she caught Moses's eye, 'just until we get a breakthrough.'

Moses didn't look impressed. 'Isn't that something we should be doing, not that old ma?'

'Yeah? Well there are lots of things we should be doing, we just can't do them all.

It was late afternoon by the time they all gathered again in the office. Dead end, that was the unspoken conclusion they came to. Their investigation was at a dead end. Earlier that afternoon Asholodu had gone back to his church, Mother Harris had been interviewed and allowed to go home and all the members of the Never-Die Church apart from Pastor Wolo and his deputy, had been released. It was a very low ending to a day that had started with such high hopes.

Gloria looked around the room. The weight of disappointment on top of the afternoon heat was heavy on the team. It reminded her how young most of them were. 'Today has been hard, I know. But that doesn't mean we give up. In fact, we need to do more before these...' There was a sigh around the room and some muttering.

'You want say something Christian?'

Christian hung his head but said out loud. 'We ready to work boss, but empty bag can't stand, you know it.'

There was a ripple of laughter in the room. 'It's true ma'am, I think we are all hungry.' Ambrose looked around the room as he spoke.

'And hungover from that party yesterday as well... anyway,' Gloria put up her hands for silence, 'I've already arranged for us to eat.' Now she had silence, 'I thought we needed to do something tonight to remember Alfred because there won't be time tomorrow so we will meet at Day Break...'

'Mouth Open Food Center,' they all finished her sentence, laughing. It was well known as one of Gloria's favourite eating places.

'... at six,' she carried on as if she hadn't been interrupted. 'Food and drinks, soft drinks only though, and then we are back on this case. You know what they say, if the criminals don't stop, the police can't sleep. That's in one hour so enough time for you all to write up a report and get it to me before we go.'

They dispersed noisily around the room, the thought of food animating them.

'If the criminals don't stop...' Moses was laughing now.

'I know, I know, but it was all I could think of.'

'You are reading too many of those crime books. Which detective is that saying from; Morse, Mappo or Madame Ramotswe?'

Gloria sucked her teeth. 'I ever get time to read books these days? And for your information Moses it's Marple, Miss Marple to you I would think.'

Moses shrugged again. 'Those interviews are tomorrow boss, you didn't forget?'

'No, I haven't forgotten, who else is interviewing apart from us?'

Moses looked blank. 'I thought we had decided there was only one suitable candidate?'

'Yes, we did, Mardea Jackson wasn't it? But we still have to invite others for the interview and we need outside people on the panel or else they will accuse us of just appointing our friends.' She was shaking her head, 'Come on Moses, this is standard practice anywhere... and this is Liberia, where we have to be even more 'transparent and open' according to that World Bank report. Have you got anyone at all, apart from the two of us?'

'No boss, I didn't want to make the thing big big. I thought we would just meet Mardea and appoint her, if we liked her.'

Gloria stared at him for a moment. 'Contact two of the other candidates, the graduate and the woman who works in the canteen if possible, and make sure they turn up tomorrow. The interviews are before the funeral aren't they?' Moses nodded glumly. 'I'll ask Marcia Reynolds to come along as the public representative. Right, well, you better go then.'

With a mixture of bribery and blackmail the interviews were set up for nine the next morning and one last call from the restaurant secured Marcia's unwilling presence on the interview panel.

Gloria opened her beer under the table feeling like a naughty teenager, but there was no way she was drinking the soft drinks she had mandated for everyone else – apart from Moses who clearly had a beer in the large plastic cup he was drinking from… and she was pretty sure that wasn't ginger beer Christian was drinking and Izena had excused herself by saying she was still celebrating her wedding and had ordered red wine for herself and Alfred, and given a glass to Clementine who had just wanted to taste it apparently. In fact as she looked up the table she could only see Ambrose with a soft drink in front of him – and he didn't drink anyway. Oh well, she thought, they were all adults and they were off duty, and she was going to be working them very hard. Fine, let them think they got away with defying her orders.

'Attention please,' she tapped her bottle, 'I'm not going to give a speech, and none of you want to apparently, so just raise your glasses to Alfred.' She lifted her plastic cup, 'To an honest policeman, loyal colleague and,' she paused, 'a hard worker.' She couldn't bring herself to say friend. Old Alfred had never approved of her or her methods or her opinions… or anything about her really, and he had made that clear on every possible occasion. But he truly had been honest and hard-working and those were praiseworthy virtues enough.

They all joined her and for a moment there was silence until Izena asked. 'Any developments in finding the man who killed him ma'am?'

'Not that I know of, but it's not our case.'

'But do they even have an idea who would want to kill him?' Lamine looked very earnest.

'Oh, we all wanted to kill him Lamine, let's talk truth now,' Ambrose was only half-joking, 'but who would want to kill him enough to actually kill him?'

'And like that.' Izena shuddered.

'I'm sure Inspector Barnyou will find all that out but I really don't believe someone is targeting police…' Gloria looked round the table again and gave up. Most of her team were not bothered about a possible threat to them as officers and the ones who were didn't believe her anyway. 'Let's eat.'

Chapter Eighteen

It was a beautiful Tuesday morning, a lovely day for a funeral, as one of her fictional detectives would say. But there was work to do before any funeral. It felt wrong somehow that in the middle of a terrible murdering spree they would be spending most of the day interviewing people and going to church but that's exactly how it was going to be.

Marcia had turned up punctually at nine looking even more glamorous than her advertising posters but without her trademark smile and no sign of her 'flashlight teeth' as the street kids referred to her American dental work. Marcia had confided to Gloria that she had spent a lot of time and money on her teeth before returning to Liberia as she 'didn't trust local dentists,' and the results were quite dazzling.

'Good morning Inspector, Captain.' She gave them both a nod of the head. 'I hope we will be starting on time, I am very busy.'

Gloria shook her head but said nothing. If she was true to her school days behaviour Marcia would tie her face for a little while and then forget and start enjoying herself.

The first candidate was Festus Garmondeh who when asked what he had been doing for the past three years since graduating declined to answer and when pressed said it was his business and no-one else's. The lady from the canteen had withdrawn her application so Moses had found a replacement, a woman who had been 'an active member of the revolution' according to her CV, which turned out to mean she had been a rebel commander in the Lofa area. She seemed to resent every question and Gloria could feel Marcia squirming when the woman demanded to know if they were just going to 'talk war business' when she asked her what experience she thought she had for the job. It was a fairly short interview.

Gloria looked at her watch. They had half an hour before they should leave for the funeral and the last candidate. Mardea was short and plump with round glasses, a severe hairstyle and an easy smile. She was very ordinary looking but she radiated confidence and ease, and when she spoke it was the same. She had only just finished her training but she had years of experience of working with NGOs and the Ministry of Education. The interview turned into more of a discussion about the relationships between police and the community and would have gone on had Gloria not stopped it by pointing out it was almost time for Alfred's funeral.

With Mardea out the room Gloria looked at the other two expectantly. They were both nodding.

'Yes, I really liked Festus,' Marcia had stood up and was gathering her things together. The other two stared at her. She started laughing. 'Damn, I couldn't keep that up. Festus, man of mystery and that other woman... jeez, I thought she was going to go for my throat. I was going to make you two suffer a bit but it's no use. I take it you both want Mardea?'

'Che, you gave me a fright Marcia. Hmm, Festus eh? If you had gone for him, my girl, you would have been interviewing him instead of me on your TV show, I can tell you that.'

'My only worry Gloria is that Mardea doesn't have enough experience to work on a team like yours. The work you do is kind of specialised.'

'We're just looking for raw material Marcia.'

'Actually we would have settled for someone who wasn't crazy, that would have been enough.' Moses wasn't laughing. 'Mardea will do fine.'

Marcia scuttled off back to her studio and Gloria and Moses headed for her car. Three small figures were draped over it.

'Hello old ma, how the day.' The speaker was a spindly child in nondescript shorts and t-shirt. He looked to be about eleven or twelve. His 'colleagues' as he referred to them were younger boys who didn't say anything.

'Hello. What you doing out here then? Someone catch you chopping?'

The boy smiled and shook his head. 'Who will catch me old ma? I too quick for all dem people.' He sucked his teeth. 'Catch me! It not possible.'

Gloria knew him but not his name. She was sure he was part of the group that hung around the shops on Benson Street. The ones who charmed, harassed, cajoled and occasionally threatened the shoppers as they came out of the shiny supermarkets and upmarket clothes shops. It was a good ploy. Anyone who could afford to buy imported meat or real Italian shoes could spare a few dollars.

'So, what you want then? I rushing-oh, so you mun talk quick quick.'

The boy raised an eyebrow and shrugged but started talking fast. 'We see you talking to those "East Coasters" down Gurley street.' East Coaster was the new slang for sex workers because, as Abu had explained to her, 'East Coast Airline planes arrive in the dark and are gone before daybreak, you hear them but you don't see them...'

'So what?'

'Ehn you give them food and money and clothes.' He sucked his teeth again. 'We all need help, old ma.'

Gloria stared at him. The 'dey say' rumour mill had obviously been going full tilt. 'Look pekin we are the police not one of those organisations you go tell all your stories to.'

Prince, Gloria had remembered his name as she was talking, looked genuinely insulted. He covered his mouth with his hand while his eyes grew big. 'O! Old ma what you say. You say we wan eat your eye? Ehh, mmm! Old ma! Tha how you talk to your children now?' It was a good performance but even the two younger boys were laughing by the time he had finished.

Gloria opened her hands. 'So Prince what is it. You wan tell me something or not?'

Prince grinned and sat back on the car bonnet. 'Ok, we just want to know why you asking those girls to help you but you not asking us. Tha not gender equality there.' He pronounced the words very carefully and both Gloria and Moses burst out laughing.

'Gender equality? My man you have been hanging around those white people's offices too much. Gender equality tha what?'

But Prince had both their attention now. 'Ah, leave that thing now old ma, I say you only talking to the girls and you not talking to us and that's against our children's rights.'

Gloria sighed, even the street kids had all the jargon now. 'What do you want Prince?'

'We want to help is all. Those girls all stay in that one street there or they go visit men to their houses.'

'Or their cars.' The small boy behind Prince was laughing.

'So what do they really know eh? If you need information you suppose to ask us.' He waved his hand at his two friends, in case she wasn't sure who he was talking about.

'What? You three?'

It was Prince's turn to look exasperated. 'Not just us, all of us. We the children are all over this town. We see everything, you know. You suppose to ask us to help you.'

Gloria looked at her watch. Even by the standards of Liberian timekeeping they would be lucky to get to the church before the funeral started. 'Let's be clear pekin. We did not give the girls clothes and money, right? If you want to help that is good but you should do it because that's also your children's rights.'

Prince shrugged noncommittally. He just needed an agreement and then they would negotiate terms.

'Come back to the office this afternoon, if you can make it. We will talk.'

By the time they had got in the car Prince and his 'colleagues' were disappearing back towards town.

'We better get a move on Moses. Foot down, come on.'

They took off with a lot of noise, windows open against the heat. They had fifteen minutes to get there.

'So now you're going to spend time talking with street kids boss? The office will be packed with them or they will just tell us anything. Why couldn't you leave it the way it was?'

'You mean us waiting for Lawrence to come and tell us something or me looking for Pascal? Not really fool proof Moses, and the fact is that pekin is right. They do know everything that goes on but they have the habit of secrecy. And we are stuck. I will try anything at this stage.' Gloria flashed her badge out the window as Moses forced the car into the tight lines of traffic. 'But I think I have an idea how to do it. Abraham Kanneh has volunteered his services on us, forcibly volunteered them actually, but why don't we let him head up our Street Kids Liaison Project? He feels important, the kids like him, we get some information and it won't cost us any money.'

'Wow, you came up with all that while that pekin was talking to you?'

'Mmm, well when you say 'all that' all I've got is what I said, not exactly a plan but maybe enough to put to AK.' Moses shrugged and focussed on pushing his way through the traffic, but even with his aggressive driving it was a full forty minutes before they turned into the church compound where hundreds of mourners were milling around. Although it was well after the advertised time there were no signs of the funeral starting. 'It really is almost impossible to be late in this country isn't it? Well no disrespect to Alfred but if this service goes on longer than three hours I will have to leave!'

They joined the team who were standing in a subdued silence near the church's main doors and a few minutes later the ushers urged everyone to come inside.

The service was long, the church hot and, despite the choir being very, very loud, when the pastor, a short man with huge bass voice, got up to speak Gloria could feel herself drifting off. The Rev Jackson was famous for his outspoken criticism of government and modern culture and he spent more time talking about the ills afflicting Liberian society than giving much comfort to Alfred's family who were weeping copiously in the front row. 'We have learned nothing from this war,' he bellowed, thumping the reading stand in front of him and making Gloria jerk upright, 'we are still steeped in sin and we don't want to change. And do you know what 'sin' means eh? Sin means 'missing the mark' and that's what we're doing, we are each and every one of us missing the mark,' his voice had risen to a crescendo and he was pointing at them, 'say it after me and say it, louder.'

The congregation thundered back 'We are missing the mark.'

'When we lust after power what are we doing?' He was walking up and down the aisle now. 'We are missing the mark' they shouted back.

'When we lust after our neighbours wife what are we doing?' He was leaning on Alfred's casket pointing at them. 'We are missing the mark' they continued to shout, some people jumping up and down now.

And then his voice dropped to a whisper. 'When we gossip and cheat and steal what are we doing?'

'We are missing the mark' they whispered back. He paused then, looked around the church and then knocked on the casket with his knuckles. 'We should learn from this man,' Gloria presumed he meant Old Alfred, 'this was a man who did his duty to his family and to society. He didn't miss the mark…'

'Well the mark didn't miss him either…' Gloria couldn't help herself, 'or we wouldn't be here.' She heard Moses splutter and then start to shake as he tried to stop his laughter. 'Just sayin' Moses.' She was about to add another comment when she heard her name being called and for an instant thought the pastor was telling her off but realised she was actually being called up to give a tribute.

She walked to the front and stared down the church. Despite her flippancy the pastor's words and the loud chanting of 'missing the mark' still echoed in her head. As she surveyed the congregation she noticed Captain Luseni off to the side, and he was crying! Luseni and Alfred hadn't been great friends. In fact, Alfred had thoroughly disapproved of him and had told him so on several occasions. So why was he crying? The same way he had been crying the night of the accident. The hairs on Gloria's neck were standing up now as she struggled to say how much Alfred would be missed and what a great example he had been, while trying to reach in her head for the answer that had come to her, prompted by the Rev. Jackson's words.

When it did come, it seemed so obvious that it left her in no doubt. Back in her seat she leant over to Moses. 'It's Luseni.' She couldn't keep the excitement out of her voice. 'It was Luseni that driver was aiming for not Alfred. He got the wrong person.'

The service was finally coming to an end and they eased past the other mourners and into the porch. Gloria had signalled Lawrence to join them. Luseni was on his team after all. 'Look, as far as I know everyone's been struggling to work out why Alfred was killed right? The murder was obviously deliberate but why Alfred? It came to me as the preacher was talking.'

Lawrence lifted one eyebrow, 'Divine inspiration?'

Gloria grimaced. 'I don't know about divine but definitely inspiration. The driver of the tanker missed the mark, it's obvious isn't it, he was aiming for Luseni not Alfred.'

They stared at her in silence. She could see the thought processes ticking over in their heads, neither wanting to be the first to support or query what she was saying.

'Look, there's two things about this case that are puzzling; why someone would want to kill Alfred and…'

'… how they knew Alfred would be there,' Moses was getting excited now. 'I remember asking myself that question because I had to drive in the opposite direction to tell his wife the bad news.'

'Exactly. That night I met Luseni on the corner, he was in bits, crying. He said he had been talking to Alfred, catching up on news, and had just walked away when the truck hit the car. So, here's the thing; Alfred and Luseni hated each other so they would not be 'catching up' that's for sure. Luseni was definitely at the car talking to Alfred but I bet Alfred had deliberately gone there to speak to him. That's the only reason he was there. And he got killed instead of Luseni.'

'And since he had just come from our meeting about the first killing, remember, all that stuff about Leopard Men, I bet he had worked out some connection between Luseni and our case and went there to confront him, you know, and prove himself to the rest of us.'

Lawrence was nodding and staring at Gloria with open admiration. 'Better tell Barnyou?'

Barnyou absorbed the information silently, nodded once and then ordered two of his men to collect Luseni and bring him to the station.

'Moses, you better go to that interview, we need to see if there are any connections with the children, and Barnyou doesn't know all the details.' She paused. 'On second thoughts I'll go to that interview and you go and talk with Alfred's family again, see if he said anything to them.'

'Today boss?' Moses was asking but clearly had already decided that he would not be doing that today.

'No, no, you're right. You can do that tomorrow. Let's just say goodbye to Alfred,' the casket was coming out of the church followed by a mass of wailing family and friends, 'and then we will go together.'

It was still an hour before they got back to the station but Barnyou had not started the interview. 'Thought I'd better wait so I got the facts right.' The three of them went into the small interview room where Luseni was crumpled rather than sitting behind the table. He looked terrified.

'So tell us, what happened?' Barnyou sat in front of him. His simple opening was enough to get Luseni talking. 'I don't know. Alfred came to see me that night. He said he wanted to talk to me. I was leaning in his window and then I heard a roar behind me. When I turned round the tanker was almost on top of us. I threw myself out the way but there was nothing I could do for Alfred.' He stared at his hands. Gloria could see he was terrified, and she didn't think it was of them.

'So what did Alfred want to talk to you about?'

'Oh, he was just asking me… you know about some case… wanted my advice.'

'My man, that old pappay had no time for you so he was not asking for your advice. What was he saying?' Gloria couldn't stop herself interrupting.

Luseni had his eyes on the table and spoke in a low voice. 'He started accusing me of having something to do with these murders… me! He was talking crazy.'

'Accusing you of what? Hurry man. If you are not guilty of anything then help us.'

'I don't know, I was going to walk away. He was saying something about some business people I am involved with but that's got nothing to do with children.'

'So who was trying to kill you then, your business partners?'

Luseni sighed and looked at Barnyou. 'When I came over to your department I was approached by some people who wanted my help, just to make things easier for them, nothing illegal, well nothing too bad anyway. You know the kind of things we all do, a few favours.'

'It's called bribery Captain and is the reason you got moved out of my department. Who are these people you were helping?' As Luseni hesitated he continued. 'If they wanted to kill you before they will definitely want to kill you now that you've talked to us.' It was an old trick to scare people into talking but no less effective for that.

'Ok, ok. I was approached by a man who said his name was Daniel. He asked me to help him with a few favours in return for a small fee. Well, my old ma is sick…' Barnyou waved his hand. 'Just stick to the story Captain.'

'This Daniel would come to me every so often and tell me what they wanted me to do. It was mostly small things, making sure some files got lost, giving them the names of witnesses in some cases, just stuff like that.'

Gloria interrupted him. 'So why did they try and kill you. You must have done something bad to upset them.'

'Daniel came to me a few weeks ago and said they had some important work for me. He started to explain that they had run into problems with some people, children actually, and needed me to sort it. I didn't wait to hear any more. I told him I wouldn't do anything against children, this was a step too far.' Gloria thought he sounded genuine.

Barnyou was shaking his head. 'And then I got all that anonymous information about your activities and you were moved out the department.'

'Yes, suddenly I was in Traffic and out on the roads again. But these people don't let you go. I failed them, I couldn't pay their money back and now,' he did look terrified, 'I've spoken to you. I am finished.' He put his head in his hands, the picture of despair.

'So who was driving the tanker? You must know something.'

He looked up at them. 'I don't. That's the worst part, I don't know anything. The driver will be someone they have forced into doing this. The real people will be hiding.'

'But the things you helped them with, we need the details of those deals. That will give us a clue as to who they are. Some kind of businessmen?'

'Ok, I will tell you everyting I know but you mun protect me. These people will kill me.' They all nodded but knew that promising protection was impossible. Luseni knew it too. He had played the system long enough to know just how corrupt it was, but he had to believe there was a chance.

'I will put a guard on the door. No-one gets in unless I say so.' Barnyou looked at Gloria who nodded agreement. 'So we better get started.' Barnyou leaned across and took out his notebook but when he looked back Luseni was staring at his hands in horror. They were covered in a red rash that was already swelling and breaking open. The red marks on his head, where he had put his hands, were also swelling and his left eye was closing as the swelling increased dramatically. They all jumped up and instinctively moved away from him. The water bottle he had been drinking from was on its side. It looked innocent enough but Gloria lifted it carefully with some paper and put it in a plastic bag.

Luseni was now hysterical with pain or fear. Both his eyes were closed and as he kept touching his face with his hands the rash kept spreading, the skin breaking open and a brightly coloured puss oozing out.

Barnyou had already shouted for a car and, ordering people out the way, they bundled Luseni down the corridor, supporting him but telling him to keep his hands in his pockets. They reached the car and got in. Gloria signalled them to go and listened to the scream of tyres as Moses drove off at speed with Barnyou beside him trying to offer comfort to Luseni, while keeping a safe distance. She turned to Barnyou's deputy who had followed them outside.

'Find out where that bottle came from, and if I was you I would check up on who has access to your department. Someone got to your prisoner right inside our headquarters.' The officer raised an eyebrow while looking over Gloria's shoulder at the crowd of sellers and supplicants swarming around the main reception.

'I'll do my best ma'am, but this place…' He left the sentence unfinished and walked back inside.

She sat on the front steps, stunned and exhausted. Some kind of poison on the bottle presumably, smuggled into the station and delivered to Luseni under the eyes of the senior officers. How had they set this up so quickly? They had only arrested the man a few hours ago. Whoever they were, they must have inside intelligence, someone who knew what they were doing, as they were doing it. She gazed at the deputy's back. It had to be someone high up.

She needed a coffee and Ma Mary's was just the place. A few minutes in the car and she was there with a cup in her hand giving herself permission to relax for five minutes.

But five minutes she didn't get. Her phone was ringing before she had taken more than three sips. It was Moses, his voice calm but grim. 'He's dead boss.'

'Ayaya, he was a useless man but that was a horrible way to die, and without giving us any information.'

'No boss you don't get it. He was shot.'

'Shot? You mean…'

'Yes boss, shot… with a gun.' He paused. 'Someone was waiting for us. As soon as we stepped out the car there were three shots, from the Pan African Plaza, and that was him.'

'The Plaza? So you were at Brown's?'

'Yes, it's the nearest clinic to the station.'

Gloria shook her head. It just got worse and worse. These people were ahead of them at every step. 'Ok, get back here. Leave Barnyou with it now. I am beginning to wonder if we are the hunter or the hunted.'

She hung up and handed the half full cup back to Ma Mary. 'I've got to go, Ma Mary. I'll have to leave this.' Ma Mary took the cup without a word and bent back to the dishes she was washing. She was used to Gloria's sudden appearances and urgent departures.

Chapter Nineteen

The whole team regrouped in their office and Gloria broke the news about Luseni. 'Ambrose, you and Lamine go over to CID and go through every case Luseni dealt with and especially the ones where files were lost, or witnesses disappeared. Cross reference anything you find with those lists you have.' They got up to go. 'And get back to me today.' They looked at their watches, it was already two-thirty.

'Ma'am…'

'Today. Just get on with it. I am sick of these people being ahead of us.'

She left Moses to divide up the rest of the work and went into her office. She stared at the photos of the three dead children. It struck her again; they looked like dolls or, not dolls… more like puppets. Like puppets which had been used and abandoned by frustrated toddlers. That was it, there was a rage in these photos, controlled and channelled but still a rage.

'Boss?' Moses had a paper in his hand. 'Dr Armah has sent his report.'

'From Luseni? Already? How?'

Moses shrugged. 'Poisons are one of his specialities apparently. It didn't take him long to recognise it.'

Gloria took the paper. It was a short statement. He identified the poison as being from the Manchineel Tree, also known as the 'little apple of death' apparently.

'The sap makes the skin erupt violently but it's not usually fatal. It can be washed off and then with some cream it usually disappears in a few weeks.' She folded the paper. 'So it was just a big trick to get him out the station and they knew we would take him to Browns. That is some organising.'

'Yes, very interesting boss but,' Moses pointed at the photos, 'doesn't help us does it.'

'I know, I know, I am trying to think this through Moses. We have connections with traditional magic or ritual killing, with professional make-up artists…'

'And Nigerians, Asholodu, the ones who were paying Luseni and the

166

couple who collected the children, well some of them anyway.' Moses had raised an eyebrow.

'And power,' she sighed, 'of course! Always power. So, what kind of picture is that building up then?'

'Nigerian crime ring?'

'Yes, but doing what? This is not just a 419 scam is it? Why the children?'

'Well boss, we know Nigerians like all that magic business and they usually target children?'

'I don't know Moses, it doesn't sound like much to go on. I mean just mention egusi soup and Abuja and any Liberian could pass for a Nigerian.' She shrugged. Staring at the photos was not going to do much.

There was a rap on the door and Izena stuck her head round. 'There is a gang of those,' she almost wrinkled her nose, 'those boys, at reception demanding to see you ma'am. They say they've got an appointment.' Izena still found it hard to accept that street kids were as much victims as the other children she came into contact with.

'I'll go down and see them. Moses call Barnyou and see if they have any idea how that poison got to Luseni.'

Prince and his two sidekicks were in reception along with two older boys. Older and harder. Prince looked uncomfortable and as soon as he began to speak one of the older boys piped up. 'Let me tell you ma, this pekin say you need informations. If you need it just ask us,' he indicated his friend who was chewing gum and staring at Gloria with cold eyes. No friendly banter here, she thought.

'And what kind of information am I looking for?'

The first boy smiled. 'You don't know the information you looking for ma?' He rolled his eyes and looked at his friend. 'You see dis for-nothing old ma. Police people eh ya!' They both laughed.

Gloria knew the deliberate rudeness was to make her mad. But why? She looked down at Prince who had his head down, staring at his feet, probably worried he was going to get the blame for bringing these two here, she thought. She noticed a bruise under his left eye.

She reached over to the taller of the two comedians and grabbed his ear by the lobe, twisting it slightly. The boy yelped and squirmed. 'Eh, old ma, I beg you, ah, old ma-ooh.' He was dancing on the spot. His friend had stopped chewing and moved back slightly. Prince was grinning.

'En you say I for nothing. For nothing business can't hurt you my man. What you crying for?' She released his ear just as Clementine came up behind them.

'Any trouble Inspector?' Prince and his two friends high-fived her.

'We were just discussing. These fine boys say they wan help us, but dis frisky one here, he wan act rude on me.'

Clementine raised an eyebrow. 'Bugabug eat your brain or what?' She looked at him shaking her head. 'You don't know Inspector Gloria eh? You mun learn quick pekin.' She passed on laughing and the boys stood in silence.

'Ok, Prince you said you were going to help so I talked to a friend of mine,' she was stretching it a bit calling him her friend but even she couldn't resist bluffing a little when she had the chance, 'so Abraham Kanneh...' at the mention of his name all five heads shot up, 'is going to come and talk to you.'

'AK? For what?'

'Yes, he will come and talk with you and then...' Gloria had no idea really what they would all do. 'Well, let him come and see you and we'll work it out.' She looked at them again. 'So, tomorrow morning then eh? I will look for you down Benson Street.'

'But how will that help you auntie?' It was the smallest of Prince's friends. He looked puzzled.

The boy who had been rude spoke up again. 'Auntie, sorry for my rudeness. If you need any information on anything you just ask us.'

Gloria nodded. She had no intention of asking them for anything. 'Just meet with AK first, ok?' They nodded and started to move away. She would have given them a few dollars but she suspected it would all be taken by the two big ones so she let them go.

She caught up with Clementine on the dark staircase. 'What do you know about those boys then?'

She made a face. 'Prince, Toto and Iron,' Gloria presumed she meant the two small boys, 'are regulars on Benson Street, they usually work the supermarket there. The other two, Original and Executive,' she sucked her teeth, 'they are bad news.'

'So that's their names?'

'Well when they demobilised they gave their names as Executive Bible and Original Bible,' she half smiled, 'don't know why but that's what was on their ID cards. Then they dropped the 'Bible' part and became Executive and Original.'

'Which one was...'

'Executive was the one cheeking you up. He's always been the boss and Original just follows him.'

Gloria made a face. 'So, not very original then. He looks tough enough though.'

'Well they were both fighters in the war, right here in Monrovia, and they,' she waved her hands a bit, 'they never recovered really. They went through different rehabilitation programmes, you know the drill Gloria - learn a trade and become a plumber or electrician, go back to school and get your High School diploma, set up a business and sell eggs or airtime for phones. Those two boys were on every programme and finished none of them. At first that wasn't so bad, a lot of the kids were like that. And besides that they were very funny. Hmm, those boys could really make people laugh-ooh.'

Gloria made a face. She couldn't picture that.

'Oh yes, they can sing, tell jokes, imitate people. They were actually on TV once doing a sketch where the ECOMOG commander ended up in a room with his Nigerian wife and his Liberian girlfriend at the same time. Very cheeky but so so funny. But nothing seemed to last with them and they just drifted on to the next thing. No School of Performing Arts for them.'

'School of Performing Arts? Is there such a...'

Clementine laughed. 'No of course there isn't such a thing Gloria, that's one of the problems. We have nowhere for kids to go to develop their talents. Small wonder they get frustrated.'

'So that's what happened to them is it? They got frustrated?' Her tone wasn't exactly sympathetic.

Clementine shrugged. 'I'm not making excuses Gloria, but life could have been different for them, that's all I'm saying. After their TV show things just got worse and worse and they were always in trouble – taking drugs, stealing, prostitution. There was even talk they were involved in armed robbery but I don't know how true that is.'

'Che, this war really messed things up eh.'

'And they were in Monrovia almost the whole time. You remember some of the nastiest killings and rapes all happened here in town so who knows what kind of terrible things they did, and have to live with now.'

'Or try and forget.' Gloria's tone was a little more sympathetic.

'Anyway I haven't seen them for a while Glo. I don't know what they've been up to recently.'

They were at the top before she heard a voice behind her. It was Prince. Alone and worried.

'Old ma please, I beg you. Let me talk with you.' He stared at her, unmoving in the sea of people washing around him. Gloria sighed.

'Ok, but you come up here, I'm not walking down these steps again.' Prince grinned and bounded up. He followed behind her into her office and sat in the visitors chair as if he did this every day.

'What happened to your eye Prince?' The bruise was big now and swollen, partially closing his eye. 'And your arm?'

Prince shrugged and with all the world-weary nonchalance his eleven years could give him said. 'It was those two goons.' Kids spent a lot of time in the video clubs and often adopted the speech of the current favourite movie. 'And they think they're so funny.' He looked at her again. 'Everyone's a comedian these days.' He said this last in a perfect New Jersey mafia drawl.

Gloria smiled. 'Well, they didn't make me laugh.'

'No, old ma, but you made him dance.' Prince's high-pitched giggle wiped years off his face. He laughed for a few more seconds and then composed himself. 'Forget those people auntie, tha life.'

'But why bring them with you, or is that what the bruises were about?'

'The thing strange auntie. I don't hardly know them. They came to me today and said they heard we were coming here to see you. When I didn't agree they beat me.'

'So, you had to bring them, I understand.'

Prince sucked his teeth. 'Not for that ol ma. They said if we didn't bring them they would do something bad to Toto and you know he is too small so…'

Gloria nodded. 'Ok Prince, but will you be ok.'

Prince laughed again. 'They will not catch us next time. But I just wanted to say we will still bring you any informations we hear.'

But Gloria had decided. This was not some game. 'No Prince, I want you to meet with AK and get on and do something. You mun not put yourselves inside this kind of trouble. Understand?'

'But Auntie…' he dragged out the title, his lips pursed.

'Enough pekin. This can be dangerous. It's not for children, even smart ones like you. You take care of those friends of yours, that's your work.'

Prince neither agreed nor disagreed but left with enough money to buy food for his friends. Gloria was running through her list in her head when Moses came in.

'No-one knows where the poison bottle came from boss. The officer who brought it in got it off one of the sellers, and they are many there. He does remember it was a boy and he was very insistent about him taking the bottle.'

'So why did the officer not get poisoned?'

'Because the bottle was out of one of those coolers and Armah says the poison would have been frozen and harmless. Luseni holding it in his hands literally poisoned himself.'

'Again,' she held her hands out, 'what is it with these complex plots. So many things could have gone wrong.' Her head was beginning to throb and she didn't normally get headaches. 'Look, I need to contact Abraham Kanneh about this project…'

'That you've just made up.'

'Yes, something like that. But he needs to go and meet those pekins tomorrow.'

Moses looked at her. 'Boss, that man needs weeks of planning and negotiations before he does anything. He is notorious. I don't think you'll get him to agree, and besides, haven't we got more important things to do.'

Gloria raised an eyebrow. It was enough. 'It's all important Moses, all of it, and this could really help protect children and maybe even get us some information. Lord knows we haven't exactly done a great job collecting any information ourselves. It's all "well we didn't see anyone" or "there were too many people around" or "well she said, or I said, or they said". Maybe those two boys were right to laugh at us, like most other people in this town…'

Moses had his hands up in surrender. 'Whoa boss, slow down. I was just saying, you know the harder the case the more things you take on. I've seen it before.'

'It would just be nice if we managed to solve a case through regular police work rather than lucky guesses.'

They were both silent for a while.

'Well, I guess you better make that call boss and give Mr Kanneh his orders. I just hope he's not planned anything else.' He turned to leave. 'I'm going to see if those guys have turned up anything from Luseni's case files.'

Gloria nodded. 'Let me know.' She looked at her watch. 'Today.'

Interviews, funerals, poisonings and shootings… and it was still only five o'clock. Well no-one was going home until they had some breakthrough or lead.

The phone on her desk rang and she jumped. She couldn't remember the last time it had worked. It was the Director.

'Inspector we need to have a press conference. This situation is out of control and the papers will be full of it tomorrow.'

Gloria guessed that by 'situation' he meant the murder of two police officers, one right inside the police headquarters, the unsolved murders of three children and their lack of any substantial lines of enquiry. What she wasn't sure about was who was going to front a press conference and what on earth they were going to say.

'Come up to my office immediately.'

Gloria put the phone down but decided to make use of it since it was working and called Abraham Kanneh's number. It rang twice before he answered.

'AK, I hope you are still interested in helping us out?'

'Oh, yes, definitely Inspector. If you've got some ideas we can discuss.'

'Well, it's more than an idea actually. I am setting up the Street Kids Liaison Project... tomorrow morning, and I really wanted you to head it up.'

'Tomorrow?' There was a faint note of surprise in his voice. 'That's quite short notice.'

'As I always say AK, if the criminals don't stop the police can't sleep.'

She could hear him laughing. 'That's what you say is it eh? I wasn't thinking of sleeping so much as planning. But what is it anyway?'

Gloria hesitated slightly. 'Well, I don't want to be too prescriptive. I want you to make this project your own, that's the only way it will work. I mean...'

'You are making this up as you go along Inspector, aren't you?' He was laughing out loud now.

'Oh yes, I sure am but...' she was laughing herself now too, 'the project is a good idea. I am worried about those kids but they could also be a real help to us. They see and hear a lot of stuff that would help us, but they don't trust us enough.'

'I know that Gloria, I was one of those kids too remember. They certainly see a lot.'

'Well the thing is I am not comfortable about using them as spies or informants, well not unless I can be sure they are safe, so your project will do both. With your celebrity status you can set up something that will help them but that will also get us some information. And football...' she tailed off. She could bluff her way through a lot of things but football with Abraham Kanneh was not one of them. 'Look, just go and meet them tomorrow. I'll be there as well and then we can discuss after that.'

Kanneh agreed without any more discussion. 'Ok, ok I'll go tomorrow and then we can talk about it afterwards, maybe even do some planning? Now, I'll let you get back to your unsleeping criminals, or police officers, or whoever it is...' He put the phone down and Gloria sat in her chair. That had gone ok, hadn't it? She wasn't sure. The unfamiliar warm feeling in her stomach was subsiding leaving her a bit confused. She had felt it with Asholodu and Ramesh and now Kanneh. Jeez, they weren't all charismatic leaders. What was wrong with her?

On the way upstairs to the Director she heard a high-pitched voice calling her name. It was Martha Dunmore. 'Inspector Gloria, at last. I have been looking for you. I believe the Director has informed you officially that you are being investigated. I have left you several messages asking you to come to my office. They were not invitations to a party Inspector. You have to attend or...' She let the sentence trail away.

Gloria looked at her. Everything about her was narrow, from her skinny body to her very annoying voice. She reminded Gloria of something. 'Messages? I don't remember getting any messages but then I have been busy with three child murders and attacks on fellow officers. You may have heard about that?'

Dunmore smiled, coldly. 'We all have our jobs to do Inspector.' Her tongue flicked out and licked her lips and it struck Gloria then. She looked like a reptile on the hunt. Cold, calculating, scaly... well, maybe not scaly but definitely the other two. 'Shall we say Friday then? That should give you enough time to apprehend a few criminals.' She took out an alligator skin notebook and Gloria felt the wave of hysterical laughter rising up from her stomach. She nodded in agreement and rushed up the next flight of stairs, collapsing against the wall as waves of hysterical laughter shook her body. This wasn't right. It had been a few days filled with murder and torture and here she was laughing uncontrollably. But each time she remembered the alligator skin notebook in Martha's long thin hands she started up again.

It was five minutes and several odd stares later before she could compose herself and go into the Director's office. She felt lighter and her head clearer. It was either the laughter or the hysteria, and on balance she thought the laughter was better for her.

The Police Director looked as calm as he always did. 'Sit down Inspector. This won't take long. I have arranged a press conference for tomorrow morning at eight. I'm hoping that might mean the rowdier elements of the press might not make it which will make your job a little easier.'

'My job sir? Why on earth am I leading on a press conference? Shouldn't it be you or Inspector Barnyou?'

'Now Gloria, let's not waste time. You know how things work here. Press conferences are just an excuse for people to come and hurl abuse at us. If you are at the front they might go easier on us.' He rubbed his hands together as if to say that discussion was over. 'So, what can you give them, positively I mean.' He looked at her expectantly.

'Not a lot sir, these people are organised and ruthless. They seem to be ahead of us at every step, in fact it feels as if they are the ones in charge.' She started to explain about Luseni's death and then remembered Luseni had been the Director's relative so he had most likely got all the details already.

'Ok Gloria,' he leaned across the enormous desk and put out his hands, 'none of that is going to be said at a press conference. Agreed?'

Gloria shrugged. Why was this becoming her problem?

'We need some good news, or at least some… light,' he raised an eyebrow, 'even the suggestion that we are on to something, but it can't be discussed at the moment. You know the sort of thing.'

'I am really not comfortable with this sir, in fact all this politics is beginning to make my eyes turn.'

The Director opened a drawer and pushed some posters across the desk to her. 'These have been plastered all over town in the last couple of hours. What do you think?'

The first poster was a crudely drawn set of figures in police uniform sitting around a table full of food and bottles of beer. The police figures were stuffing food and drinking beer while behind their backs people were committing various crimes. The slogan underneath read 'To protect and Serve'. Gloria looked back at the Director.

'And the other one Gloria.'

The second one was better drawn. Some of the police figures were recognisable; it was Gloria, Barnyou and their teams. They were all blindfolded and bumping into each other while behind their backs the figure of a child was being murdered, people were being ambushed and their pockets were being picked by small figures with old faces. The slogan on this one read 'Everything is under control'.

Gloria smiled. 'Well at least I know which phrase not to use tomorrow…'

The Director smiled too. 'Exactly. So, what can we give them? Come on Gloria, there must be something.'

'It's complicated sir.' Then she caved in. 'Ok, I will try to think of something tonight, something that's true but is at least more hopeful than these posters anyway.'

'Thank you. Just pop in tomorrow beforehand and let me know what you've come up with.' He stood up. 'Thank you, Gloria. I will let you get back to the real work now.'

Gloria wandered back downstairs bemused. Moses was waiting for her at her office door.

'Boss,' he waved some papers under her nose, 'finally I think we have something.' He was animated. 'It's the lists the team was looking at.' He ushered her into her office and started pushing the papers under her nose. Gloria stopped him.

'Just explain it to me Moses, if it's such a good lead.'

'Yes, of course boss, sorry.' He pulled one sheet from the top and pushed it across her desk. 'Ma'am,' he had gone formal on her now, 'this is the list of cases Luseni was working on or had access to.'

'We got this so quickly, how?'

'I'm afraid old Luseni was not much loved in any of his departments boss. Everyone hated him. Instead of crying over his murder they were tripping over themselves to talk about him. Ambrose collected as much paperwork as he could and Lamine just talked to people.' He paused and looked up at her. 'You are right, those boys are learning.'

Gloria looked at the paper in front of her. It had a list of cases on it. She scanned them but didn't see anything very striking. In fact, if anything the list told her that Luseni had been assigned only the most mundane cases. She opened her hands and looked at Moses.

'I know that list doesn't mean much boss.' Gloria bit back her words but Moses went on anyway. 'It's not the cases he was handling but the cases he had access to boss, that's the breakthrough. Those people were paying him to change or remove evidence on lots of cases but there's one in particular…'

He pushed a sheet across the table at her. The name at the top jumped out at her: Ramesh, occupation jeweller, nationality Indian. Jeez, what had he been up to she wondered? It didn't make for pleasant reading: the corruption of minors, the use of children in pornography, exploitation of children. Gloria looked at him. 'Ramesh? What was the proof, why didn't we know about this?'

'That's exactly it, boss. There is no case, never was. The officer who handled it told Lamine they had arrested Ramesh but their biggest problem was,' he paused again, 'under the present code, the most they could charge him with is disorderly conduct.' He shook his head. 'It is not a crime in our country to exploit children in the making of pornographic movies, as long as you keep the volume down!'

Gloria banged the desk. 'So, they were waiting for the new Children's Act to come into force so they could charge him with these, these outrages?'

'You got it boss. That's exactly what they were doing.'

'But why didn't someone tell us this when we interviewed him, and why weren't we involved in this case, these are all children by the looks of it.' She wrinkled her nose at the titles of the movies, this was bad bad stuff. 'Why?'

'Apparently Ramesh's lawyer said that they had to take action against him immediately and the case would have failed, or they had to act as if he was a free man until the Act came into force. They were still discussing it when Luseni… well, that bit you know.'

'So, his case is still pending then, they are going to wait for the new Act to come into force? Nonsense.'

'Even more nonsense boss. All the evidence they took from his photo studio – the movies and photographs – has disappeared. The same night we found the first body.'

Gloria nodded grimly. 'But if the evidence was all gone why kill the children? Do we know if those kids were mixed up with him?'

'Well, it's very likely isn't it, I mean they were even dressed for a movie set, make up and everything…'

Gloria was reeling. It had been a long day and this new information was hard to take in. Moses was still talking, animated.

'I mean what did at least two of those children have in common?' He looked at her expectantly. 'They were a nuisance, they were trouble for Wolo and Asholodu. They knew stuff and they were not afraid to talk. That would make them dangerous for Ramesh too. Even with all his movies gone those children could have made a lot of trouble for him if they had named names and places.'

Despite her tiredness Gloria could feel the excitement rising within her. Cautiously she began to allow herself to feel a little optimistic. She stood up.

'Ok, right, so that makes sense. But why Old Pa then. There wasn't enough time for him to be involved in, in this stuff,' she indicated the lurid movie titles on the paper in front of her, 'and he was sick as well. I mean what kind of use would he have been to Ramesh.'

Moses looked up at her. 'This is really bad stuff boss. Look at the titles, I mean "Death in Real Time" and "Dying for Pleasure", they are more than just pornography…'

Gloria cursed under her breath. And cursed again. And then was silent.

'He was killing these children and filming it?' She managed to get the words out although the idea seemed too fantastic even for Liberia.

'There's no proof boss but…' he held his hands up in that familiar gesture, when words are just not sufficient, 'as you say, what else would he be doing with that poor pekin? And it would explain the settings and the manner of death – it was all like a film set, wasn't it?'

'You know, it does make some kind of sense. But why put Peter in his own shop window? That is a bit dangerous surely?'

'Maybe he liked the thrill, maybe he thinks he is cleverer than us, maybe it's the double bluff… who knows.'

Gloria was nodding but her head was somewhere else. This was bizarre. They may well have identified the murderer but they could do nothing, they had no evidence at all. Just a charge sheet and some accusations that were dropped.

'Ok Moses, we have to move very carefully on this, I mean very carefully. This guy is smart and is well connected, otherwise how could he get rid of the evidence and the people. If this is true, then he managed to kill Luseni right under our noses. So,' she looked at him, 'I'm afraid it's just us again. We can't say anything before he finds out we are onto him.'

Moses looked surprisingly pleased at this. It was his preferred mode of operation.

'But we still have to continue the investigation so get the guys out collecting information but make sure none of it points directly at Ramesh. As far as we are concerned, officially he is not in our sight.' She stood up. 'The other thing is, I'm hungry now. Being angry always makes me hungry, and I am very very angry right now.' She raised an eyebrow and Moses laughed a little.

'Let's eat then.'

Chapter Twenty

They ate fufu and gravy at a small place near Gloria's apartment. And they talked. The more they talked the more connections they found between Ramesh and the case. Moses remembered Dr Armah remarking that the Manchineel tree was most common in Asia, in India in fact. Gloria pointed out Ramesh's photo studio, right in his shop.

'I mean how many jewellers have a photo studio in their shop. He probably used it as a way of making a first contact. Who is on the customer list he gave us anyway, do we know?'

Moses produced the list with a flourish and started reading from it. It was very wide ranging, everyone from Abraham Kanneh to some of Doreen Walker's girls. Costume jewellery is very popular it seemed.

'The other thing we need to find out Moses is what he was doing with these, these movies. I mean anyone buying this stuff would be wide open for blackmail.' She looked at him. 'Do we know if he was sending it out the country? Probably, I would think.' She added, answering her own question. 'But who was the internal market? If he had powerful people here buying his disgusting stuff that would give him a lot of power you know. That kind of information is worth more than money.'

Moses was nodding. 'Oh yes, for sure. But how do we get that kind of information? I can't see anyone admitting to having any of Ramesh's work in their DVD collection.'

'No, you're right, but there must be a way. This is Liberia, someone always knows. We just have to find out who.'

'Lawrence.' They both said his name at the same time. Lawrence was famous for his sources. Maybe he could ask around and get some evidence for them.

Moses stood up. 'I'm going to keep an eye on Ramesh tonight boss. If he thinks we are seriously on to him he could just leave the country. And no-one else can do it until we get some real evidence against him.'

'Do you know where he lives?'

'Above the shop, right above his own shop.'

'Ok, well I will contact Lawrence and get him onto the information gathering. But be careful Moses, this guy is bad. Don't overlook him and don't take any risks. And…'

'Keep in touch, I know.'

Gloria walked up the hill to her apartment. They had come in Moses's car and she realised that she wasn't even sure where she had left her beloved Polo. This had been the longest day. Abu was up and strumming an old guitar, his latest enthusiasm, when she went in. He managed to raise his eyebrows in greeting in between what sounded like a version of 'African Queen'; she thought that's what it was anyway. She was surprised to see it was only nine o'clock and she still had the press conference to think about.

Thoughts of Ramesh and the children whose lives he had destroyed kept intruding on her attempts to think about the press conference. She was just about to give up when the phone rang. It was Marcia. Gloria hesitated and then pressed answer.

'Gloria, at last. I've been trying to get in touch all day. I just wanted to make sure you are ready for tomorrow.'

Gloria tried to remember what 'tomorrow' was about. 'Yeah, it's been really busy Marcia. What's on tomorrow?'

'What's on? Lawdy Gloria you are very quick to forget. It's the first edition of 'Marcia,' remember now? The show you are on with…'

'Whoa, slow down Marcia. I thought this show was on Thursday.'

'Thursday? No it's tomorrow! Six in the evening, live from the studio.' Her tone changed. 'You have to be there Gloria, you promised. And besides it's all advertised and if you don't show up Judge Weah might think you are afraid.' She laughed.

Gloria sighed, loudly and long. But she knew she would have to go ahead with it. In the middle of a series of murders and just when it looked as if they might have a break. 'Ok Marcia but how long will it take?'

'Listen Gloria please, you don't have to show up until five-thirty and I promise you will be out by seven. It's just forty-five minutes of actual talking or discussion.'

'Ok, ok. I will be there. I promise.'

'And nothing controversial right?'

'Well,' she paused long enough to make Marcia worried, 'that I can't promise. Some of that depends on how the Judge behaves. And the other guests. Who are they by the way?'

'Em, I was going to tell you Gloria, it's just that the other two have cancelled at the last minute, for good reasons,' she added quickly, 'so it's just going to be you and the judge.'

'Well that sounds more like a boxing match than a discussion Marcia but…' She let the sentence hang in the air.

'No, it will be fine Glo, really, it's better this way. The whole programme will be on Women and the Law. You know the kind of thing.'

Gloria didn't but was too tired to hear any more. 'Fine, I'll see you tomorrow.'

She had just put the phone down when it rang again. Lawrence.

'I was going to call you, listen I need to tell you something, but I really can't do it on the phone.'

Lawrence grunted. 'So? This big big secret is about what?' He didn't sound delighted at the prospect.

'Well I can't tell you on the phone can I? We need to meet early tomorrow.'

He finally agreed to come in the morning before the press conference and Gloria was just about to ring off when Lawrence added.

'But I rang you Glo remember? It's about Richard and his mum.'

Gloria groaned again. Another thing she hadn't managed to do. 'Ah Lawrence it's been a helluva day. You heard about Luseni?' He hadn't, so she filled him in. She could feel his shock down the line.

'God Gloria, what is going on? This is madness eh? And the security implications too.'

'Ah, I don't think you have to worry about security, these people know what they are doing and who they are after. Mind you, having said that, you might want to keep those white gloves of yours on if you're drinking any bottled water in the next few days.' Lawrence started laughing and set her off.

'Eh Glo, this thing is not funny. These people sound really organised.' She agreed.

'Anyway, I will tell you more tomorrow. Please tell Richard and your mum I will talk to the people at the Ministry tomorrow' – when, she thought to herself? – 'and get that visit sorted out. I wouldn't mind meeting his mum again, we have some unfinished business ourselves.'

'Enough, you crazy woman, go sleep, and no more coffee!'

She sat in the dark for a few moments. The press conference. It had just occurred to her. She had been approaching it the wrong way. What to say was not the question, how to manage it was the real question. She made one last call.

'Rufus? I know I didn't wake you right? I suppose you will be at the press conference tomorrow morning?' Rufus agreed he would be there. 'Ok, now here's what I would like you to do. Just a favour and I will tell you the whole story in a few days' time.' She explained what she wanted and when he agreed she relaxed a little. She just might get through it without completely disgracing herself. And she might even get some sleep now.

Wednesday morning was bright and hot and after a surprisingly dream-free sleep Gloria was up and in the kitchen soon after sunrise. She managed to produce scrambled eggs which were still recognisable and, more importantly, edible and sat down with Abu. They didn't talk much but the eggs were all eaten by the time Lawrence arrived, crisp and fresh in his uniform and ready for a mug of Liberia's finest coffee.

'So Gloria, what's the big mystery? Well, apart from the fact that our officers are being killed while in our custody.'

Gloria sighed. 'Yeah well, more important than the death of a corrupt policeman is catching the people responsible for killing these children.' She looked at him as if weighing him up. 'Look Lawrence, Moses and I think we know who is responsible but we can't tell anyone else.' She explained what they had discussed the previous night.

'Ramesh the jeweller eh? Interesting, but you have no real evidence and you obviously have leaks in the department. Bit of a task there Glo.'

'Well, that's where you come in. Moses and I trust you,' Lawrence mouthed a sarcastic 'thank you' to that, 'and we need your help. We need to get some evidence. Even if he has managed to destroy all the actual movies and kill off the children there must be others out there. He can't have killed them all, surely! And people always know things here or they will have heard something.'

Lawrence was nodding. 'Which people though?'

'Just people Lawrence, the people you talk to, everybody.'

'Right,' Lawrence was giving her a quizzical look, 'so my task is to talk to unspecified people to gather vague information about a suspect whose name we can't mention…'

Gloria smiled and nodded. 'Yep, that's it. Oh, just listen in Lawrence, you know you can get people talking about anything.'

'Well everyone except your nephew and my sister.' Abu had left abruptly as soon as Lawrence came in.

'Yeah, but that's family so that's always going to be a bit strange isn't it!'

They both got up. 'Ok, I will do my best. Have you got time to meet up today, get some lunch or dinner, you are still eating aren't you?'

'Well only just actually. I've got a press conference now, then setting up the Street Kids Liaison project with Abraham Kanneh and finally my guest appearance on Marcia's talk show with none other than Judge Dorothy Weah.' She held up her hands. 'And in between...'

'I know, I know, trying to catch a murderer or two.'

'It's ridiculous Lawrence, I'm doing everything except my job at the moment.'

He bent down and whispered in her ear. 'But you still have to eat?'

'And keep sane so yes, please call me so we can meet up for lunch and dinner and any other meals we can think of.'

'All right, all right, let's go. I will let you know.' And then in a more serious voice, quietly. 'Look after yourself Glo, no risks this time, promise me.' He pulled her into a tight hug and for a few seconds she let him hold her and just relaxed into him. He whispered in her ear. 'Please. Other people need you as well you know.' Then he straightened up and made for the door.

'Eh, thanks Lawrence but the other thing is, I'm not sure where my car is so...'

He turned back rolling his eyes. 'Don't I get even one heart-warming exit! Ok, yes, let's go. I will personally escort you to the press conference.'

The conference room at Police Headquarters was only half-full. That was a good start she thought. The small dais at the top of the room was empty except for the new official lectern with the police badge etched in gold on it - donated by the US government who seemed to like shiny badges and plaques as much as the average Liberian – and looking out of place in the dusty airless room. At eight thirty there was still no microphone, in fact there was no electricity so even the rusty ceiling fans had stopped, and the morning sun was already heating the room.

Gloria looked at the room and announced they would start. She had decided to conveniently forget the Directors instructions to come and see him before the press conference. The loud chatter and laughter died down slightly but before she could start a voice from the back of the room ordered everyone to 'bow their heads' and launched into a long and elaborate prayer in which God was thanked for 'allowing us to see this day which many others could not see,' commended for doing 'quite a good job till now' and exhorted to 'bring light to this press conference so that truth would prevail instead of lies'.

Well that's God told, Gloria thought but she let the pious atmosphere disperse before she started. She kept her statements to a general summary of the situation so far. She listed the children murdered, the officers killed and, in the vaguest of terms, the leads they were following. In other words, as the reporter from *Pepper Bush News* complained, she told them nothing. Gloria shrugged apologetically. There really was nothing more she could say.

The questions continued for ten minutes, each reporter asking the same things, each one more irritated than the last with Gloria answering in the same evasive way. Until Rufus Sarpoh put his hand up.

'Inspector Gloria, we were called here for a press conference, why? You have said nothing we don't already know. Why don't you give us some real information.'

Gloria fiddled with the papers on the stand but said nothing.

Rufus persisted. 'Come on Inspector. Tell us about the Nigerian gangs you are investigating. I hear you have been talking a lot about Nigerians recently, looking for a couple involved in stealing children. If our children are at risk from foreign groups or individuals we have a right to know, in fact it is our duty,' he indicated the collection of reporters around him, 'to inform the public what is going on.'

Gloria's head had shot up at the mention of a Nigerian gang. She looked furious. 'Look, I am trying to do my job ok? Giving out information while we are still investigating people is not helpful. I beg you people, respect our methods and have some trust.' The hall was completely silent now. She stood up. 'I think that is enough for today. I can't tell you what to write but I urge you to make sure you are writing facts and not rumours.' Her last words were lost in the sound of chairs being pushed back and people leaving in a hurry to get the latest news on the murders into the papers and on the radio. It was a great story: Nigerian gangs stealing and killing children; I mean, it was obvious that was what was happening and the police were trying to cover it up.

Gloria managed to wink at Rufus as she swept by the crowd of reporters surrounding him at the door. She really owed him now though, she thought.

A tired-looking Moses was waiting for her. He still managed to smile and whisper. 'Nigerians?'

Gloria shrugged. 'I didn't say anything about Nigerians, that was Rufus. If they print any of that, it's their business. But, on the other hand, it gives us a bit more cover to investigate you-know-who. How was last night?'

'Nothing, he never moved. He had no visitors apart from someone bringing him food.'

'Ok, get the rest of the team working and we might need to involve other people from the department...'

Moses shook his head. 'No boss, not yet. If we tell some and not the rest it will make real problems for us later.'

After a short pause Gloria agreed with him. 'You're right, but wait now, you said someone brought Ramesh food last night. His only visitor you said?'

'Yes, I couldn't see him too well, but he looked like a young man. He didn't stay long, it looked like he let himself in, left the food and was out in ten minutes or so.'

Gloria was tapping her notebook and then flipped it open. 'Look, this is what Hassan told me the day we found Peter in that shop.' She showed him the page. 'Ramesh had a reputation for not mixing and not trusting anyone, remember? He kept the keys to the shop, he didn't have security. So, who is this person he suddenly trusts with a key to his apartment?' She raised an eyebrow. 'Maybe you could talk to Barnyou and then meet the assistant Ramesh had, the one he said he had fired. Maybe he didn't fire anyone; maybe that was just for our benefit. He must have some people working with him, he couldn't arrange all this on his own. Maybe this assistant helps with more than some food?'

'Yes, it's worth a try boss. I will get on to that now. Hmm, but what made you to think of that?'

'He struck me as one of those people who comes here and thinks all us Liberians are dishonest or stupid, or both. The very last person he would give his house keys to is a Liberian, unless…'

'It's all just for show? Part of the "film set"?'

She nodded. 'And now, in the middle of this I've to go and meet AK and those kids on Benson Street. It is crazy timing but it has to be done. Right, later Moses.'

She found her car parked against the reception wall. It had only been there one day and night and already some of the market women had taken it over. Baskets of vegetables were on the bonnet of the car and a woman and her baby were lying under the shade of the front wheels.

'Eh, ma, ma.' Gloria roused the woman and, making sure she took her baby with her, backed the car onto the street. It was hot, very hot and the smell of wilting cabbage and boiled eggs persisted even with the windows open.

It was 10.30 when she reached Benson Street her head full of plots and clues. With adrenaline rushing through her body and frustration at being here instead of pursuing the case, she didn't take in at first the huge crowd of children milling around on the pavement in front of the St Luke's Shelter. Ayaya, she thought, there must be seventy or more of them. For these kids to take time off from their 'hustling' to come here meant she had been right about AK being a crowd-puller. She hoped she had also been right in her judgement of him. If he didn't turn up now she would have a real problem on her hands.

She made her way through the crowd and into the shelter. It was a large empty warehouse so there was plenty space for them but it was dark and stiflingly hot. She recognised Moko, Clementine's colleague, and went over to him.

'Inspector, I am very happy to see you,' he grinned at her, 'we might need reinforcements if it gets a bit crazy here.' Moko was average height and average build but he had a lot of experience of working with these very volatile children.

Gloria made a face. 'Are you on your own here?'

'No, no, well not in numbers anyway.' He pointed to a small alcove off the main room where five adults were huddled together around a small table.

Not a very reassuring sight Gloria thought.

'Hmmm, do you know all the kids?'

'Almost all, there's a few from further out I think. News spreads fast. You must know them as well?'

Gloria looked around. Actually yes, she did know most of them but there were some real babies in the group she didn't recognise. In the corner, separate from the rest she saw Original and Executive, leaning against the wall and watching.

'You know them?' She nodded her head in their direction.

Moko grimaced. 'Those two are so so bad news I'm afraid. They have been from day one and they haven't changed. I'm surprised to see them here but I will keep an eye on them. It mun sound funny to say, in a group like this, but they are a bad influence…'

Gloria was nodding in agreement when Prince came up to her. The homemade badge stuck onto his t-shirt declared him to be a 'Vice-pressedent.'

'Inspector, we are here, we brought all the pekins, you see. They plenty-ooh.' He pointed around the room. 'Well most of them, some just came by themselves.' He was looking at Original and Executive. 'But some of those big boys got real bad heart, dey not supposed to be here old ma, dis ting not for dem eh? I beg.'

'Don't worry Prince, it will be fine, everything will be ok.' Without thinking she reached out to pat him on the shoulder until Prince pulled back with his trademark look of irony. He pointed at his badge.

'When is the man coming ma? I supposed to be the one to meet him and bring him in.'

'Eh, well,' Gloria looked around the warehouse where kids were milling about, the noise building up, 'very soon, I think, I hope.'

Prince nodded thoughtfully as if this is exactly what he had been expecting. 'Right, well we mun do sumtin before he gets here or these pekins will soon start fighting.' He turned to the crowd and in a surprisingly loud voice launched into 'What the Lord has done for us...' It was like magic. As if on cue they all started singing, some loudly others a bit more reluctantly, but they all joined in, clapping and swaying a bit too. Even Executive and Original had joined in. Original, with his eyes closed and his head thrown back, seemed to be really enjoying it.

It went on for twenty minutes with Prince leading them from one song to another, quiet and loud, happy and solemn. They were singing 'Higher Higher' for the third time when the heavy metal doors of the warehouse were thrown open and in walked Abraham Kanneh with what could only be described as an entourage of eight men all of them dressed in black jeans and t-shirts and gold chains. The kids went wild clapping and cheering but didn't, she noticed, try to get near him.

AK came up to her at the front smiling broadly. 'Inspector, I'm very glad you made it.'

'And I am very glad you made it. Believe me.'

'So what's the programme? Or there isn't anything organised?'

Gloria smiled at him. 'You're here, the kids are here she gestured with her open hands, 'so, just get on with it.'

The black t-shirted entourage started muttering about rudeness and one said in a loud voice that maybe they should leave but Kanneh was made of stronger stuff.

'Brown,' he called a beefy young man forward, 'gather the pekins around now, so I can talk with them. You,' he pointed to another two of his group, 'bring in the bags from the car.'

Then he addressed the children. 'Are we together? Are we together?'

The answering 'Yes' from the group of excited children subsided into almost complete silence as Abraham Kanneh began to work his magic. He asked them some simple questions about where they were from and then told them stories from his childhood of growing up in Westpoint all the way through to his international football career. He arm-wrestled the biggest boys in the room and even managed to beat the girls at nafu playing round after round until they gave up. And he made them laugh over and over without ever losing control of the room. Gloria had to admit, he was very very good.

She couldn't remember the actual details of the project AK described to the children. It was to do with football and training and... it all sounded very worthwhile. She noticed some of his followers did not look quite so happy as Kanneh volunteered them for various roles, but nobody dared contradict him out loud.

He took some questions at the end and after answering what must surely be the usual crop of enquiries about how to become rich and famous Prince piped up from the front row.

'Big brother, thank you for all the tings you tell us today but I wan ask you something. What can we do to stop the children being killed. As for me I na wan to be big big player, I know that will never happen. But,' he paused and looked around the room, 'I don't want some stranger to come kill me and then for the police people to, to, to,' he looked at Gloria apologetically, 'do nothing. Nothing.' He raised his voice. 'So all the tings you tell us, all the plans, this big project we coming do, yeah all of that is good but I beg you pappay,' he touched his forehead, 'I hold your foot. Do something to help us stay safe.'

Kanneh didn't reply straight away. He went over to Prince and shook his hand and then looked around the room.

'Yes. We will do something. I promise. And don't be mocking the police. Tha Inspector Gloria brought me here today. You all know her right?' The kids shouted back that they did, the old ma was ok and a few other less complimentary things. 'So now, me, I am working with the police. Me and the Inspector, we will do it.'

Gloria wasn't so sure about this close association but just smiled.

The session ended with the distribution of gifts; footballs, sneakers, caps and a radio for the boy who had beat him at the arm wrestling. The children were delighted, took their gifts and, satisfied there was nothing else coming, started to drift away. After forty minutes the room was empty and quiet.

'So Inspector? How was it?'

'You did well AK, really well, but you know that don't you?'

He grinned. 'Ah Inspector Gloria, they are children. They just want attention and from adults who will really listen to them. You know that's the biggest crime in this country, the fact that we ignore our children. And then we are surprised when they do bad things like take up guns and go fighting.'

'Or move on to the street to hustle a living rather than going to school, I know. And still bad things happen to them, like getting murdered! So let me tell you, I didn't get all the things you were saying but this project is important.'

'Not just a hook to get me to do something for your nephew then?'

'No, well maybe it was at the beginning but not now. If we can draw attention to these kids…'

'And learn from them?'

'Yes, and learn from them, it will be great.'

AK shook her hand. 'And it is going to cost money too Inspector but,' he saw Gloria's expression, 'don't worry about that. I will make sure we get sponsorship, I'm good for that.'

Gloria raised an eyebrow. 'You can get money out of people in this town of course with your connections.'

AK laughed. 'I certainly can Inspector. Some of our Lebanese and Indian friends will give equipment or transportation and there are some wealthy Liberian business people around too you know – LUTC, you know them?'

Gloria shrugged. 'I know the name – Liberia United Trading Corporation isn't it?'

'Well they want my face for their advertising campaign and they are prepared to pay for it.' He smiled broadly. 'I am sure sure sure they will sponsor this project.'

'And get your face in return?'

Kanneh sucked his teeth. 'Hmm, you joking right? My face on posters all round town advertising imported rice or argo oil? I don't think so, but as long as they think I might agree they will support us.'

Gloria was laughing now too. 'Not just a…'

'Pretty face? Well I'm glad you have realised Inspector, but don't go telling everyone, it's so much easier when people think I'm just that poor boy who had a talent for football.' He winked at her and turned towards his waiting entourage. 'I'll be in touch, probably quite soon. You take care Inspector.' He turned to get into a sleek SUV when she remembered what she wanted to ask him.

'Just one more question AK.' He paused but didn't take his hand off the door. 'Do you know a jeweller called Ramesh down Carey Street?' Kanneh looked blankly at her. 'Oh maybe you don't, he specialises in costume jewellery, I bet you only buy the top quality real thing.'

'Oh that Ramesh.' He laughed and then bent towards her and for a moment Gloria thought he was going to kiss her but he leaned into her ear and whispered. 'You see all those gold chains and medallions my friends are wearing.' He tilted his head in the direction of the black t-shirted group. 'All bought from friend Ramesh.' He laughed again and stood up. 'Mine is real Inspector, theirs are just good fakes, like their loyalty.' She couldn't help but laugh at that herself and waved him off with a promise to be in touch soon. There was a flurry of car doors being slammed shut and the roar of engines starting and then they were all gone in a cloud of dust.

Chapter Twenty One

Gloria found herself alone on the sidewalk, still smiling from the encounter and wondering if she had time for a coffee? She wrestled with herself briefly and then went into the small newly opened coffee shop on the corner. The interior was modern and beautifully air conditioned, but the coffee was awful. She sat with her expensive watery drink and thought about Prince's outburst. These kids were scared, of course they were, but they couldn't show it. Maybe this thing with Abraham Kanneh would really help them. He seemed to be quite serious about it and was obviously a man of greater resources than she had given him credit for.

Her phone rang. 'Boss, I am here with Collins, Ramesh assistant. I'm not sure what to do. If I bring him into the station everyone will see him.'

'Is he going to talk do you think?'

'Hmmm, talk? He's already told me he's the one who brings Ramesh his food each day and that he wasn't really fired from his job. Ramesh told him to say that. So, yes, I think he's ready to talk but he is so scary, I mean he is actually trembling right now just talking about all this.'

'What if you take him to… well, wait now, ask him how Ramesh makes contact with him?' There was a pause and a muffled discussion down the line.

'By phone, any time, but usually in the evening to tell him what food to bring.'

'Ok, so put him in the car and bring him to Daybreak. It'll still be quiet there but it's near enough if his master calls. I'll meet you there.'

She finished the disgusting coffee and drove down to the restaurant. As predicted, it was quiet. She had just sat in the corner when Moses arrived with Collins. He was tall and thin and looked absolutely terrified. As soon as he saw Gloria he started babbling and before she could stop him he was on his knees touching her shoes and begging for protection.

'My man, get up now, we just want to talk, that's all. Ah, my man, leave my shoe, sit down before everyone sees you.' Collins reluctantly sat in the shaky plastic chair with his head bowed. 'Look, this will not take too long and then you can be back home. Just talk the truth now.'

Moses opened his notebook but closed it quickly at the sight of Collins terrified expression. 'Ok my man, just talk. Here drink this.' Moses pushed the soft drink towards him. 'Tell the old ma the same thing you told me.' Collins sipped the drink. 'Well, em, I've been working for that man for two years.'

Gloria was taken aback. The man spoke in an educated accent, no Liberian English here. 'So why did you take a job like that, a shop assistant.' Collins looked at her cynically. 'Oh, surprised are you Inspector? Thought I was some grona boy did you? No, I've been to university and everything...' His tone was sarcastic. 'But there are not many jobs in this town. I went from shop to shop asking for work and that man, Ramesh, took me on.' He leaned back in the chair and sipped the drink. 'He promised me training in photography, said I would be running his photo studio before long, with a good salary.'

'And none of that happened?'

Collins laughed. 'Oh no, he kept his promise. He did train me; I was running that damn photo studio. I do have a good salary.' He looked at Moses. 'That shack you met me in today, that's not my real house. That's where Ramesh told me to stay. Because that's the price you pay for working with Ramesh, you do what you are told.' His face puckered. 'He owns me.'

Gloria could feel the revulsion in her stomach. 'Owns you? But how, the money was too good to leave or what.'

Collins stood up and lifted his t-shirt. His chest and stomach were covered in long angry-looking welts, some faded and others new and fresh. 'I won't show you the rest Inspector. It is too humiliating.'

'Ok, ok Collins. Sit down and tell us the whole story.'

It did not make for easy listening. The slow process by which Ramesh took an intelligent, decent person and by careful degrees drew them into his web of evil, implicating them, breaking them down until they were totally enslaved, was quite horrifying. He told them about the other studio, the converted container on the edge of the swamp on the road out of town and the filmmaking that went on there, the filming he was forced to do while Ramesh directed.

It was enough to make the sweetness of the drink turn sour in her mouth. 'And why are you telling us all this now if you are so afraid.

Collins looked terrified again. 'A few months ago Ramesh came to my house, uninvited. He was so friendly, really charming. Then the next day he told me he wanted my daughter, she is only eight years old. He said he was preparing a special movie for her to star in.' He started to cry. 'I didn't know what to do. He always said if I didn't do what he said he would go to the police and tell them I was the one making the movies.'

'And killing the children…'

Collins looked up. 'Killing children? No, that was never mentioned.'

'But you said Ramesh got you involved in everything. What about the killings?'

Collins looked blank and shook his head. 'I don't know anything about killings Inspector. The man is bad, evil, but killings? I don't know him to be involved in anything like that.'

'What do you mean? Of course he was; the boy in the shop window?'

Collins frowned. 'I never saw him before Inspector. Honestly, I don't know anything about killings. That man used children to make his bad bad movies but I don't know about killings.' He looked at her. 'He was killing them too?'

'Well what happened to the children after he had used them?'

Collins shook his head. 'I don't know, really, I don't. I never thought he was killing them.'

Gloria and Moses exchanged looks. That was a bit of a blow but still they could get him on Collins evidence. 'Ok Collins. You need to get back and just carry on as normal, as best you can. Just for a little while longer.' He nodded but when Collins looked up the fear was back in his eyes. 'And my daughter?'

Gloria hesitated. She didn't want to draw any attention to Collins but he knew Ramesh and he was terrified for his child.

'Look, go back home and stay there. We will come back to you as soon as we can. I promise.'

Moses got up but Collins shook his head. 'No, I will get home myself Inspector. Better no-one sees me with you. I will take care of my daughter until you get back.'

'Right Moses, we go to this container first. Get any material and evidence we can and get back to Collins before Ramesh hears about it.'

'Sure, we can do that by ourselves.' They were making for the door when Gloria felt a tap on her shoulder. She spun round and there was Original, or was it Executive, she wasn't sure, anyway one of those boys staring at her with a fixed grin.

'Old ma, how the day?'

She shook her head, the assumed familiarity really grated on her.

'What you doing here?'

'Eh ma, I work here, you know we all got to eat eh.'

'Ok, very good.' She turned away.

'No ma, I want say something. Please.' Gloria stopped. 'You still looking for information ma?' She said nothing. 'Eh ma please. I know my man there was too rude the other day but we can help you. Look…'

'No, you look. I don't know what you think you know, or what I need to know but let me tell you something. If you want to help then come to the police station and we will talk then – and I not paying money for no nyama-nyama talk, let me tell you.'

'Ay-yah, old ma, you talking too rough. We your children na.'

Gloria turned and left, leaving him standing.

'You know Moses, I've got patience for a lot of people but those two…'

'Two?'

'Yes. They are Executive and Original. They cheeked me up the other day and now he's here offering information.' She sucked her teeth. 'Information. Those two are real professional grona boys.'

Moses laughed. 'Maybe they have to be boss. "Just trying to survive, got to stay alive, the haters hate my vibe…" you know how the song goes.'

'Enough, enough, no singing please. Maybe you are right. With people like Ramesh around, it really is all about survival for these kids. Do you know where we are going by the way?'

It was Moses's turn to give her a look. 'Yes. That was the first thing I did, get the directions. It's down eighteenth street towards the swamp.'

'Good. I'm going to call Ambrose and Alfred to join us. As soon as we've been to this place Ramesh will know we are after him so they need to go and keep eye on him right now in case he tries to escape.'

The journey took twice as long as it should have due to a group of protesters at City Hall – taxi drivers who were now forbidden to park on Tubman Boulevard by order of the new mayor - but the noisy discussion on the radio about the involvement of Nigerian gangs in the murder of children helped to pass the time. Her phone rang three times but Gloria didn't answer.'

'It's the Director,' she finally said in answer to his unasked question, 'but I'm not answering just now.'

'He probably wants to know if you've caught the gangs yet…'

Gloria shrugged. 'Well he dumped the press conference on me – and if you remember I never actually said anything about gangs, it was Rufus.'

'Yes boss,' was Moses only response.

The container/studio was exactly where Collins had described. Off the road, down a barely visible path and there, on the edge of the swamp a rusting old container with a few rough windows cut out of the sides and an air conditioner at the front and at the back. There were no signs or placards – it looked abandoned.

The silence around the swamp and the heavy humid air made the place oppressive and menacing. They walked to the front and Moses produced a pair of heavy-duty chain cutters. The heavy doors swung open easily and they blinked, staring into the total darkness. It was as hot as an oven inside. Within seconds, as they struggled to open the rough windows, they were both drenched in sweat. Gloria could feel a taste in her mouth. It was as if the stale odours of sweat and fear had been cooking up inside this oven and were now lodged in her mouth and throat. She gagged and rushed for the door.

With the windows eventually open they had a better look. There were some pieces of cloth on the floor, one slipper and the most basic bits of furniture. On the back wall a large colourful cloth must have been the backdrop to most of these terrible movies.

It was Moses who gingerly moved the cloth aside to reveal a door which opened onto a small office and storage place. Much more care had been taken here with ventilation and it felt almost cool – the vents all around the top allowing the swamp breeze to blow through. There were cupboards full of video tapes and DVDs, some in cases, others scattered around. And lots of boxes filled with what she could see were photographs crammed untidily into envelopes. Gloria surveyed the room but the expected sense of triumph, of finally gaining some hard evidence, didn't materialise. She felt sick. The taste in her mouth, the heat and all this evidence of so much misery was almost too much.

'We don't have time to collect everything Moses. We need to get it all together so we can go through it later. For now we have to bring Ramesh in and get this place secured.' There was weeks of work here, she knew, identifying and tracing children, customers and other producers. God knows what they were going to find once they started. But at least they had him now.

'I'll get Lamine and Christian out here then boss?'

'No, Christian and Clementine. She is thorough and won't lose anything, and Christian is good for protection. But they need to hurry.'

Moses was looking at his watch. 'Boss, this guy is so slippery, I'm afraid he will escape us if we don't get moving.'

'We are not leaving anything here Moses, for all we know children have died because of this…'

'I know, but we can start putting it in the car. If Clementine arrives they can finish, if not we will meet them in town. Better than standing here, and the crowds are gathering already.' He pointed to a group of small children who had appeared as soon as they arrived. They had been joined by some older children and an old man was hobbling through the grass to join them. There would be a crowd soon.

'You're right, let's just do it. Clementine and Christian will need to interview all these people anyway when they get here.'

They put everything into the boxes and bags which were lying around. Even distracted by the heat and her own sweat, the stale smell from the boxes and bags kept drawing her attention to the contents. Lurid DVD covers and cheaply produced magazines. But the worst were the photographs which kept escaping from the envelopes and scattering across the floor. Many of them were ordinary, mundane pictures of children. It was as if he had collected people's personal pictures. Maybe this was how he selected his victims. But the pictures of children playing on a beach or lying in a hospital bed, children dressed up for First Communion photos or others in torn t-shirts and shorts from the refugee camps were somehow more chilling. How many more people were mixed up in this she kept thinking as they packed boxes in the boot and on the back seat. Moses had fallen silent too; he had two children of his own.

Although it seemed longer it was only fifteen minutes until they heard Clementine arrive with Christian.

'No time to explain guys.' Gloria wiped ineffectually at the sweat that ran down her face and soaked into her shirt. 'It's Ramesh, the jeweller?' They nodded. 'You need to collect everything that's left here and then talk to all these people to find out what they know about what went on here, anything at all. And tell them if they...' she tailed off. 'Forget it.' There was no point in taking her anger and frustration out on these people.

Clementine asked no questions. 'You pack the rest Christian. I'll start talking to the crowd here.' There was no discussion. 'It is all about children Gloria? And what? Movies? Photos?'

'Yes everything, it was a film studio. We just needed to get the evidence before we moved, that's why it was all hush hush. We will go and get him now.'

Clementine waved her away. 'That's fine Glo, go and get him. Really. Go now.'

They drove in silence apart from regular calls from Moses to Ambrose and Alfred. 'You're sure he's still in the shop?'

Gloria could hear Alfred's frustration on the fourth call. 'Captain, we can see him. He's actually in the window moving things around. He's been there all morning and no-one's gone into the shop so yes, he is definitely still here, unless he has a twin.'

'Ok, ok, we'll be there soon.'

'He's definitely still there boss.'

Gloria looked at him. 'I heard. Let's just concentrate on getting there. What about Collins?'

'He'll be fine as long as we have Ramesh so let's get him first.'

The shop was quiet when they got there. Ramesh was still in the window. Gloria felt a tinge of uneasiness. Her cases didn't usually end so calmly, with the prime suspect almost offering himself up. Had their luck changed or their methods improved, she wondered to herself as they got out of the car.

In the end there was no need for any drama. Ramesh had listened intently as Moses stated what he was being charged with and had asked only to contact his assistant to come and take care of the shop. Moses refused.

'Ok, now you've got him Moses, I'll take Alfred and go and see Collins. He might be happy to get the news, although we will have to arrest him now too as an accessory.'

'Of course. I'll see you at the station boss. Do you want me to wait for you?'

'No, no need. Start questioning him.'

Alfred drove to Westpoint while she explained what had been going on. Waterside market was even more busy than usual. A dense mass of people reluctantly parted just enough to allow the car to inch through until they reached the Westpoint entrance.

'Which way ma'am?'

Gloria hesitated. The heat was almost unbearable and seemed to only make the crowds even slower to respond to the car horn. 'Just pull in over there. We can park and walk.'

They left the car in her cousin's mechanic shop and started walking. From Moses's description Collins lived close by her old primary school and it wasn't long before it came into view. 'It should be just down here.' Gloria pointed down a narrow space between the school building and the old bakery on the other side. But it was already full of people. Even by Westpoint standards there were a lot of people and even more noise. She felt the all-too familiar tingling at the back of her neck warning her that something bad was happening. But nothing could have happened to Collins? They had had Ramesh under observation all day and now had him in custody. But still she was relieved when they squeezed past the noisy crowds and she could see Collins sitting on the tiny porch in front of his house. Relieved until she got closer and saw the blood on his hands and his leg. But at least his eyes were open and he was talking, although no-one seemed to be paying much attention to what he was saying.

Gloria shouldered her way onto the porch and Collins looked up at her with a mixture of pain and hatred. 'Oh, it's you Inspector, is it? Come to offer me protection? I'm afraid you are too late for that.' He pointed to his leg where a long knife was buried deep into his thigh. Attached to the knife was a small bag. 'They've knifed me and witched me Inspector, that's why no-one wants to touch it.'

'Ok, I've sent for the doctor and then we'll take you to the clinic. Don't panic. I know it looks bad but really, I've seen these kinds of wounds before. You will be alright.' Gloria was trying to stop the blood with some towels grabbed off a nearby trader.

'I will be alright? What are you talking about?' Collins was shouting now, with great effort. He looked as if he was about to faint. 'It's too late for being alright. Eh God, eh my people-ooh.' He had started shaking and Gloria put her arm around his shoulders to try and calm him. The crowds had moved back. 'Come on Collins, you will be fine, my man. Come on.'

With a supreme effort Collins struggled free of her arm and stood up. 'You don't understand. It's finished. It's all finished.'

'What do you mean? We have Ramesh, he can't hurt you anymore.'

'You have Ramesh eh? He can't hurt me eh? Well let me tell you Inspector why he can't hurt me anymore. He already has everything I value. And there's nothing I can do to stop him.'

Gloria though he must be going into shock. Maybe the wound was more infected than she could see.

'It's not this.' He pointed at the knife in his leg. 'This is nothing. Look.' He reached behind him and pulled up a shoe, a black school shoe for a girl. 'He took my daughter. And there is nothing anyone can do to stop him.'

Chapter Twenty Two

The time passed in a blur of activity. By the time reinforcements in the shape of Lamine and Ambrose had arrived Collins had already been treated in the local clinic and then transported to the hospital. Gloria had sent her uncle in the ambulance with him for security and then with Alfred had rounded up as many of the neighbours and onlookers as they could in the empty school canteen, but it was going to be a huge job interviewing them all. Collins's wife had returned from the market, where she sold fish, after he had gone to the hospital and was currently in a state of hysterics over her missing daughter. The room was hot, the atmosphere restive. The last person she expected to see was Izena, but there she was and she was in full organisational mode.

'I think I know how we can do this ma'am...'

Gloria waved her hand. 'Then get on with it, because I certainly don't.'

Within ten minutes Izena had the thirty or so people sitting on chairs or tables. She had recruited the school principal and some of the teachers and then chalked up on the board the main questions they needed to ask and set them to interviewing with Lamine and Ambrose. She and Alfred would 'circulate' to make sure the interviews were being conducted properly and to pick up any important information.

Gloria was impressed and relieved to see the process underway and then lapsed into puzzlement. Her mother and two of her aunts had arrived and it had taken a noisy ten minutes to persuade them that she was not in any danger and they should go back home. As she sipped the strong coffee her mother had brought, she kept asking herself what they had overlooked? Ramesh was a dangerous man who had threatened Collins but how had he found out so quickly that Collins had spoken to them and then been able to organise a kidnapping while under observation. They had underestimated him and now another child's life was at risk.

She wandered around the room, her mind racing. She wasn't expecting there to be much information. She knew this community well and years of neglect by the government and harassment from local police had built a wall of mistrust between it and any outsiders, especially the police. A violent crime had been committed in the narrowest of confined spaces, a community where the houses were so close you could reach into your neighbours kitchen and steal their food, and still she would bet they were going to get no useful information – either people had seen and heard nothing or their descriptions would be so wildly different as to be useless. She actually heard herself sigh and knew she had to do something.

'Izena, are you getting anything useful?'

'It's a slow process as usual ma'am,' she rolled her eyes, 'but apart from all the people who saw a monkey or a spirit do it or who were blinded at that exact moment,' she raised her eyebrows this time, 'there are a few people who saw some human beings and heard raised voices. But no faces, no-one actually saw anyone but they do say they heard a Nigerian accent. They were all sure about that. So that's good isn't it ma'am. I mean that fits in with your theory?'

Gloria groaned. Her theory? Her diversion more like. So were there really Nigerians involved or were people now hearing Nigerian accents because that's the story hinted at. 'What other details do they have?'

Izena looked at her notes. 'Mmm, not much. It seems to have been two people, two men… and that's it. Nigerian accents.'

'Ok, well done for organising this. You stay here and finish this with Ambrose and Lamine. I'm going back to the station.' She left and walked through the crowds back to the car with Alfred. 'See if you can get us back quickly Alfred, without killing anyone though.'

'Yes ma'am.' He got them onto the road. 'It doesn't look good ma'am does it. I mean another child. How can these people run rings around us so easily? I don't understand.'

'Look Alfred, for me this is all about power. Whoever is behind all this knows some very powerful people, they have to, otherwise how could they get all this information so quickly and be able to act on it. But we will get them-ooh, and put a stop to this nonsense once and for all. Come on, foot down, horn on, we are the police after all, let's use the few privileges we have.'

When they got back the office was quiet. Clementine sat alone at a desk surrounded by piles of boxes and bags. 'Hi Glo,' she sounded weary already, 'we heard about Collins's daughter.' She shook her head. 'Do we have a picture of her? I think we should get her photo out there, in the newspapers and maybe even to those boys you were talking to. Ehn they say they see and hear everything, and we need to find her before she ends up here somewhere.' she pointed at the piles of photos she had started to arrange in some kind of order.

'True, I'll get Alfred on to that, we have her school picture here. What about you? Anything so far?' She looked again at the boxes and bags and grimaced. There was so much of it.

'Well I'm trying to arrange them first so we can document them for tracing purposes later.'

Oh dear, thought Gloria, she is still a social worker. 'Clementine,' she leaned in and spoke softly so Alfred wouldn't hear, 'we don't have time to arrange everything. At the moment these are clues in this case, evidence. So, you need to go through it all quick quick and see how much of it we can tie directly to Ramesh because at the moment he is denying everything and says Collins was doing all this without his knowledge. You get it? So, anything at all, any face you recognise, any place, like his shop for example, any other adults. I mean this one,' she picked up a snap of a girl and boy in their 'Sunday' clothes standing in front of a well-known landmark, 'was taken on a Sunday I would say, in front of the JJ Roberts Memorial on Ashmun Street. Just put it to one side and it might be useful.'

Clementine didn't look convinced. 'But…'

'Clementine, you have to forget all the ones who are just anonymous faces for now. We are trying to stop this man and whoever is helping him. Ok?'

Clementine nodded.

'What about the people out at the studio, what did they tell you?'

'Nothing. Most of them are displaced from the interior, they are just squatting there. And they were afraid. There were stories of children disappearing, so they advised their own children not to go around the place.'

'Of course, As expected. Where is Christian?'

Clementine grimaced. 'He's looking at the movies in the small conference room. Somebody had to.'

The conference room was like an oven and the ceiling fan was just making it worse. Christian was staring intently at a laptop screen and writing things on a sheet of paper. He looked up and acknowledged Gloria briefly before pausing the movie. The flickering picture on his screen showed a young girl staring blankly at the screen.

'I am just rushing through them, I need to see if I know any of the people or places.'

Gloria nodded; he had got it. 'Anything?'

Christian pointed to two DVDs on the side. 'Yes, the girls on these ones now work on Gurley Street. I saw them when I went to talk to Babygirl. That's it.'

'So they are still alive… obviously. Well, carry on but get it finished quickly.' Christian nodded impassively and pressed pause again. The cries of the girl on the screen filled the room. 'Are you ok doing this Christian. This is hard.'

He didn't look up but gave his trademark shrug. 'It has to be done, right?'

Gloria made for the interview room where Moses was still trying to get something out of Ramesh. They had obviously reached an impasse because Moses was glaring at him but saying nothing. Ramesh had his arms folded and was looking anywhere except at Moses. He sat forward when she entered.

'Inspector Gloria.'

Gloria looked at him with new eyes. How had she ever thought this man interesting or sympathetic? She didn't speak, just nodded to Moses to carry on.

'Mr Ramesh is denying all knowledge of these movies or photographs boss.'

'All knowledge Ramesh, even of the studio itself? Or did it just appear by magic?'

'I don't believe in magic Inspector. Of course, I knew about the place, but it was a storage lock-up, that's all. I haven't been out there for years. As I already said Collins managed all that side of the business. I trained him in how to use the equipment and let him get on with it.'

'That's a bit of a different story from what you told us the day the body was left in your window. I think you said then you couldn't trust 'these people,' so you did everything yourself.'

'Yes, in the jewellery shop but the photo studio was different and, to be honest, I thought Collins was different – educated and honest. That's why I let him run the photo studio. And besides, since the war, business is so slow there's hardly anything to keep an eye on. He gets one or two customers a week if he is lucky, mostly just for passport photos.'

Gloria looked at Moses briefly.

'Ok, well tell us about the studio out near the swamp.'

Ramesh was beginning to sweat. He obviously hadn't taken it very seriously to start with. 'Look Inspector I bought that thing just before the war started. I did some work on it and then the war…'

'And after the war?'

'I went out there once or twice but there was no business so we had nothing to store in it and, of course, the place is not safe now so,' he looked at them, 'it's just there, empty.'

Gloria was puzzled. His account of things was fluent and now he accepted the charges were real and not some local police blunder, he was genuinely alarmed. Was it a bluff or a double bluff or... 'What about these then?' She showed him the photos of the welts on Collins stomach. Now he looked really puzzled. 'And the charges they brought against you for child exploitation. We know about those, they are still pending.'

'There is something very strange going on here Inspector. You are talking to me about illegal photo studios and exploiting children and now you show me these photos.' He folded his arms. 'I thought it was just the usual police charade but now,' his face was serious, 'you are trying to pin something very serious on me. I need my lawyer.'

'You haven't called your lawyer yet?'

'No. That man is expensive. I believed I could handle this myself. I wasn't expecting all this.'

'Well your colleague Collins says that you caused these wounds on his stomach, he also says you told him you wanted his daughter for your movies,' Ramesh was looking more and more alarmed, 'and that you arranged for him to be attacked today and his daughter kidnapped.'

'Oh my god, this is madness, complete and utter madness. Who... why... what are all these stories? I don't even know where to start with this.' He hung his head in his hands.

'Let's take a break Moses. Get him some tea or something.' They went outside.

'What do you think boss?' Moses looked quite miserable. 'I thought we would have had a confession by now, I felt certain he would break down.'

'Look Moses either we have it all wrong or he is a very good actor. Either is possible. What evidence do we actually have? So, maybe Collins is not the innocent victim after all?'

'What, and he wounded himself and kidnapped his own daughter?'

She looked at him with her cynical face. 'You ask that after all the crazy people we have met these past few years? Yes, he could have done all those things and you know that. Think how quickly he was attacked after we talked to him... maybe an hour or so. So how did Ramesh get that information so fast?' She shrugged. 'Maybe he didn't. Maybe Collins arranged it all to make sure we see him as the victim and Ramesh as the mastermind. The fact is we don't have any hard evidence either way.'

Moses rolled his eyes. 'So that's what we need to get. I'll go and check with Clementine, see if she's seen anything yet. Why don't you get yourself a coffee boss.'

Not a bad idea, she thought.

When her phone rang she was sitting in the small courtyard off the main reception with a strong dark brew. 'Hello Lawrence, I know I said Id have to eat today but I really don't think there's going to be time.'

'I'm not surprised but that's not what I'm calling about. Information? Remember?'

'Oh right, well I think we've moved on a bit since this morning. We arrested Ramesh and are questioning him.'

'Really, any luck with that?'

Gloria knew the signs, Lawrence had heard something.

'What is it? What have you got?'

'Well,' he paused, relishing the moment. 'Do you remember Miriam, from Monte Carlo.'

'Hospitality and Catering wasn't it?' She smiled briefly, 'Yes, I do.'

'Well, did you know that Ramesh offered his services a few years ago. To teach photography as a course at Monte Carlo?'

Monte Carlo again? 'No, I didn't know that. But how did you find it out?'

'Oh, I call round to see Miriam occasionally now, part of my network.'

Gloria raised her eyebrow, his network! 'Oh, really. And she told you this.'

'Yes, so I don't know if that helps.'

'It might do.'

'Well even better, they got rid of him after he tried to persuade some of the girls to 'pose' for him.'

She sat up straight. 'Really. So he has been into all this.' She put the cup down. 'Now, that is useful information Lawrence. Does Miriam know these girls? Or have they disappeared too?'

'No, they're still around, doing their thing on Gurley Street mostly but one of them works in a cook shop on the Bye-Pass. She is called Betty.'

It took Gloria precisely thirty-two minutes to drive to the cook shop and talk with Betty. She identified Ramesh from the photo on her camera and quite matter-of-factly said that yes, he had tried to get some of the girls to come to his studio to pose for him.

'Thanks Betty, now don't worry we will make sure you are safe.'

'Safe?' Betty was laughing. 'Safe from that man? That man can't do nothing ma. Tha foolish old man there.'

Sitting across from Ramesh again, with Betty's evidence and her willingness to confront him, Gloria advised Ramesh just to tell the truth. His lawyer, Vernon McKay, was staring at Gloria through his small steel-framed glasses.

'I think you'll find that it's my job to advise the client Inspector. You just ask the questions.' He bent down and started scribbling something in his notebook.

'Mr Ramesh, we have spoken to a young woman today who is willing to testify that you tried to persuade her and other young women to pose for obscene photos or take part in movies. We know you were already arrested for this.'

Ramesh looked at the lawyer who nodded slightly. 'I made some mistakes Inspector. My business was failing, after the war and everything, people couldn't afford gold and fine things. My wife and my sons went back home, I was alone, but I needed to support them.' He sighed. 'Anyway, I got talking to some people one day who came for passport photos. They were joking, kind of, said I should expand my business. They gave me money.' He stopped again and looked up. 'I'm not a bad man Inspector. I've got a family, grandchildren. But when I couldn't pay these people back their money they started putting pressure on me. They said they needed girls… and I was going to help them get some. They got me the job in Monte Carlo so I could…'

Gloria looked over at Moses. This was a confession but not at all what they had been waiting for. 'So you could get them some girls right?'

He nodded. 'But… I hated doing it, and I wasn't even good at it. Those girls at Monte Carlo are tough. Eh, they almost drove me crazy and then they tricked me and threatened me.'

Gloria remembered the list of his customers. 'So that's why they were coming to your shop, they weren't buying anything were they?'

Ramesh snorted. 'Buying! Hmm they were blackmailing me. A gold chain here, some rings there. That's why the shop is almost empty. And then the people decided I wasn't giving them what they wanted, and the next thing I knew I was fired from Monte Carlo and under arrest.'

He really didn't sound like a criminal mastermind. It sounded as if he had been thoroughly used by everyone. She couldn't muster much sympathy for him, but it didn't look as if he was going to be much use for the case.

'You know what Ramesh, you need to tell us everything you can about these people and I mean everything.'

'But it was different people, that's the point. The first group were Indian UN peacekeepers, that's why I got talking to them. Then it was some Nigerians, at least that's what they said, peacekeepers again. They were the ones who threatened me. After that I would just get messages through people, including Collins.' He stared at her. 'Yes, Collins used to bring me messages from them, but he said he was afraid of them, of what they would do to his family. He persuaded me to keep going along with it all.'

Gloria thought he was going to cry at this point but he didn't. He just looked resigned. 'I don't know what to think any more except that these people, whoever they are, are more powerful than anyone – and that I am finished, I'm ruined.'

Vernon McKay stood up abruptly. 'A word Inspector please.' Gloria indicated to Moses and followed the lawyer out the room.

'The man has been fooled Inspector, not the first foolish foreigner and definitely not the last in our country, foolish and unlucky, but I don't think he's the one you are looking for.' He gazed at her over the small round glasses.

'Are you trying to make a deal or something? I don't see much to work with here. He's been fooled but face it, he was exploiting those girls.'

Vernon coughed a little uncomfortably. 'Eh, ok. Well, there's not much more I can do for him really. I'll give him some numbers to call, there are plenty lawyers in this town.'

Gloria shook her head. Professional ethics eh! Vernon must be worried about his payment and was ditching Ramesh as a lost cause. She shrugged. 'That's your business counsellor. I need to get back to work. Excuse me.'

A quick confab with Moses and they decided to turn Ramesh over to Barnyou. He might get some more details out of him but they weren't too hopeful. 'And make sure someone is keeping an eye on Collins, get him in here as soon as he is patched up. And,' she paused for breath, 'we need to search Ramesh's shop again, thoroughly, and talk to the other shop owners. Now.'

Clementine had lost her pained expression when Gloria went back up. Instead she looked animated. 'Look Gloria, you were right. I needed to look for a pattern instead of looking at the individual faces.' Gloria didn't remember saying that but was encouraged.

'So what did you find?' She could see two untidy piles of photographs spilling over the sides of the desk.

'Simple. All of these,' she pointed to the first pile, 'were all taken before the war, as far as I can tell. Look,' she picked up the top ones, 'these buildings were destroyed in the fighting, and here's one of Nancy Doe at a graduation ceremony and here,' she picked up a pile of them, 'look.' They were different views of a smiling group of people on a beach.'

'The Liberian Music Awards 1989! Wow, yes, these people are all gone or were killed in the war right?'

'Right, so there are two piles Gloria, before the war and after the war and they are very different. The ones taken before the war are just snaps of groups, events and individuals. There's nothing offensive at all, just sad.

But these ones,' she pointed as if she couldn't bring herself to touch them again, 'these are all taken in that shed and they are all of young girls, some children. All taken post-war and all bad.'

'Did you come across any of 'our' children?'

Clementine nodded. 'There.' She tipped the edge of a pile of photos.

Gloria lifted them up and flicked through them. There was Rose before and after make up but looking defiant and then scared and finally vacant. 'This is how she was dressed when we found her body. These must have been taken just before she was killed. When he had finished breaking her spirit.'

The rest of the pile had other children, and a pile with Peter on them. They were too painful to look at. He had been tortured and photographed at each stage. There were none of Old Pa.

Gloria and Clementine looked at each other.

'Right,' Clementine spoke first as she stood up, 'anything else I can do now?'

'No, go and breathe some clean air and then we'll meet in the office. I'll give you a shout.' She made for the door and then turned back. 'And get Christian out that room. I think we've enough evidence for now and he needs some clear air too.'

Chapter Twenty Three

The whole team were in the office an hour later. Gloria looked at them. They looked tired and bruised. They had been on this case just over ten days but it really did feel like a lifetime. And they were just about holding it together. It felt like a complicated evil mess and there was not much light at the end of the tunnel yet.

Moses stood up but Gloria waved him to sit down. 'Look at the wall. All of you.'

They turned wearily to the maze of photos, notes and diagrams stuck on the back wall.

'There is an answer there somewhere and we are going to find it. This is the moment when we are tempted to give up, remember the 'dark before the dawn' song we all sang during the war. They nodded, with the exception of Lamine and Christian. We have a huge amount of information. Now we need to make sense of it. So, let's focus. The jewellery shop, anything?'

Alfred and Ambrose shook their heads. 'Really, nothing at all ma'am. All very neat and tidy but almost nothing in the shop, a few gold chains and rings but nothing of any worth. The photo studio the same – tidy and empty.'

'As if he was getting ready to leave ma'am.' Ambrose piped up. 'His apartment was the same.'

'What about the neighbours?'

Alfred took out his notebook. 'Hassan said he kept to himself, didn't really trust people but in the last few months they had seen strangers going in and out and a lot of those girls from Gurley Street hanging about. He says they all knew the business was not doing well, they could read the signs.'

'Ok, that might corroborate Ramesh's story.' She outlined for them what he had said. 'So, now we follow Collins. He's the one who appears all the time, but we thought he was the victim and now,' she waved her hands vaguely, 'well it looks as if he definitely has a more active role.' It looked as if he was involved but not alone, he would need serious connections for this kind of operation. 'Look, I need to go to a meeting now,' they would find out soon enough she was going to appear in a chat show, 'so you all carry on. Grill Collins, go over everything again.' She stared at the wall and the photos of Asholodu, Euphemia Harrris, Pastor Wolo and the rest. 'Just go over it all again. And nobody leaves until I get back.' There were no murmurs of dissent.

Twenty minutes later she was at the TV studio.

The new studios were colourful, modern and air-conditioned. Gloria was welcomed by a young receptionist and taken to a small room to have make-up put on. She never used it herself so it was a strange and an oddly soothing sensation having someone rub and brush and pull at her face. Marcia appeared towards the end of the preparation and they went in silence to the main studio which was bright and noisy. There was even a studio audience, eight rows of strangers all talking and laughing, proud to be on Liberia's first talk show. The set itself was simple; a few chairs, a small table with a vase of tall flowers and some bottled water – and Judge Dorothy Weah in a smart suit. She smiled at Gloria and stood up.

'Inspector Gloria, nice to see you again. How are you?'

Gloria eyed her for a few moments before replying she was fine. They sat down in silence then, aware of eighty sets of eyes watching them. That was all the instructions they got. The lights were lowered, the audience hushed and then some loud music blared out and an invisible voice boomed excitedly 'Here's Marciaaa...' A single spotlight picked Marcia out as she appeared from behind the giant letter 'M' and followed her down the stairs, while the audience cheered and shouted. She looked both glamorous and composed in a simple but very stylish African print dress. She paused at the bottom of the steps, surveyed the audience and then smiled.

'Welcome to the first ever Marcia show,' there were loud cheers, 'and what a show we have for you tonight. Two of Liberia's best-known women here in the studio to discuss the law and what it means in our country today.'

Gloria squirmed slightly in her seat. She did not feel comfortable. The show did not feel right. Glitzy music, a cheering audience, a glamorous presenter – and they were going to discuss the law! But Marcia was now introducing a local band, the Broad Street Boys, who launched into their new single.

'One law for you,
One law for me,
No law for we,
It depends who you be,
Mama Liberia, our country cannot change...'

She came and sat in between them, trailing a cloud of perfume with her. 'As soon as the clapping stops we go straight to the discussion. I'll ask the questions and make sure it all keeps flowing. And remember, make nice eh!'

The last bars were still fading away when Marcia jumped in. 'So, ladies and gentlemen, we will have the chance to ask our guests anything we want – later,' she added this hurriedly as several hands in the studio went up, 'after our main discussion.' She turned to them with a very earnest expression. 'So, law in Liberia today, is it in crisis and what can we do about it? Judge Weah let's start with you, what do you think?'

Judge Weah leaned forward and looked at the crowd. 'Robbery, kidnapping,' she turned to Gloria, 'the murder of children. Are we in crisis? You bet we are, and we don't even know it. Why just today I saw some posters downtown,' she was still smiling but it was a cold smile, 'posters of our police force. Did you see them?' The audience cheered and laughed. They had seen them. 'So, are we in crisis? That's not even a question now. It's answers we want. It's safety we want. It's honesty we want.' The crowd were clapping her every sentence. Gloria noticed how Judge Weah had managed to identify herself with the general public and turn it against the police, and against her in particular.

Marcia turned to her, the picture of innocence. 'Inspector Gloria, I'm sure there's some things you would like to say.

Gloria tried to keep her features calm. 'I agree with the judge – something needs to be done. But I am surprised that she wasn't able to offer any solutions. I mean the new Children's Act,' she paused and looked at the judge, 'you do know about it judge don't you? But,' she pushed on without giving her any time to reply, 'the fact is that this Act to protect our children and punish the offenders has been stuck in the Legislature for months. Why? Any ideas judge why your friends up the hill there will not sign it into law.'

'Because they the same people abusing the children-ooh.' The voice came from the back row of the audience and set them off again. There were calls and stamping of feet.

Gloria looked at the judge. 'Why are you not using your influence to get this act passed. Not a word. Not a single word from any of our law experts to encourage the government to put some fire behind this.'

'You don't know what we are doing Inspector.' Dorothy's tone was angry although the smile never left her face.

'So tell us, now is your chance.' Gloria was aware she was taunting her but the judge had started it. 'I thought so. As quiet on this as you are on the law itself I see.'

'Well Inspector, let's be fair,' Marcia leaned into Gloria and laughed, 'the judiciary are there to interpret and apply the law not to make it.'

But Gloria was well past being fair. She looked at the audience. 'Well we have an audience here, let's ask them what they think, or what they want to know.' There was clapping and cheering from around the studio.

Marcia shook her head, trying to keep control of the studio. 'We will. But first of all,' she held up her hand to the audience who were on their feet now, 'first of all let us just establish some facts.' The noise continued and Marcia signalled frantically off camera but nothing happened. She waved her hands again at the audience, less sure of herself now. 'My people, come on, let's listen to the speakers first.' But she was pleading now rather than directing and that was never a good signal to send to a Liberian crowd. She looked over at Gloria who leaned into her.

'Sorry Marcia, but where did you get these people? They are never going to listen to you… or us. You need to clear the studio, I would say you have about three minutes before you lose control completely.'

The sentence was just out her mouth when there was a deafening bang and a flash of light. The audience froze, then screamed and stampeded in all directions, including towards Marcia and her guests. There was a moment of complete panic before Gloria stood and hooked one arm through Marcia's left arm and the other through the judge's and physically lifted them up off their seats, propelling them towards the door at the back of the studio, the audience behind them like a wave about to engulf them. Gloria glanced back and saw a sea of panicked and angry faces; she could feel their breath and their spittle hot on her neck. They were not going to reach the doors, and even if they did the doors were closed and probably locked to keep any uninvited guests outside. It was a moment's thought before she pushed Marcia with all her might off to the side where the director's booth was and then as a second even louder explosion rolled around the studio, causing the crowd to pause momentarily, she grabbed the judge with both arms and dragged her into the bathroom to the left of the main set, collapsing with her in a heap on the floor as the crowd thundered by towards the entrance. Gloria thought the judge was ok, if a bit dazed, and left her propped up on the bathroom floor while she went out to see what was happening. It was a mess but not the carnage she had been expecting. The doors at the back of the studio stood open and most people seemed to have got through although there were a few sitting on the ground holding heads or legs where they had been injured. She felt for her phone but could see police and medical people already outside – of course, the show was going out live so police and medical personnel from the nearby clinic had seen it all happen.

'There's a woman in that bathroom too,' she said to a tall man in a white coat, 'please take a look at her.' Then she went to look for Marcia. It had all happened so fast she had no idea if Marcia had escaped the crowd or not. But she had. Shoeless, torn dress and very dishevelled she was already directing people to check the studio for damage.

'Gloria,' she grabbed her arm, 'thank you, thank you. I don't want to sound dramatic, but I think you saved my life. That mob…'

Gloria nodded, she had no breath left to speak now and a jabbing pain in her side where she and the judge had collided with the toilet seat, was now throbbing. She sat down heavily on the desk and looked around. There was no smoke or fire. And then it struck her. There were no people.

'Where the director and the camera people go?'

Marcia shrugged. 'Looks like they all got out.'

'Wait now, those camera people and the director who were in front of us when the show was being filmed? How is that possible?' Gloria got up and looked around the studio. Apart from the overturned chairs there was no damage, no holes or fires.

'Marcia, how many people worked here, on this show I mean?'

Marcia looked dazed. 'Just a few. It was a bit of an experiment having a live show in the evening, usually they just broadcast movies in the evening.'

Gloria nodded. 'I know that, so how many?'

Marcia thought for a moment. 'Eh, just the director, two camera people and an extra person for odd jobs. So, four then.'

Gloria was back in action now. 'And you knew them, I mean you hired them?'

'Me? No.' Her emphatic answer telling Gloria they were not the people she would have chosen herself. 'The station provided them. They were not very good.'

'Hmm, I can see that.' She shook her head. 'I can see this was no explosion either, just a panic to try and cause harm. But to who now? Me or you?'

Marcia was pulling at her long hair anxiously. 'Well it would hardly be me Gloria. I haven't done anything yet. It must have been you and this case you are working on. Trust you to bring trouble right on my programme.'

Gloria smiled. 'Well at least…'

'Do not say my first show went with a bang Gloria. Not funny.'

'At least it will get you noticed is what I was going to say. I better go and check on the judge but you should go home.'

Marcia sucked her teeth. 'Go home, you are joking. This is a great story – explosion on live TV on my first chat show. And no damage and no-one seriously injured so I can use this for all the publicity it's worth.'

Gloria smiled. She was tired and aching and, she hated to use the word even to herself, stressed. The sight of the usually pristine Marcia getting ready to use these circumstances to promote herself was actually quite consoling. It also gave her some energy. 'Go for it girl, and in the meantime get me the names and details of the studio crew. I think I need to pay them a little visit.'

A mere twenty minutes later and Gloria and Moses, who had arrived without even a phone call, were on their way to the station to interview Marcia's crew – minus the director who had apparently disappeared.

Judge Weah had been escorted home, shaken but unharmed – and ungrateful to Gloria for saving her. The other injured people had been treated for minor cuts which apart from one broken leg, had been the only injuries.

An examination of the studio had backed up Gloria's original theory – there had been no explosives just several large 'fireworks' as the local station commander referred to them. He was a tall thin man who was one of the few surviving pre-war police officers.

'In Nigeria they call these ones government bombs – big noise no impact – they use them in army training and sometimes in riot control,' he looked at her smiling, 'I did some training there when we were being re-structured. At least now I've used some of my training.'

Gloria smiled and left him to clean up the scene and interview the audience.

She and Moses arrived at the station just before seven. 'Are you sure you are able for this boss? It's been a hell of a day.'

Gloria rolled her eyes. 'So what, you think I should go home and sit and rest or something?'

'I'm just saying something boss.'

'Yeah, yeah, I know but better to keep going I think. And these idiots might finally tell us something useful!'

She was at the end of her energy and her patience, her side was still aching and she knew she was dusty and dishevelled. Not the ideal conditions for conducting an interview, she thought grimly to herself. She had never hit anyone in the course of her duties but if it was ever going to happen, today would be the day.

As it turned out she needn't have worried. The three suspects were terrified. 'We don't know nuttin old ma, nuttin.' The first one had started speaking before she or Moses had even sat down. The other two were silent but they didn't look as if they would resist very long. Gloria held up her hand and the first man stopped in mid-sentence. Three pairs of eyes were glued on her as if trying to predict what she might do. She looked at each of them in turn, scrutinising their faces.

'Let's keep this short then. I ask y'all some questions, you give me honest answers and we finish. Agree?' They nodded in unison, eager to co-operate. Gloria opened a file and took out some photos. 'So, who are you working for?' They looked at each other. 'Short questions, short answers. Remember? We agreed?'

'Ma, we not so much working for anybody. We just got small money to put those things around the place, they said it was just for fun.'

'So who gave you the small money to do it, is what I'm asking. Who?'

'Tha Dunbar ma. The boss to the studio place.'

'The Director?'

'Yeah, tha him tell us to do it.' They shrugged, a bit more relaxed now. Gloria nodded slowly. 'Ok, so you know nothing else about this?'

'Right, old ma, nothing.' They were all three of them nodding now, pleased their ordeal was going to be over.

'Wrong, actually. You want for me to believe you just did this and didn't ask no more questions.' She sucked her teeth and sat back. 'I don't think so. You already start lying to me eh? Ok, we will wait.' She turned to Moses. 'Take them back to the cells, let them wait there while they remember anything else they want say to me.'

There was a moment of panic then. Not a lot of noise but as if they had all three shivered at the same time. Gloria had never seen suspects who were so terrified of being held in the cells. They certainly didn't look like career criminals.

'Look ma, this situation is not easy for us.' It was the third man of the trio who had been silent up until now. He twisted his hands together. 'You need to speak to our director. He the one.'

Gloria glanced at the file in front of her. 'Nathaniel? Tha you?' He nodded. 'Let me tell you about my busy day eh? About children being kidnapped and killed. And then you can tell me why your particular situation is not easy. Or,' another look at the three of them, 'you just tell me what you know right now and I decide if I'm going to charge you with attempted murder or if you can go home. That's quite easy isn't it?' Her tone had hardened. 'I just want to find a murderer or two and put them away. Ok?'

There was a deafening silence across the table. This time the three men looked completely blank – it was an expression Gloria had seen several times that day as people denied any involvement in the killing of the children. 'But, but…' Nathaniel was spluttering and shaking his head. One of the others had started crying. 'Murder? Children? No ma, I beg you, you mun not put those things on us. Ayaya, I knew sef we were not supposed to get involved with that man. I knew it.'

'What man?' Moses jumped in. 'Tell us now. What man you talking about?'

'One big Nigerian man?' As soon as he had said those words Gloria knew she had them.

'One Nigerian man eh? Right, his name, now. Stop messing around and tell me.'

'Tha big pastor ma.'

'He were too worried about his TV show.'

'He wanted to make sure the other woman didn't make it.'

'He like money-ooh.'

'But he know plenty big people too.'

They were tripping over each other to give information now, talking louder, interrupting each other. Gloria held up her hands. 'Wait, wait, wait. Che, first nobody talks then you all talk together.' She pointed at Nathaniel as he seemed to be the most articulate.

'You talk, you two keep quiet. So the Nigerian man is who?'

'That pastor man, Asholodu? He that on boards all round town with his big face.'

'Right, Asholodu. So what did he tell you to do? He want to injure me? Embarrass me in public or what?'

Nathaniel looked puzzled. 'Tha your friend he was scared of ma, not you.'

'The judge? But why?' She looked at Moses.

'No, no ma, not the judge. Marcia. He were really scared of her.'

Gloria almost laughed despite her tiredness. 'Marcia?'

'Yes ma, he say the show was not godly, the woman was not supposed to be talking all kinds of things on TV. He was so worried that…'

'Marcia's show was going to be more popular than his.' Moses finished the sentence shaking his head.

Gloria remembered the billboards around town. Marcia and her new show on some, Asholodu and his ministry on others. Like candidates in an election. She shook her head, the weariness flooding back. 'So he just wanted to spoil the show?'

'Yes ma, that's what he tell us.'

Gloria stood up, frustrated beyond anything. 'Ok, you will have to make a statement, but not here. Moses, can you get someone to take them back to that commander, I forget his name, anyway this is his crime not ours.'

Outside the cells she paced up and down. A ratings war. That's what she had been mixed up in. She might have guessed. She remembered laughing about what might happen if they ever brought reality TV to Liberia. Well now she knew, if a ratings war was this close to being a real war then lord knows what would happen if they ever brought in any of those other shows.

Moses passed her with the three men in tow. He still looked wide awake and he had missed a whole night's sleep. How did he manage it? Then a thought struck her.

'Moses,' she called after him, 'do you still have those lists of Ramesh's customers?'

He paused and called over his shoulder. 'Yes, on my desk. In the in-tray on the right. You'll find them all there.' She knew he was telling her not to upset his meticulously tidy desk.

'Thank you. I'll be careful, don't worry.'

Exactly as he had said, the lists were there. Gloria paused for a moment to marvel at the rest of his desk. It was clear except for his notebook and a pen, the in-tray and a small memo pad. In sharp contrast to her own she thought. She had stopped telling people that she knew her way around the mess on her desk and that the piles and piles of paper were really her own filing system. They weren't. It was just an out-of-control mess which meant she had to keep asking people for documents they had already given her. She shrugged. There just never seemed to be time.

She sat at Mardea's empty desk and read through the lists again. Ramesh had for some reason kept meticulous notes about his customers. There was the name she was looking for, Matthew Asholodu. One gold cross and one silver cross, and not imitations either judging by the price. Coincidence? Gloria didn't think so. There were many high-class jewellers in town where Asholodu could have bought his crosses so why Ramesh, she wondered. How were these people linked?

Chapter Twenty Four

It was now nine o'clock but it felt a lot later. The stifling night heat was barely disturbed by the small breeze coming through the open windows and the lights and the fan were both attracting and repelling the giant moths and flying cockroaches which had got in. And exhaustion like a heavy wet blanket covering them all. Gloria looked around the table and saw tiredness and frustration – and a deep unwillingness to leave. Even Izena who liked regular hours and routines was still poring over piles of papers, going through lists and forms, making notes on a notepad made soggy by her sweat.

'I was going to say it's getting late, but I think you know that.' One or two of the faces round the table registered a smile, the rest just stared blankly. 'I know some people want to stay but I really think everyone should go home and get a few hours sleep and we will meet here early tomorrow. No,' she held up her hands, 'no special cases Alfred, everyone goes home now. But just think about where we are up to,' she looked at them one by one. 'We have Ramesh definitely involved with these children, we just don't know how much. Two,' she was counting off on her hand, 'Collins, victim, accomplice, mastermind? We don't know yet.' Collins had maintained his victim stance during further interviews, citing his daughter's disappearance and the physical marks on his body as proof he had suffered as much as anyone. 'Asholodu –we know he's crooked, crafty and connected to our case through Peter and perhaps through Ramesh, where he bought his gold chains and crosses.'

'And he's Nigerian.' Alfred threw this one in. 'Well, it is significant,' he added defensively as some of the others laughed, 'people keep talking about hearing Nigerian accents around these children.'

'No, you're right Alfred, it is important. Three, we have the other people directly connected to the children: Mother Harris, Wolo, the carers out at the Children's Village and then the mysterious Nigerian couple. Four, the way these crimes were committed with make-up and costumes, the bodies placed in particular places.' She put her hand down. 'The thing is there are a lot of bad characters to choose from in this one, a lot of people doing things they should not have been doing and desperate for others not to find out. But the murders speak of something bigger than just covering up a crime; the planning and staging are different from all that, a real enjoyment in the crimes themselves, like a show.' She raised an eyebrow, sensing that she was losing them. 'Anyway, what I'm saying is we need to keep looking at the big picture here. There's a connection we are missing.' She stood up to signal the meeting was over. 'Home, now, everyone. Including you Moses,' she had seen him heading back to his desk, 'I mean it.'

Moses pointed at a folder on his otherwise clear desk top. 'I'm just taking this home. Not to read,' he added quickly when he saw her mouth open again, 'for security. I don't want to leave it lying around here.'

'Ok, tomorrow then.'

'Ma'am,' it was Izena with a little pile of sticky notelets, 'these are all the people who called wanting to see you. Well these are the urgent ones.' She handed them over and left.

Gloria sighed. Having told everyone to go home she now found herself alone in the office. She looked at the memos. The top one said Martha Dunmore – and nothing more. Gloria couldn't remember if she had missed a meeting with old 'lizard woman' or was just being reminded to attend one. She put it to one side, the non-urgent side. The second said that Mrs Adebayo had called three times and urgently wanted a meeting. No doubt she's furious that we keep talking about Nigerians as being involved, Gloria thought. Better call her, but not tonight. There was one from Sr Margaret which said simply 'CSA. Not urgent.' I bet she dictated that to Izena, Gloria smiled. Typical Margaret, but reassuring too. There were a few from family members which were definitely placed on the non-urgent pile. The last one said that Doreen Walker had called twice and requested that the Inspector get in contact as soon as possible, no matter how late or early. Gloria rubbed it between her fingers. She was tired and sore but still, for the reluctant Doreen to leave a message like that must be significant. She put it in her pocket.

It was only when Gloria locked her door and went down to the car park she remembered she had no car. She hesitated but she was tired and hot and the thought of joining the crowds still waiting for a taxi or the bus made her even more tired.

'Lawrence,' it had been an easy decision to call him, 'is your invitation to eat still on?'

'You need a lift right?'

Gloria looked at her watch. It was already after ten. 'Eh yeah, it's been a very long day but I do still need to eat though. I mean as well as needing a lift.'

'See you in ten.' The phone clicked off.

The front of the police headquarters had been built in the grand style: a wide approach road circling around a roundabout originally full of flowers and bushes – now empty except for a dilapidated statue in the middle. She had never really looked at it and wandered over to see if up close the statue was identifiable. The lights from the main entrance barely reached past the steps so the area was dim. She had a restless energy that often took her over in the middle of a case, it meant she was past any chance of sleeping tonight. She could barely even keep still. And she couldn't blame the coffee this time, she had hardly drunk anything today.

As the lights from Lawrence's car came sweeping up the drive and hit the statue. Gloria saw the movement. It was brief but she was certain there was someone trying to hide behind the ruined remains. She strained her eyes into the dark and when the lights hit the statue from the other side she saw him. Or at least she thought she saw him. It was that boy again – Original or Executive, she still didn't know which was which. She crossed over to get a better view, her shoes scuffing over the dusty soil, but by the time she reached the statue all she could see was the back of a figure running away. She hesitated but in the end tiredness got the better of her and she went back to Lawrence who had parked the car right in front of the steps of the main entrance.

'What are you doing?' Lawrence looked fresh and wide-awake in contrast to Gloria's dusty uniform and dishevelled.

'Oh nothing.' She was too weary to start and explain. 'Right, shall we go somewhere dark then?'

Lawrence looked at her, one eyebrow raised.

'I mean my appearance, that's all.' Gloria laughed. 'After the day I've had a dark place, some food and…'

'… a cold beer, I know.'

'That's all I want right now.'

'Maybe you should pay a visit to Mrs Fernandez, get some tips on, you know…'

'My appearance? Really Lawrence? That's what you think I should do is it? At the end of a day like today.' She folded her arms and sat back, feeling aggrieved that she was being criticised for looking a bit dusty, having just survived an explosion on live TV.

'Well anyway, I enjoyed the show by the way. All ten minutes of it.'

'Luckily no-one got hurt too badly, except me maybe,' she winced as the pain in her side jabbed her again. 'And of course, the damage to my appearance!'

'Do you want to go to the hospital then?' He looked anxiously at her. She wasn't sure if it was concern for her health or the thought of having to drive to an Emergency ward at this time of night that was most disturbing him.

'No,' she shook her head, 'It's a bruise that's all. But try and find a food place on Gurley Street. I might try and pay someone a visit.'

Lawrence laughed again. 'You do know that visiting Gurley street at this time of night could really spoil your name, don't you?'

Gloria laughed. 'Always a big worry of mine of course.'

The streets were busy. Post-war and post-curfew Monrovia loved to buzz around at night. Gurley Street was in full swing when they got there although some of the bars were beginning to quieten down. 'Shall we try Ricoh's?' Lawrence knew the area better than Gloria. She nodded.

No-one gave them a second glance as they went in – which meant they had been seen and noted. There were a few empty tables and they sat down at one close to the bar. A man came over to them. Was this Ricoh himself, she wondered. Was there even a real Ricoh? He slapped Lawrence's hand in a high five and nodded over at her. They started a conversation in which Gloria heard that the food would take about twenty minutes because they needed to make it fresh for them. She interrupted to say she was going to see someone and would be back in ten minutes.

The alley leading to Doreen's house was near and Gloria once again stumbled in the dark, remembering to avoid the huge open drain hole, down to Doreen's little haven of peace. A single bulb hanging over the door was the only light and the courtyard was empty, doors closed. Maybe it was too late to go knocking on people's doors then. While she stood there undecided a small shutter next to her elbow opened and she heard a hiss.

'Is it you Inspector?'

Gloria leant down and looked in. 'It's me, but if it's too late...'

'Go around the back. I will open the door.'

Going around the back involved climbing over two large flower planters, ducking under some low-hanging barbed wire and stepping through a gate into the back yard. It was also dimly lit, this time with kerosene lanterns which were giving off more smoke than light. Gloria felt very uneasy. This didn't feel right at all. She remembered that no-one knew where she was. She had simply told Lawrence she was going to see someone. She got out her phone and found his name in her contact list. One press and she could call him.

Doreen Walker appeared silently from the shadows. She looked smaller, older, somehow diminished. 'Inspector, I am so glad you came. I have a problem.'

'Ok Doreen,' Gloria went to sit down but Doreen wouldn't let her. She beckoned Gloria to follow her but instead of heading for the back door, as Gloria had expected, she made for a set of stairs in the corner, holding her lantern in front of her like some ghostly guide. Gloria shivered and then gave herself a shake, grateful for the jabbing pain in her side which shook her out of this strange feeling.

The few stairs led down into the pitch darkness but as soon as Doreen opened the door at the bottom, light flooded out. Bright, electrical light, thank goodness, so bright she had to blink several times for her eyes to adjust. The room was cool, cold even after the sticky heat of the night outside, and as her eyes adjusted Gloria saw it was comfortably furnished. Then she saw the girl.

Curled up in a ball of fear, shivering with cold or terror, eyes wide open, staring at her. 'Please help me, ma. Please.'

'This is my problem Inspector.' Doreen's voice was harsh. 'This girl was brought to me this evening. But look at her, I ask you. She look like she ready for this kind of life?'

'She's a child Doreen. You are in serious trouble.'

Gloria bent over and started talking to the girl who just stared back at her with scared eyes. She took in the Westpoint school uniform the girl was wearing and the single school shoe at the side of the bed and knew it was Collins's daughter.

Doreen was still talking but Gloria was on the phone, first to Lawrence and then to Moses. Then she sat down hugging the child, the single blanket wrapped around her.

'Inspector, that is why I called you. I knew this was not right. I don't take kidnapped schoolgirls here, I help young women.'

'Yes, I've heard all that before Doreen. Just give me the details of this girl, that's all I want right now.

'The details? Ok I will give you the details. The housegirl came to tell me there were people at the door who had to see me. It was late in the afternoon, not a time I ever see people but they insisted. It wasn't even a man, a boy really, standing at my front door with this poor creature wrapped up beside him. He said to me. "This is for you. You will see success." And then he left.' Doreen picked up some things from the table; feathers, a beaded bracelet and a small cow skin pouch. 'She was wearing these.'

Gloria looked at them. Cheap ornaments?

'It's Gboyo Inspector. I would recognise it anywhere. Child sacrifice.' She said these words through clenched teeth as if the words themselves could bring her harm. 'I lived in Harper for a few years Inspector. I know Gboyo when I see it.'

Gloria had heard of Gboyo of course, everyone in Liberia knew about the practice of killing people, taking their body parts and then offering them as sacrifices to bring power, wealth and success, but Gloria had never actually come across it herself. 'So they dress the children up before killing them?'

Doreen nodded. She was clearly very rattled by the whole experience. 'But why dress this one up and then send her to me. I don't need this kind of thing for success. I am already successful. I don't like it Inspector.'

Gloria covered the girl's ears. 'Doreen, this girl was kidnapped right in front of her father today, we suspect by people already involved in the killing of those other children. Now, she hasn't been killed but is being used to send a message to you or me or somebody. We need all the information you can give us.' She bent down to the girl and spoke softly. 'You are ok now, the people have gone to fetch your pa, he will soon be here.' She felt the girl stiffen under her and start to cry again.

'Go and watch for my people Doreen, make sure they find the place.' Doreen went off frowning. Despite her fear she was still resentful of being given orders in her own house. She hated all this attention on her house, her life and especially her business. With her departure Gloria peeled the blanket back a bit and looked at the girl. 'Let me turn this air cool down a bit, it's very cold in here.' She turned it down and then took the blanket off the girl completely. She didn't even know her name, couldn't remember if she had ever even heard it. She was eight, she remembered that much, and small for her age too. She looked tiny. Gloria lifted her up. The sleeves of her school blouse slipped up and Gloria could see marks and bruises on the top of her arms. Some looked old but one or two of them looked very recent.

'What your name child?' The girl looked at her blankly. 'Your name now. How they call you?'

'My name Korpu.' The whispered response was given without her even lifting her head.

'Ok Korpu. Just sit and relax. Your pa is coming now.' Again the child stiffened and when she looked up at Gloria she was ready to cry again. 'What is it Korpu? You don't want to see your pa?' The child gave a barely perceptible shake of the head.

Before she could respond Gloria heard the noise of people on the stairs and Lawrence appeared, looking anxious and ready for action. 'Are you ok?' He looked around the room. 'Who's the child?'

'Long story Lawrence. Her father is on his way here with Moses but he can't see her until we have the whole story. There is something very funny going on here.' But she just finished saying this when Moses came into the room with Collins behind him. The little girl squealed when she saw her father, but not with delight, her whole body stiffening with fear. Collins looked uncertain and then started to cross the room to his daughter slowly.

Gloria stood up, the girl behind her. 'Everybody just stop. This child is in shock and will not be speaking to anyone,' she held up her hand, 'not even you Collins. Until we find out what happened here. This lady here,' she pointed at Clementine who had arrived at the same time as Moses, 'is going to take Korpu somewhere safe. The rest of use are going to talk.'

Collins put up no resistance to this and stood meekly out of the way as Korpu took Clementine's hand and climbed the stairs.

'Where's Doreen?'

'The lady who met us at the door?'

'Yes, that one. Where did she go?'

There were blank looks all round. 'Get up there and get her Moses.'

She turned to Lawrence. 'How was the food?'

He laughed. 'Well the two mouthfuls I had were very nice. It's still there.'

Despite the exhaustion, the adrenaline rush, her frustration and anger Gloria was hungry. And the night was not over yet.

'I'm going back to the station.'

'So why don't I get some food and bring it there? My little contribution to solving crime.'

'Big contribution you mean. Especially after you've dropped me back at my office first?'

Moses came back with the news that Doreen had been found trying to leave her house by another door. She was on her way to the station now too.

'So, I guess we better get down there. Moses, call Clementine and tell her to examine the girl carefully. She had bruises and marks on her arms. They didn't look accidental to me. And you saw the way she reacted when Collins came in. I'll talk to Doreen and you start with Collins.'

Chapter Twenty Five

It was the early hours of Thursday morning and most of the team had drifted back to the office as word spread of the new developments, the only ones missing were Lamine and Mardea. There was a subdued buzz of excitement.

Doreen Walker had stuck to her story. She had refused the offer of a lawyer saying she didn't need one and maintained she had no idea who the person was who had brought Korpu to her, no idea why the girl had been brought to her and, like everyone else in this case, denied any connection with the murders.

But she was connected. She had to be. Nothing in this case had been by chance.

Collins, after his initial hesitation at Doreen's house, had gone back to his righteous indignation pose as the main victim. A hard position to take given his daughter's reaction to him and the marks on her body which Clementine had detailed, even going so far as to look for a doctor at that late hour to verify what she had found. Korpu's legs and arms, her stomach and back were covered in welts and bruises, some of them similar to the ones Collins had shown them in his stomach. At first, he had said the kidnappers must have done it and then when Clementine pointed out how old some of the wounds were he tried to say that Korpu was a frisky girl and he had to discipline her.

A 2 a.m. team discussion should have been difficult but it wasn't. Finally the team sensed they were on to something. 'So we add Doreen to our list now. Clementine, I want you and Moses to question her again. She is guilty of something, why else was she so panicked when they brought that girl to her? And that room in the cellar? She has used that room before.'

'Trafficking.' Clementine looked around the table. 'Didn't you know that?' Nobody said anything. 'But everybody knows that's what she's really into. Trafficking young girls out the country, mostly to Europe.'

Gloria was stunned. 'Trafficking? And what, she's just allowed to get on with it is she?'

Clementine frowned. 'Well you're the police Gloria, if you don't do anything who is going to? Don't tell me, you didn't know anything about it?'

'There have always been stories boss, about Doreen I mean,' Moses had opened his notebook, 'I was going to discuss her with you after this case. The problem is they have just been stories, no evidence. Not a single person, parent or guardian, has ever made a complaint about her or reported a missing child so there wasn't much we could do.'

Gloria shook her head wearily. 'Right, let's focus on the facts then. Doreen is sent a child and goes into a panic. Why? Especially if she's been taking children before.'

'Too young ma'am,' Izena had spoken without thinking and now looked up, 'for her work I mean, I'm sure the girls she takes are fourteen or fifteen.' She looked at Clementine who was nodding. 'An eight-year-old would be more trouble that she was worth.'

'Okay, true enough, so what is going on here?'

'Ma'am?' Ambrose had tentatively put up his hand, she nodded to him. 'Every one of these children has led us back to someone doing wrong; Wolo, Asholodu, Ramesh, Mother Harris, Collins and now Doreen Walker. Back to powerful or influential people, people who would normally be beyond our interference.'

There were nods around the table. Some vigorous as if some people were beginning to make sense of it, others more hesitant.

'Yes, we do have a very impressive list of people to investigate, but we're investigating them for corruption, cruelty and exploitation, not for murder and it's the murder we need to focus on.'

'But surely they are linked ma'am,' Ambrose was animated now, 'every one of those people is capable of murder as far as I'm concerned.'

Gloria nodded. 'I agree. Of course they are, to cover themselves, but these murders are different aren't they? There has to be someone else behind it all?'

There was a silence then. It was true they had pieced together some of the puzzle, but she suspected they had only been given the pieces someone wanted them to have. The missing pieces were still being held by someone else.

'So, amongst our list of suspects which of them is the criminal mastermind?' There was another pause around the table. 'Exactly. The only thing these people have in common is their preoccupation with their own businesses and activities, mostly with making money in any way they can. I haven't seen any signs that any of them could be interested or capable of stringing together this elaborate set of murders.'

'What about Collins? He is certainly smart, I think he very neatly implicated Ramesh for a start. And if he is capable of torturing his own child…' Moses said this with force.

'And inflicting those wounds on himself?' Gloria threw that one in and there were nods around the table again. 'But what connection did he have with Wolo or Asholodu?'

'Well, we don't know yet boss but we are still investigating.'

Gloria sat up then. 'Right, I agree we follow up on Collins, but Alfred I want you to lead on that with Ambrose.' Alfred looked delighted. 'The rest of us are going to focus on the frustrating possibility that there is someone else involved here, something even bigger than all these characters. And we have very little to go on. In the meantime, let me say what I said five hours ago. Everyone go and get a few hours sleep otherwise none of us will be fit for anything. And we need to have our wits about us. Clementine,' she turned to her, 'What's happening with Korpu.'

'She's safe Gloria. I will make a better arrangement tomorrow.' Clementine stood up. 'I'm going to her now before I go home.'

'Good, we should all go now. See you back here in the… well, in a few hours' time. Alfred, are you ok to keep questioning Collins?' He nodded, standing up and indicating to Ambrose.

'And I will go back to Madam Doreen. I think I can manage her. I'll see if I can get a better description of the person who came to her door.' Moses had also stood up, not giving Gloria any time to respond.

The room emptied again and Gloria sat on alone. The jumbled images of the day passed in front of her but she couldn't see any pattern. Her side ached and she was so hot and grimy, she really wanted a shower, a coffee and some paracetamol, but only the paracetamol was available. And at the back of her brain, just eluding her, the piece of the puzzle she couldn't quite reach. She stretched and put her hands in her pockets for the paracetamol and found a small, crumpled card she had forgotten about. 'Domestic Angels,' it read, 'Making Your Home Happier.' Domestic Angels. They had cropped up a few times but they had overlooked them. She remembered that she and Moses had not even gone to their offices that day just because they were legitimately registered.

She went down to the interview room where Moses was settling in across from a defiant-looking Doreen Walker.

'Just one question before you start Moses. Doreen, what do you know about an agency called Domestic Angels?'

Doreen's mask of defiance slipped completely for a moment, her head shot up and she stared at Gloria and then at Moses. 'Domestic Angels? What is that?'

But Gloria and Moses had seen the look and they both jumped in.

'Domestic Angels Doreen. What do you know about them? Tell us, before we find out for ourselves.'

Doreen shifted in the chair. 'Well yes, I have heard of them of course, they are well known in town here.'

'Yes, but what do you know about them?'

'Inspector,' she looked at Gloria pleadingly, 'please. This is dangerous stuff, for everyone. You don't know.'

'I don't know but I know you are in serious trouble and that you need to tell me what you know right away before any other child gets harmed. Now.'

Doreen looked to be at breaking point, she was sweating and tearing at the thin handkerchief in her hand. Finally, she looked up. 'Ok, but only to you. I mean it.'

Gloria looked at Moses. 'I think you need to go and ask our friend the same question.' She raised her eyebrow. He nodded grimly. 'I think so too boss.' He stood up. 'I'll leave you to your chat.'

In the silence that followed his departure Gloria stared at Doreen and waited. 'Ok I will tell you this, but I will not say it again and I will deny I ever said it.' Gloria nodded. Just talk, her brain was screaming at the woman. 'You know my business and how I try to help…'

Gloria held up her hand. 'Enough Doreen. Just the facts.'

Doreen licked her lips and took a sip of the water in front of her. 'So, my business is doing well but a few months ago someone came to me. They said they were from these people, Domestic Angels. They said they were looking for young girls for their business. Of course, I have my contacts but I was surprised how much money they wanted to give me for these girls. I mean, they said they wanted to train the girls to work in people's houses but of course it was looking strange to me.'

'So you knew they were doing something different with these girls but the money was too much, right?'

Doreen put her head down. 'I didn't know, not for sure and anyway once these people started it was hard to stop. They started to threaten me, they said they would expose me to the authorities, that they had evidence…' She looked genuinely upset. 'Inspector I was afraid, once these people get you… I was too greedy, that's the truth, and I…' She wiped her nose and then sat up straight. 'Anyway, I just stopped, I couldn't do it anymore. For a few weeks nothing happened. I stayed quiet and then… this happens.'

'You mean Korpo?'

'Yes, that young girl turns up on my door, dressed like a sacrifice. That was the warning, I know it. That's why I called you. I couldn't deal with this myself – a small girl like that. Anyway, that's what I know and I am finished now because those people will not stop until I am destroyed.'

'Who Doreen, who are these people?'

'Oh,' she stopped and looked at Gloria, 'well I don't really know. The first one I met was a woman, she spoke good English, dressed nicely – but she wasn't the boss, I knew that, she was just delivering a message, and she looked really nervous. After that I didn't see anyone. I would get a message, some man would come and collect the girls from my place out of town and then money would go into my account.'

Gloria nodded. Sounded like the same story as with Ramesh and even Luseni. She left Doreen and walked quickly down to the even smaller interview room where Moses was just coming out with a new gleam in his eye.

'Boss…'

'He knows them too, right?'

'Absolutely, and he is so scarey.'

Gloria smacked the wall with her hand. 'Jeez Moses we missed this…'

'I know I know, but now we have something. We need to check with all the others too. This is the connection between them all, I'm sure of it.'

Gloria checked her watch again. It was after four. The others would be back soon.

'You need coffee boss.'

'And you need sleep.'

'Well at least we can get coffee. The sleep can wait.'

They drove to Gloria's apartment, the roads finally quiet in the pre-dawn darkness. Coffee and some stale bread Gloria found in the otherwise empty cupboards, a change of clothes, or a wash in Moses's case, and they were back at the office by five-thirty. Gloria started writing on the board again and when she turned round the entire team were back. It didn't look to her as if anyone had slept much but they were all alert and reading what she had written.

'Domestic Angels. This could well be the clue we have been missing, or we missed rather,' she put up her hands, 'I missed.' There was a buzz around the table again. 'But right now we need to focus on finding out what the connection is. So, all the paperwork we have, everything, we need to go over it again. There has to be a common name we have overlooked. So, before we…'

'Mrs Fernandez.' The name hung in the air for a moment. They all looked at Izena who was shuffling the papers in front of her. 'That's the common name.' She looked back at them over her glasses. 'I sent everyone an email yesterday. Doesn't anyone read anything?'

Chapter Twenty Six

Izena's attempts at establishing an information system had been thorough – and completely premature. She had emailed everyone the results of her research but in the frenetic activity of the past couple of days no-one had even thought to check their emails. Emailing, when you could get a connection, was just for keeping in touch with friends and family abroad, wasn't it?

'Ok Izena, let's forget the system for now, just run through what you discovered.'

Izena, still smarting from the fact that no-one had read her email shuffled her papers again. 'Well, let's see. Ok, I went through all the information we had to see if anything jumped out at me and all the names we have on the board were there but there was only one name that was everywhere, Fernandez,' she looked up and shrugged, 'her name always cropped up. That's all I said in the email.'

'No, Izena,' Gloria could feel the hairs on the back of her neck rising, 'tell us, go on, step by step, but hurry.'

'Well, em...' Izena looked a bit nervous now, 'let me check. Ok, according to Ramesh's list of customers Mrs Fernandez used to buy all her wedding decorations from him and her cosmetics. Ehm... what else... she teaches at Monte Carlo of course and I found out she also did some volunteer work at the Healing Garden place and, oh yes, she is seriously involved at that Domestic Angels place you were talking about.'

'What!' Gloria and Moses exchanged looks.

'Domestic Angels, the place you just mentioned. She worked there. I checked all their work permits at the Ministry of Labour and Domestic Angels is registered as her main employment. In fact, I would say she is some kind of director there, it's hard to tell from the way the business is set up, but she is more than just an employee. But no,' she looked at Gloria as if anticipating the next question, 'she's not the owner, it's part of some trading group.' She looked at her notes again, 'LUTC – they are involved in many things: importing rice, exporting timber and diamonds, they run stores and restaurants, gas stations and a transportation business…'

'And lots of charitable donations…' Gloria was shaking her head as she spoke. 'LUTC. That's the third time that name has cropped up recently.' She looked at Moses. 'So, who is actually behind it, who is the owner?'

Izena started shuffling her papers. She hadn't followed that line of enquiry, it hadn't seemed so important. She scanned a printed sheet to the bottom and then stopped, her hand over her mouth. 'Oh,' she gulped, 'the chairman is… Africanus Varley.' She pronounced this last name slowly as if she was eating some bitter soup. There was a stunned silence around the table. 'I'm sorry, I was just focussed on the Fernandez name. I didn't think the company was so important, and I didn't have much time.' Her voice trailed away briefly. 'But… him again! It is important, isn't it?' She was talking quietly, unnerved by the expressions she could see around the table.

There was a pause and then Gloria held up a hand. She spoke calmly but the set of her mouth showed the effort she was making to suppress her anger. 'Thank you Izena. And no need for sorry. You did better than us. We didn't even look at Domestic Angels. But,' she looked at them, 'who is the one person we know capable of manipulation on this scale. Eh?'

'But ma'am, we can't just put Varley in every investigation. There was nothing tying him to any of this.' Moses looked at her.

'There would have been if we had investigated properly, I'm sure of it.' Gloria put up her hands. 'Let's think about this logically. We have Africanus's name in the mix now, and for me that makes sense but…'

'We've got nothing on him, no motive, no real connection, in fact, apart from him owning LUTC…' Moses looked frustrated. He shrugged. 'Boss I think we have to deal with what is in front of us right now, not this…' His voice tailed away when he saw Gloria's face.

'If you had let me finish Moses, you might find I agree with you.' She glared at him, and then around the table. 'As he says we need to work with the evidence we have and that evidence, at the moment, points towards Mrs Fernandez. So, we bring her in and push her for answers. Izena, you and Ambrose try and find out any connection between her and Africanus Varley.'

Moses interrupted her. 'Boss. This is a bit of a guess but when you interviewed her the first time didn't she say she had been here a long time, remember we were surprised by that, and that her husband had worked with some company.' Gloria sat down and pulled out her notebook, flicking the pages in a hurry.

'An import/export firm is what she said, but not the name of it.' She looked over at Izena who was already digging through the pile of papers in front of her. After what seemed like an eternity, she pulled out a yellowing paper from the bottom and pointed to it. 'LUTC registration from 1987. Chief accountant is listed as A. Fernandez.'

She stood up. 'So, she told us right to our faces that first time we met.' She felt like banging the table in frustration – but didn't. 'Ok, let's start moving. First priority is to bring Mrs Fernandez in. I'll go with...' she shook her head at Moses who had already stood up, 'Alfred. Moses you need to coordinate the questioning along these new lines. And get all the rest of them in here: Asholodu, Wolo, the whole lot of them. Let's throw Mrs Fernandez at them and see if we get anything back.' There was a lot of chair-scraping as the team hurriedly started moving in different directions, relieved to be active again.

Alfred kept trying to make conversation in the car, but Gloria was preoccupied; a connection to Africanus Varley at this late stage was not what she had been expecting. She still couldn't see how it fitted together but fit together it did. She sighed wearily as she tuned back into Alfred's conversation.

'So ma'am how are we going to do this?'

'We're bringing a middle-aged Indian woman in for questioning Alfred. We will knock at her door and invite her to join us in the car. How does that sound as a plan?'

Alfred nodded in silent assent. He knew when the boss was vexed and silence was usually the best strategy.

It was just at the large exit doors in the foyer, quiet and empty at this time, that she saw a very familiar figure trying to slip through the side door. Jeez, it was one of those boys again – Executive or Original, she wasn't sure which. 'Alfred, that boy there, catch him for me please.' But even as Alfred started towards him, the boy was through the door and into the pale grey dawn. Alfred hesitated and Gloria called him back. 'Leave him. Those boys are everywhere just now but we will get them later.'

Monrovia was waking up and despite her tiredness Gloria could still appreciate the brief freshness of a Liberian morning, the breeze from the ocean, the first delicate light on the ocean and the smells of new bread and fried fish. Her mind was racing though, trying to make sense of this new information. Mrs Fernandez? She took out her phone. 'Moses, I've just had a thought. Can you send someone behind us now, maybe Christian and Ambrose? Just let them follow us.'

Mrs Fernandez's apartments were quiet too. A few cars parked in front and a taxi idling, probably waiting to take a customer to the airport. The taxi was blocking the entrance and they had to wait a few minutes while an elderly couple fussed with an improbable amount of luggage and then haggled over the fare before getting in and driving off. Gloria's temper was at boiling point by the time they reached the front doors and, perhaps more for her sake than for Alfred who looked very relaxed, she said. 'Now remember, we are just inviting her to the station to answer some questions, that's all. Nice and easy, she was quite nervous the last time I was here.' She had just finished saying this when she heard a sharp crack and then another. It was the sound of shattering glass that jerked her out of her shock. She turned to Alfred in time to see him crumple silently and fall, blood already spurting from his head. She reached out and grabbed him, simultaneously trying to pull him into the front hall. Another crack and the remaining glass panel in the door shattered sending shards everywhere. Gloria crouched in the corner over Alfred's body. She was shaking, trying to see the wound and stop the blood and at the same time call for back up. With the clean handkerchief her mother had always insisted she carry, she pressed down on the blood pouring from Alfred's forehead. His eyes were closed and his breathing quick and shallow.

Then she heard the running. Someone was coming towards them and she had no weapon and a dying colleague in her arms. Not on this fine fresh morning, surely not. She knelt in front of Alfred in a feeble attempt to protect him and pressed her phone. It would be too late for help but if she could at least speak to Moses he would know what was happening.

'Ma'am? Are you ok?'

The familiar voice startled her and she looked up and saw Ambrose in the doorway. Just for a moment relief left her speechless then she blurted out. 'It's Alfred.'

Ambrose very calmly moved her aside and lifted Alfred. They went out, Gloria supporting his head, trying to hold the makeshift bandage in place.

'But the shooter…'

'Christian got him, we were just behind you. It's crazy, he was just standing at the gate. Young boy too.' They were at the car now and Gloria knew the imperative was to get Alfred to hospital. Everything else could wait.'

'You'll have to drive Ambrose, and fast…'

Ambrose just nodded and sped to the gates. He paused long enough to shout something at Christian, who was using his belt to restrain the shooter, and then drove on. But it was also long enough for Gloria to see the shooter's face; she stared in shock at the young man being secured by Christian. It was Executive, or Original, – one of those boys staring sullenly ahead. What on earth was going on?

She had no more time to think about it as Ambrose raced onto Tubman

Boulevard narrowly missing a large NGO jeep. She kept pressing on the wound and talking to Alfred. The head wound didn't look as bad now but there was still a lot of blood. She lifted his shirt and saw the second wound. Oh god, she thought, it is bad. 'Ambrose, you're going to have to go faster.' She heard the screech as Ambrose put his foot down and the car strained forward the last short distance to the gates of the Catholic Hospital, did a half spin and then sped up the drive to the Emergency entrance. The next ten minutes were a blur of activity as medics put Alfred on a stretcher and wheeled him inside. Gloria slumped on a bench outside talking to Moses.

She told him about the shooter, shaking her head. 'We have missed something important here Moses. Did you send someone to bring Mrs Fernandez in?' He had but her apartment had been empty.

'She had just gone boss, there was a warm cup of tea and hot porridge still on the table. Your shooter gave her the time she needed. We are looking for her now along with Inspector Barnyou's people. How is Alfred?'

'He's in intensive care with what looks like half the senior medical staff in attendance, I never knew Alfred was so famous.' She heard Moses give a quick laugh. 'There's nothing I can do here. I'm going to leave Ambrose here and Izena is on her way.' She paused. 'The head wound is just a graze but he took a bullet in his side too and he's lost a lot of blood. They are still trying to assess how much damage has been done internally but it doesn't look good to me Moses. And we just sauntered in there, I thought we were just going to question some middle-aged woman.'

'Really boss? Why did you ask for back up then?'

'Well, I just had a thought that maybe we had underestimated her and her role, but I never expected a sniper for God's sake.'

'Still, if you hadn't you might both have been dead. Christian said he was walking towards you when he brought him down.'

Gloria shook her head again. Those few moments of utter powerlessness would stay with her for a very long time. 'I'm coming back to the office now.'

She met Izena on the way out. She was accompanied by her mother and several brothers and she looked ashen and unkempt. 'Where is he ma'am? Is he going to be alright?'

'They have stabilized him Izena. It's serious but the doctors are very hopeful. Go in, Ambrose is in there.'

'Which doctor is attending him?' Izena's rather imperious mother looked set for battle. 'I think we might have to move him to a better establishment.'

Gloria rolled her eyes then bit her tongue She knew her exhaustion might lead her to say something she would regret. 'Just go and talk to the doctors Izena, half the hospital is in with him.'

Back at the office anxiety and anger levels were running high. The shooter, Original he gave his name as, admitted to everything: driving the truck that killed Alfred, poisoning Luseni and then shooting him, kidnapping Korpu – and then as if it was an afterthought, the murders. He sat very calmly and described how he and Executive had taken the little girl and Peter and Old Pa and killed them. He kept talking and grinning and eventually Gloria left the room. The Director was standing outside.

'How is Alfred?' Gloria shrugged. She was too full to speak. 'Look if you need anything, let me know.' Gloria remembered to breathe again and nodded at her boss.

'But you have a confession Gloria, right?'

She nodded. 'Looks like it.'

'And?'

'Well he is giving all the right details so yes, I am fairly sure he and his psychopath friend did the killings…'

'Good, eh, well not good but…' the Director was actually rubbing his hands together.

'Not even nearly good sir,' she looked at him, frowning. 'It's more of the same problem we have had with this case - answers but no solutions.' She held up her hand. 'I believe he and his friend did all this killing and mayhem but not alone and not for themselves; the make-up on the children, the poison on the bottle, the dressing of the bodies… none of this was their doing. There is someone else who has been pulling all the strings on this.'

The Director, as always, looked disappointed that another neat solution had been snatched out of his hands. 'But he's not telling you anything? About anyone else being in control of the whole thing?'

'Not a thing, claims they did it all between them.'

'So you are focussing on this woman now then? Fernandez?'

'We were, well we still are but there are also links to Africanus Varley sir.' She paused as the Directors face fell. 'Look, I know you don't want to hear this but it's the only thing that makes sense, who else could bring all these people together and his company has a connection with every one of our suspects…' her voice trailed away, as she saw his face tighten in irritation and a great tiredness swept over her. What was the point? 'Anyway, right now we are searching for Mrs Fernandez sir and this boy's friend.' Back on safe ground the Director's face relaxed again.

'Good, good Gloria. Keep the investigation on track, get it finished. That's the priority, that and young Alfred's recovery. Leave the… ehm… the speculation until we get this wrapped up.'

Gloria choked back her response but the Director was already walking briskly away from her and anything she said would have been addressed to his back. She leaned against the wall letting the heat and exhaustion flow around her and through her. Clearly he thought her obsession with Varley was distracting her from the case at hand. Who knows, maybe he even blamed her for Alfred being shot. She stood up straight and allowed her clenched fists and her shoulders to relax. Ok, she needed to focus on the suspects in front of her, so that's exactly what she would do – for now anyway.

She went back into the interview room where Original was still holding court. 'Where do we find your friend?'

Original paused and looked at Gloria. 'Hmmm, you won't find him, you police people are stupid.'

'No, you are the stupid one pekin. Your friend is in danger, whoever got you to do all these bad bad things is not going to be happy that we have caught you, even if it did help Mrs Fernandez to escape.'

Original looked at her warily but then shook his head. 'There is no-one. I did it. I was just attacking you this morning, I've been following you for a long time. So,' he sat back and folded his arms, 'anything you want do, you mun just do it.'

In the event they didn't have to wait long. The call was from Clementine. 'Hi Gloria, thought you would want to know this; I'm at the hospital and they have just brought in that boy Executive. He is in a bad way.'

Gloria went out to the corridor. 'What's happened to him? Can you make sure he doesn't leave until we get there?'

'Hmm, leave! It's not possible Gloria. He is covered in huge, I don't know what they are, like open sores, everywhere, he is in agony. I would be surprised if he leaves here at all.'

The poison! 'Clementine, listen, go and talk to him, ask him where Mrs Fernandez is, their boss. I know she is the one did this to him. And Clementine, please please take some pictures and send me them right now.' She heard Clementine splutter. 'I'll explain, really I will.'

She rang off and got Moses out of the interview to go to the hospital. The photos arrived ten minutes later. They were horrific. The boy was covered in a mass of sores, his face and hands hugely swollen. But the call that followed confirmed her worse fears. 'He's dead Gloria, sorry. He couldn't speak even if he wanted to. It was horrible.'

Gloria shook her head. 'But I've seen that poison before Clementine. It is painful and ugly but Armah told us it was not fatal.'

'Maybe not Gloria but the bleach he drank certainly was.'

'Bleach!'

'The doctor says he drank some corrosive material – he thinks bleach, given the blistering around the mouth.'

'And the poison?'

'It was just a distraction really…'

'Or part of the show.'

'The show?' Clementine sounded shocked.

'None of these deaths have been simple Clementine. Jeez, what a mess.' There was a pause. 'I'll see you later.'

Gloria knew what she was going to do now. She went into the interview room where Original was slumped in the chair, and without a word put the photos of his friend in front of him. Even on the small screen of her phone the pictures were shocking. Original's face didn't change but his eyes started moving wildly from side to side. He licked his lips and looked up at Gloria. 'How you do this, you think I don't know tha trick here.'

Gloria twisted her lips. 'Trick eh? Ok, you will see your friend soon enough if you live long enough. That poison can get anywhere you know.' Original dropped the bottle of water he was holding. 'Oh yes, you know that trick don't you. Right, well I leaving you now. See you later, maybe.'

She opened the door and told the young officer to keep an eye on him but he couldn't keep it up. 'Old ma, wait, wait.' Original was sweating, staring at his hands, examining his skin. The realisation of what might happen to him was beginning to sink in. 'You have to help me, please.' For a boy who had been so immersed in death he seemed very scared by the prospect.

'So what, tell me something and I can help you.'

Chapter Twenty Seven

It took Original an hour to detail his and Executive's part in the whole sorry tale. They met Mrs Fernandez on the set of their TV show where she had volunteered to do the make-up. 'The ol ma talk to us so nicely, hmmm, she say she wan help us, promote us. She tell us we mun be careful because the other people will just use us and steal all our money. So we started to go around her and she give us small money and then she give us some kind of tea to drink, she say it will make us strong... and tha true-ooh. When we drink the tea we feel so strong, we know everything.' He gestured with his hands. 'So, tha it there.'

'Tha what there. What about the killing? She just tell you to kill people or what?'

'The killing? Tha not really killing. The ol ma explain everything to us. She was just testing us, teaching us. She say we have to do so many things before we ready for our career, things the other people don't know and won't teach us.'

'The little girl, what happened with her, why you kill her?'

Original screwed up his face, trying to remember. He shook his head.

'The little girl whose body you left on the roof of the stadium.'

Original smiled. 'Oh yeah, that one. Oh, she was frisky, very frisky. The ol ma took her from those church people and wanted her to be working for her too but the girl refused. So we dressed up like some kind of animals. We scare her bad way...' He laughed out loud at the memory. 'When we finish with her the old ma dress her and tell us to put her on the roof. She was very happy with us that day.'

Gloria's stomach was churning at the images he was conjuring up as well as at his complete detachment.

'And Peter, the Nigerian boy. Was that funny too?'

Original's face darkened. 'No, that was not good. The boy was so nice, polite everything. He worked to the ol ma's place there. But one day she said she couldn't do nothing with him and she couldn't afford to have him just there eating so we should get rid of him.' He hesitated. 'Peter begged us, he was on his knees crying and crying but we ourselves were scary from the ol ma.' He closed his eyes, this was not a memory he relished. 'Executive shot him quick quick just for it to be finished. The ol ma was not pleased with us.' He opened his eyes again and shrugged. 'What to do.'

'So where do we find her now, the ol ma?' Original looked blankly at Gloria and shook his head. 'Where you used to meet her?' But Original looked completely drained now and just stared back emptily at her.

Moses stopped writing. 'We've got everyone out looking for her boss, we're checking all the organisations we know she worked with and all the places she might go to but I think she's way too smart to go to any of those places.'

'She is smart smart, and the one controlling her?' She looked at Moses with raised eyebrows. 'Did she really manipulate Asholodu, Wolo and Collins, Ramesh and Doreen, and all the others we don't know about yet? Just with the help of two boys? Seems incredible to me.'

Moses shrugged. 'Well she's been here a long time, she worked or volunteered with a lot of different organisations and groups so just imagine how much information she could collect – a quiet Indian woman that people hardly remembered? Easy for her to find out where vulnerable children are and to use our other suspects' greed or their badness to control them. Look at all of them, Asholodu and his church business, Doreen and trafficking, Collins and his movies, what a collection and they all thought they were so smart but she was way way smarter, lured them in and snared them.'

'I know Moses I know, but snared them with what? Where would she get the big money to lure them in with?'

Moses looked at her, exhaustion now visible on his face. 'I'm not saying there aren't other people involved boss, but she is the one who carried it all out. Right? We can agree on that? So, maybe we need to focus on finding her, that's all.' He went back into the room and she saw him offering the boy some water.

Yes, that's all, thought Gloria and then what? Mrs Fernandez was not going to be an easy person to tie to any of these crimes. No-one as smart as that was going to leave an easy trail, if they found her at all. She jumped when her phone rang and Abu's strained voice came through.

'Aunt Glo, there's a woman here to see you, she says she wants to speak to you, that it's important.'

Gloria's heart sank. Not again, in her own home. 'Ok Abu, put her on, let me speak to her.'

'No, she just says you should come home, and you should come on your own.' Abu sounded puzzled rather than scared.

'Right, right, I get it Abu. Now listen. Don't drink anything or touch anything she offers you. I will be there in a few minutes.'

Gloria hesitated before leaving a message for Moses about where she was going. What if Fernandez had other informants apart from those boys, maybe even in her own office? She wrote a few lines on a sheet and went into the interview room to hand it to Moses. 'This needs to be filled in today, remember.' Moses looked up at her. 'I'm just going to get a drink of tea and then I'll be back.' It was a very simple code she had used before with Moses who knew well her devotion to coffee. He nodded nonchalantly and put the paper down.

She closed the door behind her. And then she was running down the corridor to her car, her mind racing, her heart pounding. The ride to her apartment took forever and she was bursting with frustration and anxiety by the time she got there. The door was open and when she went in Abu was sitting looking bemused at an album of photos Mrs Fernandez had on her lap. There was an empty glass in front of him. Mrs Fernandez smiled at her. 'Inspector, very good of you to come.'

'What did you give him to drink?' Gloria walked towards her but Fernandez held up her hand.

'Really Inspector, you should sit down. I mean now. We don't have much time and I am here to help you.'

'Tell me what you gave him first. Then we can talk or whatever.'

'Oh, it's just one of my special teas. It won't do any harm, well not immediately.' The wide smile was back on her face. 'Let us talk first.'

Gloria reluctantly sat down. Abu looked a bit dazed now, his eyes were closing and he was swaying slightly in the chair. 'Ok, but how do I know you won't kill him.' She tried to keep the panic out of her voice.

'Kill him! My dear Inspector I came here to-day to tell you that I didn't kill anyone so why would I do something as stupid as that right in your own house. The tea is just so you will listen to me,' her voice hardened, 'I insist you listen to me.' She held up another bottle with a rusty coloured liquid in it. 'And then when we agree I will give Abdul this and he...'

'Abu,' Gloria glared at her, 'his name is Abu.'

'Yes, yes of course Abu. Who will be fine as long as he drinks this in the next few minutes, and as long as I don't spill it on your rug.' She had loosened the cap and was holding the bottle at an angle.

'OK, whatever you want. But I know the story and how clever you are at manipulating and using people. Congratulations.'

'But don't you want to know why Inspector?'

'No. I really don't. In fact, I already know. And before you say anything, I know you are going to tell me it wasn't about the money, right?' Gloria glanced quickly at Abu who had fallen back in the chair, his eyes closed, and quickly continued. 'Yes, you were making money by exploiting people who were exploiting children right - blackmail, trafficking, movies, information and lots and lots of money I presume. But,' she looked Mrs Fernandez straight in the face, 'you're not in charge here are you. You are definitely not the boss or the brains are you? Hmm, how would we describe you? Africanus Varley's servant? Puppet? Plaything?' At the mention of the name Mrs Fernandez froze, a look of absolute shock mixed with fear on her face. She tried to say something but couldn't get the words out. Gloria continued, forcing her voice to keep strong, even as she watched Abu slump down completely in the chair, unconscious.

'So who invented all the little dramas around your victims? Was that you? Are you the director or were you just doing what your master told you to do, step by step, detail by detail?'

Mrs Fernandez's frozen smile relaxed a little and there was even the beginnings of a smile on her face. 'Good try Inspector. Very interesting story but really, I'm just a poor Indian widow trying to make a living here, and to help out where I can. I don't know these big people you are talking about.' She was smiling broadly now. 'The only thing I know is that you want to pin these crimes on me because I'm an easy target; a foreigner, a woman… a helpless woman who volunteers her time helping poor unfortunate children.'

Gloria stood up slowly. 'So, this paper which mentions the fact that your husband was the chief accountant for LUTC holdings in Liberia for over ten years means nothing right? Africanus Varley's right-hand man for ten years but you say you don't know Varley?' She held up the other hand which actually held only blank papers. 'And the signed confession of your boy Original? That certainly paints quite a different picture of you.' Gloria was talking but had kept her eye on the small bottle in Mrs Fernandez's hand but before she could make a dive for it Mrs Fernandez had stood up too, her face darkened with rage. She flung the bottle across the room where it smashed against the wall. Gloria lunged at her bringing her down and scrabbled frantically to save the liquid which was draining away into her carpet.

Moses's arrival saved her any more efforts. Gloria pointed at the woman, unconscious on the floor and then at Abu who was now slumped in the chair. Moses nodded and made for Fernandez while Gloria with Ambrose and Christian, lifted Abu down the stairs and into the car.

Chapter Twenty Eight

Several frantic hours later and Gloria was sitting on Abu's bed watching him be sick again. The induced sickness the doctor assured her was just a precaution but he didn't think there had been any poison in the tea Abu had drunk, just a strong sedative. If there had been poison he would not have made it to the hospital. Abu looked as miserable as if had been poisoned.

'Well I told you not to drink anything Abu, jeez, one day you might actually listen to me.'

'But she insisted and I didn't want to be rude. I thought she was just some old lady.' He retched again, his stomach empty now and then stared at her before asking quietly. 'What about Alfred Aunt Glo? I heard the nurses say he was shot.'

Gloria smiled. 'Izena texted. They have operated on him and the doctors are sure he's going to be alright. He might not be coaching for a while, but he'll be back.'

Abu leaned back on the pillow, his relief obvious, and then looked at her again. 'So that one old lady is responsible for all this shooting and killing and stuff?'

'It's complicated. She is certainly responsible but there are a lot of other people involved in the shooting and the killings. As well as trafficking, pornographic movies, slavery...'

'Wow, that old ma? But how she manage?'

Gloria shrugged, she was beyond exhaustion and the day was far from over. 'Well she controlled some people, including those two boys, and she managed to get information on a crowd of other rogues but I am sure she was taking orders from...' she broke off and stared at Abu. 'Wait now, you are ill, and I'm not supposed to be telling you these things anyway. This is police business.'

Abu snorted. 'Police business! Aunt Glo your police business almost got me killed again!'

Gloria laughed. 'Well technically Abu you were in no danger of dying as she never gave you poison but…' she stared at him, clammy and wretched-looking under the thin bed sheet, 'It's true you are suffering because of the case so I suppose I could tell you what I know, and take your mind off your stomach for a while.'

Abu sat up expectantly.

'Right, so I believe she was taking orders from someone else – from Africanus Varley in fact.'

Abu's face clouded. 'Him again? Che, he really is bad. But her, the ol ma, why she do all those wicked things?'

Gloria shrugged. 'For money, for power, you know, control over other people. In fact, maybe power was the main thing. I'm sure Africanus Varley is the overall boss but I think she loved controlling those children's lives.

Abu was staring at her. 'And you keep telling me to grow up and be more adult… adults are crazy Aunt Glo, so so crazy people.'

The noise at the end of the ward made Gloria look up in time to see her mother, who had arrived with what looked like the entire family, arguing loudly with the small Spanish nun who ran the ward. 'My dear sister, I know there is no visiting during meal times but as we ourselves are bringing my grandson his meal,' she held up several large plastic bags, 'the meal time cannot yet have started, so I must be allowed to go in.'

Gloria laughed as the nun, recognising defeat, backed off with a muttered 'Well don't stay long please and try to keep the noise down' and her mother advanced towards them talking at the top of her voice.

'Right, pekin, talking of crazy adults, your grandma and uncles are here to see you so I have to go. I have a case to close and a story to unravel.' She stood up. 'You might want to close your eyes for a while.' But Abu had already done that, looking for all the world like he was fast asleep.

She greeted her mother and left the ward wondering which would break first, her mother's ability to sit and wait or Abu's talent for acting. She was pretty sure this was one competition Abu was not going to win.